Classic Sports Cars

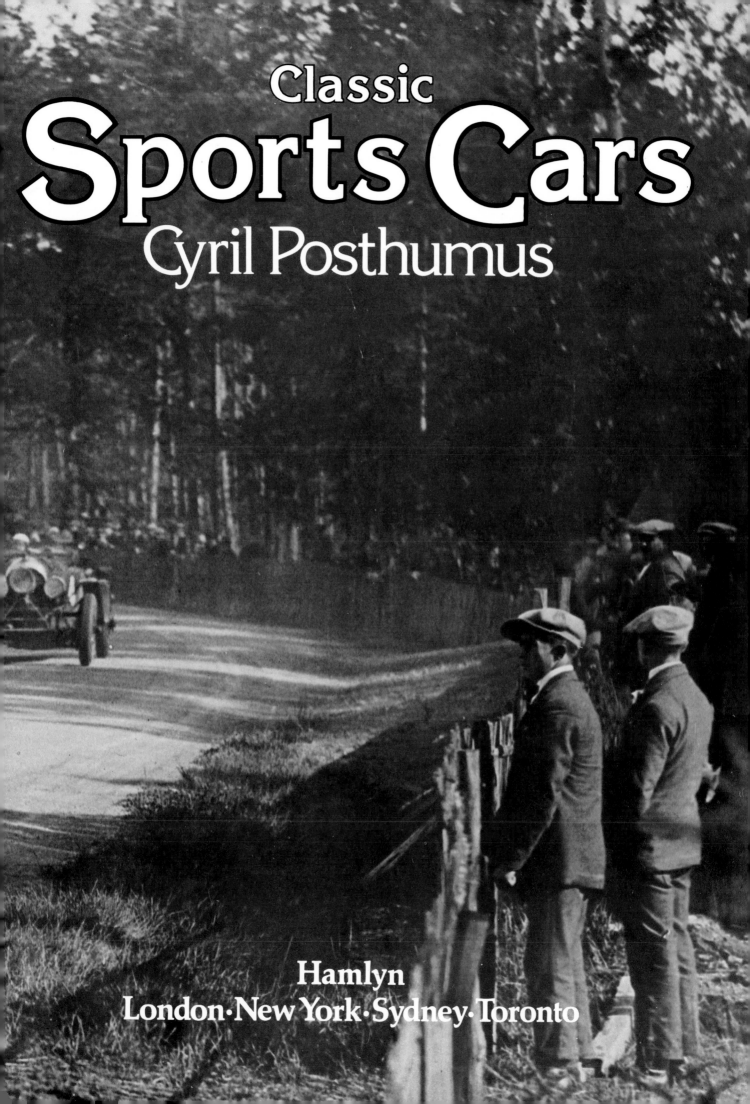

Classic
Sports Cars
Cyril Posthumus

Hamlyn
London·New York·Sydney·Toronto

The publishers are grateful to the following for the
illustrations in this book: James Allington; Associated Press;
Autocar; Hugh Bishop; Alice Bixler; Neill Bruce; Briggs
Cunningham Automotive Museum; DPPI; Ford; G. Gédo; Geoffrey
Goddard; David Hodges; Jeff Hutchinson; Leigh Jones; LAT
Photographic; Mercedes-Benz; *Motor*; National Motor Museum;
Bill Oursler; Cyril Posthumus; Publifoto; Renault; Robert
Roux; Maurice Rowe; Shell; Nigel Snowdon; F. David Stone;
Gerry Stream; Francis Tainturier; Colin Taylor;
Technical Art Werbe GmbH.

Side elevation drawings by Malcolm Ward.

Published by The Hamlyn Publishing Group Limited
London · New York · Sydney · Toronto
Astronaut House, Feltham, Middlesex, England

ISBN 0 600 32045 6

Printed in Hong Kong

Contents

Foreword

After writing *Classic Racing Cars* it seemed logical to follow up with *Classic Sports Cars,* but Oh, how different and how much more complex the subject! Racing cars are simple, tangible things made to carry one person fast; sports cars carry two or more, can be open or closed, or either, can be raced or rallied and sometimes both, and might be production, GT, prototype or sundry other things. They may qualify as "classics" for their design and looks, for how they performed on the road, for what they did in competition, or for a combination of all these—and if there seems undue emphasis on racing and rallying in the ensuing pages, it is because success in competition is, and always has been, of paramount importance in proving a car.

Which brings up another point; the reader with a fair idea of what is, and is not, a sports car may wonder at the inclusion of such "fringe" subjects as the CanAm McLaren, Chapparal, Porsche 917, Maserati "Birdcage" or Renault-Alpine "Turbo". I can but reply that these are all descendants of the former "sports-racing" class, now lost in the Sargasso of modern FIA regulations which have attempted to differentiate between production-based and specially built two-seater high-speed cars.

Most of the cars in question, moreover, have competed in the Le Mans 24 Hours race, that world-famed sports car classic of the past, but today a battleground between "special production", "series production GT", "two-seater racing" and other categories even more puzzling than the "prototypes" they have replaced.

That apart, I would stress that the subjects included are but a selection of classic sports cars, and not by any means all of them. Alvis, Morgan, Riley, Amilcar, Salmson, . . . all are unquestionably classic sports cars, and I apologise to adherents for their omission due to lack of space, taking comfort only in the fact that most of them have already been well documented.

C.P.

Sports cars- the early years

The genealogy of the sports car is almost as difficult to trace as the species itself is to define—and efforts to do that adequately have enlivened the opening chapters of excellent books on the subject. The term "sports car" seems to have been coined around 1921, but the genus goes back to the first decade of the 20th century, when cars ceased to be primitive, found reliability, and began to be fun.

Combining lively performance with the ability to carry at least two people in relative comfort, the sporting motor car represented a kind of "half-way house" between the racing car and the touring

Precursor of the sports car: Jenatzy's 9·2 litre Mercedes "60" which won the 1903 Gordon Bennett race. The lofty seating and steering column betray its touring origins, but good engine flexibility, well-balanced chassis and excellent steering ensured victory

car, and both types contributed vitally to its evolution. Other things counted too: the mounting popularity of voiturette racing in reaction to the ultra-large, ultra-costly "unlimited" racers, the birth of long-distance road contests —forerunners of the modern motor rally—and, above all, the spirit of adventure and independence so joyfully embodied in a good, fast car.

He could not have realised it, but when that ebullient Belgian, Camille Jenatzy, took a Mercedes 60 to victory in the 1903 Gordon Bennett Trophy race in Ireland, he was driving a direct ante-cedent of the sports car. A disastrous fire at the Mercedes factory at Canstatt had destroyed the three special racing 90hp machines built for the great race, which was less than a month ahead. The manufacturers scouted frantically around for substitutes, securing the loan of three private 60hp road cars, one from the American Clarence Dinsmore

and two from the Paris distributor, M. Charley.

The change was fortuitous, for the 60 proved itself eminently more suited to the job than the faster but more erratic 90, and Jenatzy outpaced Panhard, Mors and Napier opposition to win by over 11 minutes. The other two Mercedes had to retire, but not before one had turned in the fastest lap of the race. Yet these 60s were basically touring cars, built to carry a driver and four passengers in luxury. Their five-seater tonneau bodies, lamps, mudguards and other impedi-menta had been removed from the chassis at Canstatt, bucket seats for driver and riding mechanic had been fitted, together with a pair of light front wings, and all three were then painted in Germany's national racing colour, white.

Moreover, the trio were *driven* from Germany, across England and over to Ireland, and later driven home again—

an amazing demonstration of sports car-style stamina in 1903. At the time, the Mercedes 60 was probably the world's fastest production car, and certainly one of the best handling. Its engine, with overhead inlet and side exhaust valves, all mechanically operated, measured 140 × 150mm (9,230cc), and gave 65bhp at 1,060rpm, making it an over 60mph car even when carrying luxury touring coachwork. In a later age, the proud manufacturers might well have produced a replica "Gordon Bennett" sports model for sale, but in 1903 the cult of the specifically sporting road car had yet to come.

In contradistinction to the Mercedes, which was a touring car converted for racing, quite a few redundant racers became embryonic sports cars after a degree of "taming". One such was the 1902 60hp Paris-Bordeaux Mors, which the Wolseley company rebuilt for Montague Grahame-White into an open four-seater with lamps, wings, honey-comb radiator and a "cloverleaf" tail. Racing Panhards, Darracqs and others were similarly converted, while S. F. Edge of Napiers varied the theme by offering replicas in their catalogue of the 1908 "Grand Prix" six-cylinder Napier for road use. Owing to a dispute with the Grand Prix organisers over its quickly-detachable wire wheels, the Napier did not contest the race, and it is not certain whether any "replicas" were actually sold.

Other notable conversions from track to road trim included a 90hp 1906 Grand Prix Renault on which its owner killed himself, and a 1908 Grand Prix Itala. This was a muscular 100hp car which submitted to four-seater touring body-work in 1912, and which still graces the British vintage racing scene today, ironically now wearing a replica version of its original racing bodywork. Such "wolves in sheep's clothing" were expensive, exciting and difficult for laymen to handle, although in expert hands they probably ran as well as their touring brothers, the difference between racer and road car being a lot less over 70 years ago.

At the other end of the social motoring scale was another antecedent of the sports car—one, moreover, that more people could both operate and afford. This was the voiturette, a light, inexpensive small car dependent on a good power-to-weight ratio for its nimbleness when carrying two people. The prior need to save weight and cost meant a simple single or twin-cylinder air-cooled engine and spartan equipment, making the voiturette essentially a sporting

machine for young, agile people, while its low price attracted a considerable clientèle. And as Grand Prix engines grew ever larger, a smaller, cheaper racing category for voiturettes was welcomed by manufacturers with fewer resources, among whom Sizaire-Naudin and Delage were prominent.

In 1906 the French journal L'Auto had promoted a Coupe des Voiturettes contest aimed expressly at encouraging development of inexpensive light cars of brisk performance, that could be used both on road and track. The regulations limited single-cylinder engines to a bore of 120mm, and twin-cylinder engines to a bore of 90mm, while to prevent undue skimpiness in chassis construction a minimum weight limit of 700kg (1,543lb) was imposed. The competition, held near Rambouillet, comprised a six-day reli-ability trial in which cars had to cover 200km per day at a set average, followed by a 140-mile road race.

A stock single-cylinder 120 × 110mm Sizaire-Naudin won the event from a single-cylinder de Dion-engined Delage, the winning car being interesting, both for its curious three-speed final drive devised by a floating propellor shaft with single pinion and three sets of teeth on the crownwheel, and for its indepen-dent front suspension by a transverse leaf spring and vertical slides. Designer Maurice Sizaire was a pioneer in using castor oil as a lubricant and in lacing the petrol with ether, and could tune the long-stroke single so that it "chonked" over gently without a miss.

Identical cars were built at the rate of two per day at the modest Sizaire-Naudin factory at Puteaux, and early in 1907 Naudin further demonstrated the ability of their voiturettes by driving another stock example to win the 185-mile Sicilian Cup race over two laps of the very demanding Targa Florio mountain circuit. When the French Coupe des Voiturettes event was repeated later in 1907, the organisers reduced the bore limit from 120 to 100mm, but rashly left the stroke unrestricted. Sizaire-Naudin quietly lengthened the stroke on their singles to 150mm and won the event a second time. Engineers of the time deplored this step towards freakishness, but Kent Karslake, in his splendid book Racing Voiturettes, wrote of several of the cars, including the Sizaire-Naudins, that they "appear to the eye of a later generation as very neat little sports cars in an era when the sports car is not generally recognised as having been invented".

Certainly if the requisites of a sports car are that it be as practical as a road

car, yet can give a good account of itself in competition, and will handle and corner well, then the little Sizaire-Naudin of 1906–07 and one or two of its voiturette rivals such as the first Lion-Peugeots and the Delage qualify as important forerunners of the breed. Unfortunately, Sizaire's bold elongation of the stroke began a rot in the Voiturette class, bringing freak long-stroke singles and narrow-angle vee-twins in grotesque high-bonneted cars, evoking much criticism where formerly praise had been fulsome.

Soon strokes were to rise to beyond 200mm, but meantime a significant saving move by race organisers in 1908 was to admit four-cylinder engines, albeit with bores limited to 62mm maxi-mum, at the same time stipulating more generous body and chassis dimensions to restrain the drift away from the sporting road car image. Several "fours" appeared that year, the design sophisti-cation of at least two of them high-lighting the crudity of the ferocious long-stroke "one-lungers", even though they could not match their pace. One was the Swiss Martini, the other the Italian Isotta-Fraschini, both having clean little monobloc engines with overhead valves operated by a single overhead camshaft, and shaft final drive.

Although the Martini was the first four-cylinder finisher in the Coupe des Voiturettes, its design, regrettably, was not followed up, whereas the little Isotta-Fraschini was marketed later in 1908 as a sporting road car, being exported during the next few years to the USA, Australia and elsewhere. Its engine dimensions were 62 × 100mm (1,207cc), the cylinders being cast in a monobloc, and a ball-bearing crankshaft allowed rotating speeds approaching 3,000rpm. High-tension magneto igni-tion, automatic lubrication and a single I-F carburettor were used, and an inter-esting feature was the lightweight rear axle casing, formed from two halves in pressed steel, welded together—a process hailed as "innovative" when used on the 1922 Grand Prix Fiat, 14 years later.

Aluminium figured strongly else-where, and wood-spoked wheels were employed on the production model with 1½ litre engine. Long semi-elliptic springs, rear hub brakes and a total weight of 680kg (1,499lb) completed a charming precursor of the small sports car. The Italian magazine Motori, Cicli e Sport in September 1908 was moved to comment: "Although the small Isotta-Fraschini car may have the appearance of an attractive plaything, it is a master-piece of precision . . . agile and light,

Appearing, in Kent Karslake's words, as "a very neat little sports car", a single-cylinder Sizaire-Naudin voiturette with independent front suspension by single transverse leaf spring, seen at the Gaillon hillclimb meeting in 1907

but compact and robust. This small, swift vehicle induces a feeling of intoxication in the driver . . . all the pleasant sensations which the automobile normally provides being infinitely multiplied. . . . Those who have already travelled in an ordinary double phaeton or limousine discover in the small car with its two narrow seats a new sense of liberty, agility and absolute independence. . . The driver is in direct contact with the animated mechanism of this car, in which one has in full the feeling of possession and dominance over the vehicle, and in which one has almost the illusion of flying. . ."

All of which seems a fulsome Latin way of describing the pleasures of a typical small sports car. Here, perhaps, was the world's first car marketed with

sporting intentions. One of the mechanics working on the Isottas in the paddocks at Dieppe and Compiègne in 1908 was Alfieri Maserati, an eminent future manufacturer, and undoubtedly the pretty little Italian voiturette also attracted the attention of another future manufacturer, Italian-born, German-domiciled Ettore Bugatti. Indeed, so jewel-like was the Isotta that its design, when under study in the 1950s and 1960s, was attributed to Bugatti, whereas in fact it was the work of one Stefanini, under the guidance of Isotta-Fraschini's technical head Giustino Cattaneo.

Isotta-Fraschini were old hands at overhead camshafts, as it happened, building their first engine so-equipped in 1905, while Bugatti himself produced a 10·3 litre four-cylinder ohc engine in 1907 for the Deutz marque of Cologne. Before leaving their employ in 1909 he laid down the design, and built the prototype of his immortal Type 13, the first car to bear his name. It closely resembled the "baby" Isotta, having virtually the same bore and stroke, the same shaft-and-bevel driven enclosed ohc, a similar

ball-bearing crankshaft, separate four-speed gearbox, semi-elliptic springing, and similar light metal fabricated rear axle. It, too, revved to 3,000rpm, giving 22bhp, and the main differences were confined to Bugatti's unusual arc-formed "banana" tappets, which also figured on his Deutz units, and a wet multi-plate clutch.

After leaving Deutz, Bugatti set up his own works at Molsheim, in German Alsace, in 1910, and put the Type 13 into production with slightly larger 65 × 100mm engine (just as Isotta did) and plain main bearings. Three chassis lengths were offered, and reversed quarter-elliptic rear springs replaced the semi-elliptics from 1912. Whether the Type 13 owed anything to the Isotta-Fraschini or not, the latter for all its promise barely lasted four years, whereas the Bugatti was listed from 1910 to 1925, and won innumerable friends for its high-revving but ever sweet engine, superb steering, lively performance, general zest and good workmanship. It was a pioneer small sports car, not in the cheap 1930s idiom, but as a small-scale

Purpose-built: The 5·7 litre Austro-Daimlers which finished 1-2-3 in the 1910 Prince Henry Trial had a lean and hungry "sports car" look, with "tulip form" open 4-seater bodywork, rudimentary wings and Rudge-Whitworth detachable wire wheels. The winning driver was Dr Porsche

---

edition of a larger top-quality product.

The four-cylinder clause that saved the dignity (and the future) of the Voiturette racing class was instrumental in bringing forth, not only the comely Isotta and Martini cars in 1908, but an even more important sporting model

---

Routing rivals of up to 10 litres, this light 2·1 litre four-cylinder 10/20 Opel with characteristic "tulip form" bodywork won the 1909 Prince Henry Trial in Germany, driven by Wilhelm Opel of the famous German motoring family

two years later. This was the four-cylinder Hispano-Suiza from Spain, a 2·6 litre car with an unusual T-head side-valve, long-stroke engine of 65×200mm bore and stroke, which routed the freak singles and twins by winning the 1910 Coupe de l'Auto and other races. This voiturette formed the basis of the famous "Alfonso" Hispano-Suiza, one of the earliest and most successful of sports cars.

The voiturette category was to make further important contributions to the blossoming world of sports cars right up to 1914, but meantime a new kind of automobile contest had taken a firm hold in Germany, and was producing some outstanding designs of decidedly sporting character. Students of art may recall the name of Hubert Herkomer as a London-based portrait painter of some prominence about a century ago; students of motoring, however, will

scarcely be aware of him as the father of rallying. Yet Professor Herkomer, who came from Munich but became a naturalised British subject, certainly helped inaugurate the competitive motor tour which has grown through the years to become today's international motor rally. The first Herkomer Trophy Trial was held in 1905, cars in various capacity classes from 16 to over 60hp competing over 566 miles of Bavarian roads.

Marks were given for speeds on the level and up hills, for reliability, comfort and appearance, but sheer horsepower clearly counted most of all, and three big Mercedes took the first three places. The "Herkomer" was staged again, over different terrain, in 1906 and 1907, emphasis moving firmly towards the speed and hill climbing abilities of the contesting cars. A Horch won in 1906, and a big Benz in 1907. The Germans having acquired a taste for such events, a new series was inaugurated with the patronage of Prince Heinrich (or Henry) of Prussia, brother of the Kaiser. Called the Prince Henry Trial, it again put emphasis on performance, with a handicap based on the number of cylinders and the bore thereof, in an effort to give smaller-engined cars a chance.

This did not prevent a 7·3 litre Benz from winning in 1908, but a light 2·1 litre Opel won in 1909, and in 1910 three 5·7 litre Vienna-built Austro-Daimlers took the first three places, roundly defeating a big Opel and a bigger Benz. These Austro-Daimlers were very enterprising, with their overhead valves operated by an overhead camshaft à la Isotta-Fraschini. The winning car, moreover, was driven by its designer, Dr Ferdinand Porsche of future world eminence, who nursed his "Prince Henry" Austro-Daimler into small-scale production, some 200 being built by 1914. The lessons it taught were not unheeded, nor was it the sole inheritance from those pioneer German rallies.

Britain, having made a late start in automobile production through its own backward, horse-orientated legislation, her earliest cars were well-built but lacking in design enterprise. By about 1907, however, the brighter British makers were feeling their feet. Napier had already proved the six-cylinder principle, and the Rolls-Royce was established as the apotheosis of high quality manufacture. Soon other makers, having learned the basic motor-building trade, emerged from the ruck and began to show individuality.

One such was Vauxhall, born in 1903 of a London engineering firm based at

TT race in 1906 with their 22hp four-cylinder model. In 1911 a 7·4 litre six-cylinder side valve Silver Ghost with four-seater touring body travelled from London to Edinburgh and back on top gear alone, then lapped Brooklands at 78·2mph. One of the "London-Edinburgh" replicas, superbly hand-some with long low bonnet, and lean coachwork and wings, won the 1913 Spanish GP for touring cars, and in 1913 and 1914 Rolls-Royce tourers with four-speed gearboxes, aluminium pistons and other aids made best performance in the Austrian Alpine Trial. No Rolls-Royce was a sports car, but these fine looking, fine performing open models were certainly classic sporting cars.

On the other side of the Atlantic, before the USA became involved in the First World War, there were those famous protagonists, the Stutz and the Mercer. Both had sturdy side-valve four-cylinder engines, the Mercer Type 35 "Raceabout" an eight-plug 4·9 litre unit, the Stutz "Bearcat" an eight-plug 6·4 litre unit. The Mercer, extant from 1911 to 1917, was lower, shorter, lighter and better styled; the Stutz, which came on the scene in 1914, was more powerful, sturdier, easier to start and less expensive. Both were popular with monied young bucks in the warmer, drier American states; neither Raceabout nor Bearcat had any real weather equipment, although both affected the "monocle" screen for the driver, leaving the flies and dust to the passenger.

Both had exhaust cutouts and 70 mph maximums, and both enjoyed a waiting list of buyers. With their lusty engines they must have been enormous fun, even if the famous rivalry between exponents of each has probably been exaggerated through the years. A later Mercer with L-head and four speeds appeared in 1915 but it could not eclipse the classic T-head Raceabout. Lesser opposition to both makes came from Locomobile, National, Marmon and others, generally wearing the same "uniform"—two bucket seats, raked steering column, sparse mud-guards, bolster fuel tank and monocle. To American classic sporting car fans, Mercer and Stutz are as Bentley and Vauxhall to their British counterparts, loved, revered and cherished for the classics they are.

Vauxhall, close by the Thames. The early Vauxhall motor cars were remarkable for their use of an early form of integral chassis/body construction, coil instead of leaf springs for suspension, and the indulgence of a three-cylinder model. None of this lasted long, and after the firm moved to Luton in 1905, "bread and butter" convention reigned until the appointment of 24-year-old L. H. Pomeroy as assistant chief engineer. In those days of many makes and small outputs, success in competition was a vital asset to sales and reputation, and the pushing young Pomeroy saw his chance when the RAC held a 2000 Miles Trial in Britain in 1908.

In the absence on a long overseas holiday of the chief engineer, he took a standard 20hp 3 litre Vauxhall with a five-bearing, four-cylinder side-valve engine, and wrought such improvements upon its porting, carburation, balance, lubrication and other responsive factors that he raised the output from 23½bhp at 1,800rpm to 38bhp at 2,500rpm. There was no time to alter the erect four-seater *Roi des Belges* style touring body with its vast "scroll" back, but with the aid of carefully chosen gear ratios the Vauxhall made the best performance of all cars in the 2000 Miles Trial, imbuing the Luton works with a new and keen competitive spirit.

The 3-litre Vauxhall became a force to reckon with in hill climbs and sprints, and with Pomeroy extracting a further astonishing 22bhp from its rugged power unit, the directors felt emboldened to

contest the 1910 Prince Henry Tour in Germany with three specially prepared cars. These had lowered chassis bearing clean, doorless open four-seater bodies, and two achieved non-stop runs, securing Tour plaquettes. Thus was born the Prince Henry Vauxhall, a near-replica of the Tour car catalogued as "a light carriage suitable for fast travel-ling or speed work". How useful would the simple term "sports car" have been.

Vauxhall soon raised the engine capacity to 3·96 litres, the resultant 75bhp giving a road speed of over 70mph and a 95mph lap speed at Brook-lands track, where a special single-seater set many outstanding records. The "Prince Henry" was the direct forebear of that unforgettable classic British sports car, the 30/98 Vauxhall.

The Prince Henry had some significant contemporaries, also competition-bred. The compatriot Talbot and Sunbeam marques also shone as fast tourers or competition cars while, like Vauxhall, they both stuck to side valves in their pre-First World War production models, thereby achieving enviable standards of reliability coupled with unexpected performance. Brooklands track, the first purpose-built racing circuit in the world, was largely responsible for the speed and stamina of these makes, sustained high revs teaching engineers an awful lot about the durability (or otherwise) of their engines.

Even the august Rolls-Royce marque turned towards competition in those days. They won the second Isle of Man

Hispano-Suiza Alfonso

It was strange that a trendsetter should come from Spain, rather than France, Germany, Britain or Italy. The pioneer Spanish motor industry was small and largely domestic, yet out of two obscure Barcelona marques, La Cuadra and the Castro which succeeded it, came Hispano-Suiza in 1904. Meaning simply "Spanish-Swiss", this romantic-sounding concern was founded by two Spaniards, Damien Mateu and Javier Castro, and a young Swiss engineer, Marc Birkigt. Their first products, catering for a small, exclusive market, were of high-quality four-cylinder touring type, advanced in having their engine and gearbox in one unit, and shaft rather than chain final drive.

One of Hispano-Suiza's most distinguished patrons, King Alfonso XIII of Spain, was a great motor sporting enthusiast who decided that his country should have its own major road race, the Catalan Cup, in 1909. At that time Grand Prix racing was in suspension, and the premier class was for so-called "voiturettes", with bore and stroke restrictions ranging from 100 × 250mm (1,957cc) for single cylinder-engined cars to 80 × 192mm (1,920cc) for twins, and 65 × 140mm (1,852cc) for four-cylinder units, together with a dry weight of 600kg (1,323lb) minimum.

A Spanish voiturette race with no Spanish participants was unthinkable, and Hispano-Suiza came up nobly with a 65 × 140mm water-cooled four based on one of their smaller production models, and employing a T-head with large-diameter side valves operated by two camshafts in the crankcase, a three-speed gearbox, shaft final drive and artillery wheels. Three of these ran in the Catalan race, but were too new to place better than fourth. The trio then finished 5–6–7 in the Coupe des Voiturettes at Boulogne, indicating that at least they had found reliability.

For 1910 Birkigt found more speed. The stroke restrictions were removed, so he increased it in the Hispano-Suizas to 180mm, at the same time equipping them with quickly-detachable Rudge-Whitworth wire wheels for the second Catalan Cup, when one car finished third. The stroke was then further

increased to 200mm, giving 2·6 litres for the Coupe des Voiturettes, again at Boulogne, where one Hispano-Suiza driven by Zuccarelli won the race, and the others placed third and sixth. Thus a conventional four had at last defeated the freak long-stroke singles and twins and, more, a Spanish car had defeated the French in the season's biggest race.

A few weeks later the Hispanos scored another win in the Ostend voiturette race, and with this double *réclame* the company decided to commercialise their success and market a light sporting road edition of their racing voiturette. For this car, designated the 15T, Birkigt specified a larger bore of 80mm in conjunction with a 180mm stroke, giving a capacity of 3,604cc. This gave an output of about 55bhp at 2,300rpm, which was transmitted through a multi-plate clutch, a three-speed gearbox in unit with the engine, and an open propellor shaft with bevel final drive.

The engine/gearbox unit also served as chassis bracing, Birkigt dispensing entirely with a subframe, while the very large, flat honeycomb-type radiator was supported on the front frame cross-member. The chassis had pressed-steel side members and semi-elliptic springing front and rear, and braking was by rather small hand-operated internal expanding brakes on the rear wheels, and a sturdier pedal-operated transmission brake with broad ribbed drum. King Alfonso took delivery of the first car in 1911, and drove it over the rough, twisty roads of those days some 250 miles from San Sebastian to Madrid at an average of close on 50mph. Greatly pleased at its performance, he permitted it to be called the "Alfonso XIII".

That same year Hispano-Suiza opened a new factory at Levallois, in Paris, certainly a more central location for car production, both for labour and material supplies than Barcelona. The comely Alfonso was among the first models to be built there, finding a ready international market among motoring sportsmen and selling well in Edwardian Britain at a chassis price of £425—not so cheap as it sounds, when an average British mid-sized car such as a Humber, Rover or Singer cost little more than

£325 completely bodied and equipped.

Its RAC rating was 15·9hp, coincidentally the same as the post-war 3-litre Bentley whose characteristics it anticipated to a degree. Despite its side valves, the long stroke engine gave it a long-legged gait, with effortless cruising at close on 60mph, excellent pick-up, and remarkable top gear flexibility, enabling the car to come down to around 8mph without a change-down. Even so, the three gear ratios were very wide, requiring frequent use, while the light but precise gearchange, in an outside gate on the right-hand side, made this more a pleasure than a chore.

The makers claimed a maximum of 77mph, and Brooklands lap speeds of 81·51mph and 78·5mph were achieved by two privately owned Alfonsos in 1914. The steering was high-geared, requiring but $1\frac{1}{4}$ turns lock to lock, while the handling and general balance were excellent. Despite its large radiator area, the Alfonso tended to overheat, and would boil in traffic. A vee-radiator was used on racing Alfonsos in 1912, and a few cars so fitted were supplied to French customers. A variety of special sporting bodies could be fitted by outside *carrossiers*, including a very pretty two-seater with swept, flat-section wings and an elegant tail, while a bolster-tanked version and a "cloverleaf" three-seater were popular in France.

From 1912 two wheelbases, 8ft 8in and 9ft 10in were available, the respective chassis weights being 1,456 and 1,680lb. The longer model enabled coachbuilders to fit more spacious four-seater "torpedo" bodies, and closed models were also built. After 1912 the multi-plate clutch gave way to an excellent cone-type, a four-speed-and-reverse gearbox became available, and three-quarter-elliptic rear springing was adopted. Most Alfonsos were built at Levallois, then at Bois-Colombes when Hispano-Suiza moved to a bigger factory there early in 1914. By then the design had become outdated, and Birkigt had already introduced other models with overhead camshafts before the First World War broke out.

The beloved Alfonso, one of the world's first sporting cars, did not

Above: *Supporting the contention that "the racing car of today is the sports car of tomorrow", the 2·6 litre T-head side valve four-cylinder Hispano-Suiza which won the 1910 Coupe des Voiturettes at Boulogne provided the basis for the later 3·6 litre "Alfonso" road model*

Below: *A 1912 Hispano-Suiza "Alfonso", rakishly Edwardian with slender wire wheels and spidery mudguards, poses before a more modern, less personal form of transport. This particular Alfonso, accurately restored, belongs to the National Motor Museum at Beaulieu*

survive the war, after which Hispano-Suiza's name, widely respected for the excellent V8 aero-engines they had built in 1914–18, rose to the very summit with the magnificent big six-cylinder and V12 luxury cars the company produced into the 1930s.

Specification

Engine: 4 cylinders in line, fixed head; 80 × 180mm, 3,620cc; sv in T-head, operated by two camshafts; single Hispano-Suiza carburettor; Bosch h.t. magneto; cast-iron pistons; tubular connecting rods; 4 plain main bearings; 57bhp at 2,300rpm.
Transmission: Multi-plate clutch; 3-speed gearbox in unit with engine (4-speed gearbox fitted after 1912); open propellor shaft final drive.
Chassis: Pressed steel side members; semi-elliptic springing front and rear (¾-elliptic at rear after 1912); transmission brake and internal-expanding brakes on rear wheels.
Dimensions: Wheelbase, 8ft 8in (9ft 10in also available after 1912); track, 4ft 0in (rear track on long-wheelbase cars, 4ft 3in); approx. dry weight, 1,460lb (short wheelbase), 1,680lb (long wheelbase).

Vauxhall 30/98

Surprisingly the 30/98 Vauxhall, unlike its eternal rival, the Bentley, never raced at Le Mans, nor won a major motor race anywhere, yet competition bred it, and was the very lifeblood of this splendid Vintage sports car. It came into being quite precipitately at the whim of a prosperous North countryman, Joseph Higginson, whose talents ranged from textile engineering to inventing the Autovac, and making fast climbs of Britain's famous Shelsley Walsh hill in Worcestershire. Driving a big French 80hp La Buire, he had ascended in 64·2sec in 1912 and, seeking to improve on this performance with fewer litres, he asked L. H. Pomeroy of Vauxhall Motors if he could produce a car capable of breaking the Shelsley record, set at 63·4sec by H. C. Holder (Daimler) in 1911.

With the 1913 meeting a bare eight weeks away, Pomeroy agreed, at a fee of £2,000. He then indulged in some bold if barbaric expediency, which only a brilliant engineer such as he could contemplate, and get away with. He took a Vauxhall C-type "Prince Henry" engine —a conventional but potent 4 litre, 95 × 140mm four-cylinder side-valve unit—and converted it into a sprint special for which he would guarantee only a two-minute life. The bores were opened out to a precarious 98mm, leaving wafer-thin cylinder walls, and an unmachined C-type crankshaft was then tortured in a steam press, the throws being *cold*-stretched 5mm to gain a 150mm stroke. Thus were prototypes built!

While making one such engine, Pomeroy put through another for the works driver A. J. Hancock to use. Higginson's was fitted into a 1912 Coupe de l'Auto racing-type chassis, and clothed with a rakish aluminium sporting body able to carry four people. It weighed about 2,020lb, wore a new, flat-fronted radiator with the famous Vauxhall flutes in place of the traditional fluted vee of the Prince Henry, and in general was a very striking piece of fast Edwardian machinery. It was delivered to Higginson within six weeks of his order, giving him time for a preliminary try-out in the Waddington Fells hill climb in Lancashire, which he promptly won, watched by Pomeroy himself.

Then came Shelsley Walsh, and a story-book triumph for Higginson and

Top: *Ancestor of an illustrious British sports car, J. Higginson's prototype Vauxhall 30/98 on the line at Waddington Fells, Lancs, in 1913, when it made fastest climb of the day, first time out*

Right: *From the 4½ litre side-valve power unit of the first E-type 30/98s, the OE with overhead valves operated by tubular duralumin pushrods was evolved in 1922. The engine here is of 1926 vintage*

the new Vauxhall, with a record climb in 55·2sec, 8·2sec faster than the old figure. An elated Pomeroy returned to Luton, and in 1914 the new car went into very limited production, at a formidable £900 for the chassis alone. They called it the 30/98, although just how this designation originated is not certain, since the RAC rating was 23·8, not 30hp, and the overall output was nearer 90 than 98bhp. Some contend it was Pomeroy's frivolous retort to a powerful German rival, the Mercedes 38/90, but whatever the origin, the 30/98 as a fast tourer was destined for fame and relative fortune.

The First World War interrupted its early production, but with the return of peace the model soon established itself as the fastest catalogued British car, with 100mph guaranteed in stripped racing form. The first production model, the E-type, was built up to 1922, its long-stroke side-valve 4,525cc engine driving through a dry multi-plate clutch and a massive separate four-speed gearbox with a high (3:1) top gear. Chassis design was conventional, with semi-elliptic springs front and rear, and a sub-frame of pre-war concept for the engine. The torque from 90 horsepower in a 2,690lb car meant highly impressive acceleration, flexibility and top gear performance, and private 30/98 exponents reaped a rich harvest of hill climb and sprint successes in the early post-war seasons.

Early in 1923 a new pushrod overhead valve version of the 30/98, the OE, was introduced. The new head on the old lower half, plus the innovation of duralumin connecting rods, meant an extra 22bhp despite a shortened stroke, making the big fours from Luton smoother and more refined. However, their brakes on the rear wheels and transmission only were scarcely advanced on those of the Prince Henry of ten years earlier, and were not up to a road maximum now well in excess of 80mph.

Late in 1923, front brakes with cable operation were at last fitted, while almost at the close of the 30/98's production life, in September 1926, hydraulically-operated front brakes were standardised. By then a balanced crankshaft with bigger main bearings had further mellowed the Vauxhall's lusty four-cylinder "thump", and with well over 100bhp now, plus a new, closer ratio gearbox, the 30/98 had become vastly more refined than its illustrious namesake of 13 years earlier. It had lost nothing in speed, however; the fastest lap at Brooklands track by a side-valve E-type was 106·19mph in 1925, while the fastest OE lap was at 113·68mph in 1936.

General Motors of Detroit took over Vauxhall late in 1925, and although they did not end 30/98 production until mid-1927, the whole policy of the marque had changed, and a unique sports car departed. It is surprising that, in all, fewer than 600 30/98s were built, some 270 of them E-types and the rest OEs. That over 100 still survive, and perform nobly in Vintage car events, testifies to their rugged construction and to their inimitable charm. Aesthetically the 30/98 was immensely pleasing, enhanced by the handsome radiator well set back, a bonnet often left in bare, polished aluminium, well-proportioned bodywork, and the purposeful large-diameter wire wheels. Vauxhalls themselves produced some of the most attractive coachwork, and perhaps their four-seater "Wensum" design on the OE chassis, with vee-screen, cloverleaf tail and bold convex-curved mudguards, epitomises the car at its most handsome.

Epitome of the early Vintage era; the 30/98 Vauxhall E-type in handsome 1922 "Wensum" open 4-seater form with clover-leaf back and elegantly swept wings—a classic 80–85mph sports car in normal road trim

Specification

Engine—*E-type:* 4 cylinders in line, fixed head; 98 × 150mm, 4,525cc; sv; Zenith carburettor; Watford h.t. magneto; 5 plain main bearings; 90bhp at 3,000rpm.
OE-type: As above, but with detachable head; pushrod-operated ohv; 98 × 140mm, 4,224cc; 112bhp at 3,300rpm.
Transmission: Dry multi-plate clutch; 4-speed gearbox; open propellor shaft with torque stay.
Chassis: Pressed steel side members; semi-elliptic springing front and rear; transmission brake and internal expanding brakes on rear wheels on E-type (1914–1922); transmission brake and internal expanding brakes on front and rear wheels on OE-type (1923–1926); hydraulic operation of front-wheel and transmission brakes on OE-type (1926–1927).
Dimensions—*E-type:* Wheelbase, 9ft 8in; track, 4ft 6in; approx. dry weight, 2,670lb.
OE-type: Wheelbase, 9ft 9in; track 4ft 6in, later, 4ft 8in; approx. dry weight, 3,250lb.

Lorraine-Dietrich

The name Le Mans looms very large in the story of the sports car. It was not the world's first 24-hour race, nor at times was it the most significant or sensible, but overall no other race can approach its influence on the evolution of the high-performance road car. As a test of automotive durability it commands world-wide acclaim, and a good performance there reflects on sales of the particular car or marque, even on the prestige of its country of origin. With Britain, France, Italy, Germany and the USA all taking keen interest at different phases of its history, Le Mans rates as an immensely important International contest.

At the beginning, in 1923, the new race was for catalogued four-seater road cars, and these were much closer to standard than in later years. Among the marques trying their luck were Lorraine-Dietrich, an old-established Alsatian concern, with a trio of 15CV "torpedo" tourers. These had 3·4 litre six-cylinder engines based on a 15CV model introduced in 1920. Its designer was Marius Barbarou, a Frenchman with a distinct bias towards motor racing, even though the 15CV was intended for hard road work. He prescribed a 75 × 130mm, 3,446cc engine with overhead valves operated by curious exposed "needle" pushrods, aluminium pistons, a three-speed gearbox with central change lever, and a substantial chassis with cantilever-type rear springing and Sankey-type steel artillery wheels.

The basic concept was very American, even to employing Delco coil ignition and left-hand drive, but the handling and performance proved surprisingly good, and the engine was exceptionally flexible, saving on gear-changes and earning the model the nickname "la grimpeuse" or "the climber". In Britain it was called "The Silken Six". Durability was remarkable too, some 15CV owners claiming well over 120,000km (75,000 miles) before needing to take the engine down. Thus Barbarou had little difficulty in persuading the makers to pit their tough motor car in what promised to be a tough motor race—the first Le Mans, in 1923, when two finished 8th and 19th.

If disappointed, Barbarou was not discouraged. Instead he introduced a new sporting edition of the 15CV for 1924, boosting engine performance with twin carburettors, twin ignition, larger valves and raised compression. The chassis was lowered and shortened, Rudge-Whitworth wire wheels and four-wheel servo-assisted brakes were fitted, and handsome light sporting four-seater bodywork installed. It was catalogued as the "Sport", and three works-prepared cars ran at Le Mans in 1924, still retaining left-hand drive. This time things were much better; two Lorraines finished second and third behind a Bentley, although the third retired when leading.

The year 1925 was better still, one Lorraine winning outright at record speed, and another was third. The year 1926 was best of all, with three Lorraines sweeping home first, second and third, all averaging over 100kph, while one car also set the lap record at

Le Vainqueur: A ghosted drawing by G. Gédo of the 3½ litre Lorraine-Dietrich that beat the Bentleys at Le Mans in 1925 and 1926. This rugged French sports car featured six cylinders, pushrod ohv, Delco coil ignition, a 3-speed gearbox, cantilever rear springing and left-hand drive

114·44kph (70·95mph). The Société then marketed a "clients" replica of the Le Mans winner, a sleek and elegant machine with the same open four-seater bodywork, the same neat tail, the distinctive L-D vee-radiator with stone-guards, and the long, swept, unvalanced mudguards that typified the Le Mans car of the 1920s.

As rugged as the race winners, the replica could reach 90mph compared with their 93mph along the Mulsanne Straight at Le Mans. The engine was finished in black stoved enamel, the left-hand drive remained, and a strong point of the car, inherited from Le Mans, lay in its braking, with four large-diameter drums and a Dewandré-Repusseau servo motor. By 1928 a four-speed gearbox became optional, and more luxurious cabriolet and coupé bodywork became available. Production of the 15CV Sport continued until 1932, and a late, unexpected but welcome success for a weighty and now dating design was 22 year old Jean-Pierre Wimille's second place in the 1931 Monte Carlo Rally with a fabric coupé, beaten only by Donald Healey's 4½ litre Invicta.

Specification

Engine: 6 cylinders in line, fixed head; 75 × 130mm, 3,445cc; pushrod-operated ohv; twin Zenith carburettors; dual ignition; 4 plain main bearings; 75bhp at 3,600rpm.
Transmission: Dry single-plate clutch; 3-speed gearbox in unit with engine (4-speed gearbox optional from 1928); torque tube final drive.
Chassis: Pressed steel side members; semi-elliptic front springs, splayed cantilever rear springs; friction dampers all round; four-wheel brakes with servo-assistance.
Dimensions: Wheelbase, 9ft 5¾in; track, 4ft 7¼in.

Below: *The de Courcelles/Rossignol Lorraine-Dietrich makes a pit stop during the first Le Mans 24 Hours race of all, in 1923. It finished a modest 8th. On the right is a Vinot-Deguingand*

Alfa Romeo sixes

The name Alfa Romeo has been synonymous with sports cars for well over 50 years, making it the more ironic that so illustrious an Italian marque sprang from humble single and twin-cylinder utilitarian cars and taxis—and of French design at that. Like several other makers, Darracq of Paris sought to exploit the boom market conditions in Italy early in the century, and opened a factory there. After a brief sojourn in Naples they moved to Portello, on the edge of Milan, late in 1906, thereafter learning the hard way that the ''10/12hp'' attributed to their most powerful model just was not enough to cope with Italy's rough hilly roads.

This realisation, plus a sharp recession in 1908, saw Darracq-Italiana's hopes fall to zero, but in 1909 a new all-Italian group raised a substantial bank loan, formed the Soc. Anonima Lombarda Fabbrica Automobili (ALFA), and took over the idle Darracq factory. By 1910

they were building sturdy four-cylinder side-valve cars more suited to the terrain, and these found a ready market. By 1911 an ALFA car had contested its first Targa Florio race; it did not finish, but the fierce competitive urge which impelled the marque to such greatness began thus early.

During the First World War, ALFA was acquired by a Milan engineer and businessman, Ing Nicola Romeo. He made mining gear, railway wagons, tractors, compressors, ploughs and many other things, and by 1919 he was making cars at Portello as well, renamed Alfa Romeos. The young marque quickly showed its sporting inclinations with a fine new six-cylinder model called the Tipo RL, for which ALFA's pre-war designer, Giuseppe Merosi, was responsible. It was produced both in touring and sports forms from 1922 to 1927.

The engine, of 76 × 110mm bore and stroke and 2,994cc volume, was of

pleasingly clean external aspect and sturdy construction, and the same basic unit featured in the touring RLN (Normale) and the faster RLS (Sport). The specification included a cast-iron head, four plain main bearings, dry sump lubrication, magneto ignition and (on the Sport) twin carburettors. Transmission comprised a multi-plate clutch, a four-speed gearbox in unit with the engine, and an open propellor shaft to an underslung rear axle. The frame was typically ''vintage'', with semi-elliptic springing and friction dampers all round. Rudge-type quick-release wire wheels were fitted, and apart from early production batches, braking was on all four wheels plus transmission.

The RL Sport Tourer, which was marketed in Britain as the 22/90, wore a handsome vee-radiator and elegant sweeping wings, enhanced by some elegant open bodywork. It was a fine handling car with excellent roadholding

Left: *The heart of the vintage Alfa Romeo RL series, or 22/90 in Britain, was its 2,994cc six-cylinder engine with pushrod ohv, twin carburettors, dry sump lubrication, and basic 71bhp output. The design was notably clean externally, with plain, polished valve cover*

Below: *The vee-radiator adds to the elegance of the Weymann saloon-bodied 22/90 marketed in Britain by the London Alfa Romeo concessionaires. The large-diameter four-wheel brakes were excellent, especially with servo-assistance, while the roadholding was outstanding*

and rugged construction, marred only on Britain's easier roads by its Alpine-bred gear ratios, giving little over 50mph in third gear. With a power output of 71bhp at 3,500rpm, the car soon underwent further development for racing. A shorter, lighter chassis, boosted engine with special seven-bearing crank-shaft, and racing-type bodywork were used, and Alfa Romeo's first major race victory, in the 1923 Targa Florio in the mountains of Sicily, was scored with a 3·1 litre car of RL Sport basis.

Other victories were scored that year at Cremona, Mugello, Savio and Polesine, the last two by Enzo Ferrari, then a racing driver and later eminent among manufacturers. In 1924 Ferrari won again with an RL-based Alfa Romeo in the Coppa Acerbo at Pescara, but by then the company's main racing was concen-trated on the P2 Grand Prix cars of immortal fame. In 1925, however, the RL sports car was somewhat updated, gaining 12 more bhp and losing some 300lb in weight, which raised its maxi-mum speed from 75 to 81mph. In this form it was called the RLSS (Super Sport), a model which stayed in produc-tion until 1927 carrying a wide variety in bodywork. By then its designer, Merosi, had left Alfa Romeo, and push-rod ohv had become very much *demodé* at Portello.

Alfa Romeo had made tremendous advances since 1922, their supercharged

eight-cylinder 2-litre twin-cam P2 racing cars winning two major Grands Prix in 1924, and two more in 1925, when they gained the World Championship title. Chiefly responsible for their design was Vittorio Jano, who earlier had worked with Fiat on their racing cars, and was well indoctrinated with the virtues of overhead camshafts. His first non-racing design for Alfa Romeo was an advanced 1½ litre six-cylinder single overhead camshaft unit which powered a lively touring car, the Tipo 6C Turismo of 1927.

The 62 × 88mm engine had a five plain bearing crankshaft which con-tributed to its very smooth running, and produced some 44bhp at 4,200rpm, enabling it to propel even a long-chassis five-seater saloon at over 60mph. A twin-cam edition was inevitable from Jano and a performance-minded marque such as Alfa Romeo, and his Tipo 6C 1500 Sport appeared early in 1928. This offered a brisk 54bhp at 4,500rpm, in a low-built, semi-elliptically sprung chassis with 9ft 6in wheelbase. Jano's next step was to fit a Roots-type super-charger, raising output to 76bhp and maximum speed to over 90mph, and the engine with its shapely finned manifolds and aluminium cam covers expressed sheer artistry both inside and outside.

Such a car, the "Super Sport", simply had to be raced, and with a choice of Europe's finest drivers, 1928 brought a

Among the fastest of the six-cylinder pushrod ohv sports Alfa Romeos of the Vintage decade was the RL SS (Super Sport) "Gran Premio" spyder of 1926–27, possessing a maximum road speed of well over 80mph

welter of successes for Alfa Romeo, including outright victories in the Italian 1000 Miles race (the famous Mille Miglia), Belgian 24 Hours, Boillot Cup and the Six Hours race at Brooklands. The eternal quest for more performance brought an increase in capacity on all six-cylinder engines for 1929. The twin-cam supercharged "1750" was now an exhilarating 85bhp, 95mph road car, bearing some glorious bodywork in Latin style, typified by the Zagato "Spider" flared two-seater. Like the famous 1926–27 Grand Prix Delage, its chassis, either with 9ft or 9ft 6in wheel-base, virtually undulated over bumpy roads, being designed to allow a degree of flexing, while the balance and hand-ling, in conjunction with finger-light high-geared steering, was superb.

Race victories fell thick and fast to the fleet red Alfas; the Mille Miglia, Irish GP and Belgian 24 Hours in 1929, and the Mille Miglia and Belgian "24" yet again in 1930, when the Italian team also came to Ulster and scored a vastly impressive 1-2-3 in the TT race. At a time when, elsewhere in Europe, big

Bentleys and even bigger Mercedes-Benz rated as the ultimate in sports cars, these smaller, more agile Alfas were a revelation in precise handling and efficient high performance. Despite the apparent complications of twin cams and superchargers they were outstandingly reliable without the need for frequent servicing and attention which might have been expected.

By 1931 factory attention at Portello had turned fully to the new Jano-designed straight-eights. Small scale production of the six-cylinder 1750s continued until 1933, however, and many examples still survive today, cherished by their loving owners for the works of mechanical art they unquestionably are. The spectacle of those superb twin-cam blown cars in racing action cannot be re-enacted, but fortunately their glorious sound can still be heard. Pat Braden, vintage secretary of the Alfa Romeo Owners' Club of America, wrote of it as follows:

"It is rhapsodically indescribable. Each moving part including, I think, each ball in every bearing in the camshaft drive, makes its own audible report; a mechanical fugue that is deafening at 4,000rpm. Superlatives pale in the reality of those sounds. But then the whole car is that way, and every time I slide into it and start it, the ennui of everyday living vanishes, and the thrill is fresh and new once more."

Italian classic: The Tipo 6C 1750 Alfa Romeo of 1929 with 1,752cc six-cylinder twin ohc super-charged engine. It is seen in Super Sport form just after winning Italy's 1,000 mile Mille Miglia road race, driven by Giuseppe Campari. The striking spyder two-seater bodywork with distinctive sweeping wings is by Zagato, who set a styling fashion widely admired

Blown twin-cam: the exquisite Jano-designed 1½ litre six-cylinder twin ohc Tipo 6C "Super Sport" Alfa Romeo, X-rayed by Max Millar of The Autocar in its 1929 competition form when it won the first Double 12 Hours race, held at Brooklands track

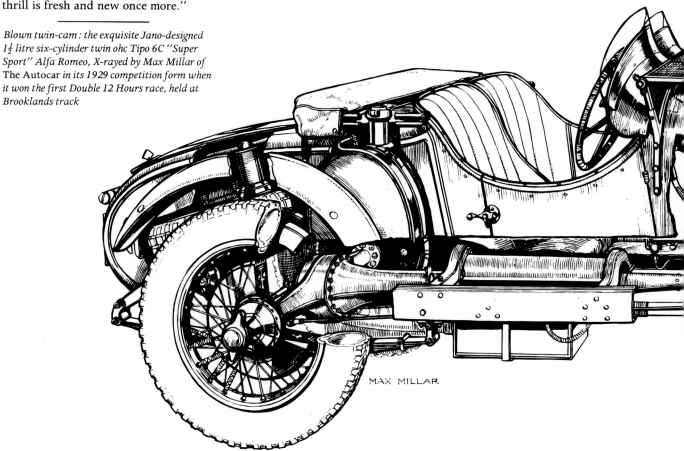

MAX MILLAR

Specification

Tipo RL

Engine: 6 cylinders in line; 76 × 110mm, 2,994cc; pushrod-operated ohv; twin carburettors; magneto ignition; 4 plain main bearings; 71bhp at 3,500rpm (RL Sport); 83bhp at 3,600rpm (RL Super Sport).

Transmission: Dry multi-plate clutch; 4-speed gearbox in unit with engine; open propellor shaft.

Chassis: Pressed steel side members; semi-elliptic springing front and rear; transmission brake and internal expanding brakes on rear wheels up to September 1923, on all four wheels thereafter.

Dimensions: Wheelbase, 10ft 3in; track, 4ft 9½in; approx. car weight, 3,920lb (RL Sport), 3,580lb (RL Super Sport).

Tipo 6C

Engine—*1500 Sport:* 6 cylinders in line; 62 × 82mm, 1,487cc; shaft-and-bevel driven 2ohc; single carburettor; coil and distributor ignition; 5 plain main bearings; 54bhp at 4,500rpm.

1500 Super Sport: As above, but with Roots-type supercharger, 76bhp at 4,800rpm.

1750 Sport: As 1500 Sport, but 65 × 88mm, 1,752cc; 55bhp at 4,400rpm.

1750 Super Sport: As 1750 Sport, but with Roots-type supercharger; 85bhp at 4,500rpm.

Transmission: Dry multi-plate clutch; 4-speed gearbox in unit with engine, torque tube final drive.

Chassis: Pressed steel side members; semi-elliptic springs front and rear, friction dampers; internal expanding brakes on all wheels.

Dimensions: Wheelbase, 9ft 6in or 9ft 0in; track, 4ft 6in.

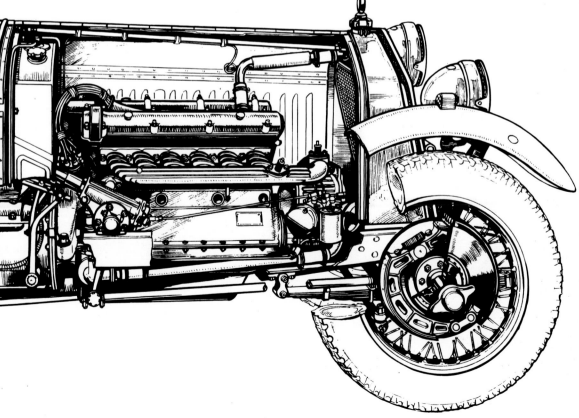

Bentley

The 3 Litre

One of the saddest things about the Cricklewood-built Bentley—Britain's great "Wearer of the Green"—was its short life span of a mere 12 years, compared with M.G. (over 50), Jaguar (over 40), or Lotus (nearly 30). Yet no marque packed more adventure into its career, nor more aptly epitomised the classic between-the-wars sports car. The fact that Walter Owen Bentley ("W.O."), a lover of steam locomotives, built his cars *strong* may have drawn cutting comments such as Ettore Bugatti's concerning "the fastest lorries in Europe", but it also meant they won Le Mans 24 Hour races, not once but *five* times and, further, that their cars lasted a long time, as evidenced by the large number still around, over 50 years after they were built, keeping the great name evergreen.

The idea of a fast sporting car for fast, sporting people developed in W.O.'s mind during the First World War, when

Starting a tradition: The first Le Mans 24 Hours race was held in 1923—and a 3 litre Bentley took part, a lone British entry against one Belgian and 31 French cars. Driven by Duff and Clement it finished 5th after delays through a holed fuel tank, but the same car won in 1924

he was working on the Bentley rotary aero-engine used in Sopwith Camels and other prominent fighter aircraft. When peace returned, Bentley Motors Ltd was founded and built a prototype chassis with four-cylinder 3-litre engine just in time for the 1919 Olympia Show. Some engine parts had still not been delivered, however, so they simulated the sump, cam casing and one or two other components in wood, and the keen interest shown was ample encouragement to plunge into production.

The first 3 litre Bentley sold was delivered in September 1921. Its engine, 80 × 149mm in bore and stroke, was redolent of 1914 racing practice, having a single shaft-driven overhead camshaft operating four narrow-angled overhead valves in each cylinder head. Ignition was by twin magnetos and eight sparking plugs, and aluminium pistons and a five-bearing crankshaft featured. About 70bhp was realised initially at 3,500rpm, the exhaust emitting a stirring "four cylinder thump", the thrust passing via a cone clutch and a separate four-speed gearbox to a spiral bevel final drive.

With its engine set well back in a typically "Vintage" chassis with semi-elliptics all round, rakish open body-work, Rudge wire wheels, swept wings and beautifully proportioned vee-

radiator, the 3 litre Bentley was a bewitchingly handsome sporting machine, superbly made, and with a performance living up to its looks. In roadholding, liveliness and acceleration, particularly in the middle range, it seemed absolutely born to be raced; and raced it was, without delay, for W.O., a pre-war racing man, well knew the value of racing both as a design testbed and for publicity.

Beginning in 1921 with sprints and hill climbs, Bentleys won their first races at Brooklands track, then placed second, fourth and fifth and won the team prize in the 1922 Isle of Man TT. Next, private owner John Duff and Woolf Barnato took the British Double 12 hours record at Brooklands at 86·79mph, a feat encouraging Duff to tackle the new French endurance race, the Le Mans 24 Hours, in 1923. He finished fourth, and went back there in 1924, a single British car against 40 French ones—and won outright.

Although Bentleys had assisted Duff in his Le Mans efforts, they took an official interest from 1925, running their own car alongside his. However, Bentley lost the race to the French Lorraine-Dietrich team, both that year and in 1926, when the surviving car, fighting for second place but almost

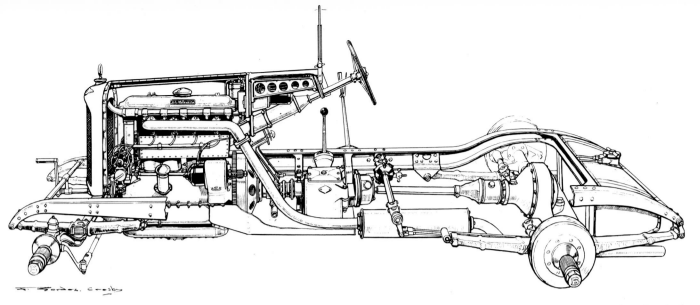

The chassis of the first Bentley, the 3 litre, laid bare to show disposition of its four-cylinder single ohc engine, separate 4-speed gearbox and open propellor shaft final drive. Over 1,600 3 litre Bentleys were built between 1921 and 1927, many still surviving today in rugged good health

brakeless, buried itself in a sandbank only 20 minutes from the end. 1927 saw the epic White House corner mix-up, when two French cars and all three Bentleys—one a new 4½ litre car—crashed into each other, and S. C. H. (Sammy) Davis extracted his battered 3 litre from the wreckage, made for the pits for jury repairs, rejoined the race, and won.

That dramatic victory, achieved despite a twisted chassis, cracked steering arm joint, bent front axle, battered wing and broken headlamp, brought splendid publicity for the marque Bentley, but it was the 3 litre's last Le Mans, the car being superseded in racing by newer, larger models. On the production side, however, the 3 litre was built until late 1928, over 1,600 being sold in three wheelbases, and bearing very varied bodywork, ranging from open two-seaters to lofty saloons, by the best of British vintage coachbuilders. And like every Cricklewood-built Bentley, each one had a five-year guarantee, in testimony to W. O. Bentley's confidence in the longevity of his cars.

Specification—3 litre
Engine: 4 cylinders in line, fixed head; 80 × 149mm, 2,996cc; single shaft-driven ohc operating 4 overhead valves per cylinder; single carburettor (twin carburettors on high-performance models; two ML magnetos; 2 plugs per cylinder; 5-bearing crankshaft; 80bhp at 3,500rpm (up to 1925), 85bhp at 3,500rpm (from 1925).
Transmission: Cone clutch; separate 4-speed gearbox; propellor shaft final drive.

Chassis: Pressed steel side members; semi-elliptic springing front and rear, friction dampers; rear-wheel brakes only to mid-1923, 4-wheel brakes after mid-1923.
Dimensions: Wheelbase, 9ft 9½in (Short Standard, TT and Speed model), 10ft 10½in (Long Standard), 9ft 0in (Super-Sports); track, 4ft 8in; approx. car weight, 2,912–3,192lb (Short Standard, TT and Speed model), 3,700lb (Long Standard), 2,970lb (Super-Sports).
Le Mans Cars: As above, but approx. 88bhp at 3,500rpm; wheelbase, 9ft 9½in.

The 6½ Litre
Like that other eminent designer, Dr Ferdinand Porsche, W. O. Bentley preferred big, relatively unstressed engines to small, busy ones. He had envisaged a smoother, more powerful Bentley ever since seeing the 3 litre chassis overloaded with heavy-four-door saloon bodywork. This indicated a widening in Bentley clientele from the sporting types who enjoyed open sports cars, to include many who enjoyed brisk performance in more civilised forms, with doors, windows and a roof. Production of a longer-chassis 3 litre was but a part-answer, excess weight diminishing its performance, and in 1924 W.O.'s thoughts turned to something better able to combine luxury with Bentley-style performance.

Six cylinders would mean smoother power impulses, and with this and cost in mind, his first step was to add two cylinders to the 80 × 149mm 3 litre engine, producing a prototype six with slightly shorter stroke and a capacity of 4¼ litres. With a ponderous saloon body and an ugly radiator as disguise, the car, registered as a "Sun", was taken by W.O. and others for extensive testing in France. There, by sheer chance, they met an equally experimental Rolls-Royce, a prototype of the Phantom 1, and the resultant impromptu race revealed their respective speeds to be

almost identical. W.O. therefore decided that the new Bentley six needed more litres, and upped the bore from 80 to 100mm, getting a capacity of 6,597cc.

For rigidity an eight-bearing crankshaft was employed, and the cylinder block and valve gear followed 3 litre pattern, although the vertical camshaft drive was replaced by three-throw coupling rods and eccentrics, driven through a gear-wheel off the crankshaft at the rear of the engine. This was an expensive but effective means of reducing mechanical noise. The engine was also mounted on rubber bushes to diminish vibration, well before Chrysler "invented" the system with their "Floating Power" of 1932.

Development of this design brought few problems other than of finance—a weak point with Bentley Motors—and the first 6½ litre Bentley was shown at Olympia in 1925. Three wheelbases were available, and large diameter brakes with servo assistance coped with an 85mph car weighing well over 2 tons. First deliveries began early in 1926, but some 2½ years elapsed before a sporting version, the Speed Six, appeared in October 1928. This differed from the standard model in wheelbase, 11ft 8½in or 12ft 8½in being available, and with twin vertical SU carburettors and other refinements power output was some 13bhp up on the normal 147bhp. Self-wrapping brakes and a modified radiator were fitted, and the Speed Six emerged as a fast, expensive grand tourer for long-distance travel, with a 92mph maximum. Perhaps its most memorable feature was its astonishing flexibility, achieved through sheer abundance of power.

When, after 1928, opposition at Le Mans made it clear that Bentleys needed more power and speed, W.O. turned to the Speed Six as the most logical source. A special short chassis with 11ft wheelbase was made, and new single port block and induction manifold evolved, while raised compression, different valves, stronger connecting rods and special rockers all contributed to the 200bhp realised. The competition Speed Six proved immensely successful, winning Le Mans for Britain both in 1929 and 1930, and also the 1929 Six Hours and 1930 Double 12, both at Brooklands, while track versions placed 2nd in the 1929 500 Miles race, and won that race outright in 1931—after Bentley Motors had gone into liquidation, one of the saddest victims of the world trade depression.

Specification—6½ litre

Engine: 6 cylinders in line, fixed head; 100 × 140mm, 6,597cc; ohc with three-throw coupling rod drive, operating 4 ohv per cylinder; twin SU carburettors; ignition by single magneto and Delco coil; 2 plugs per cylinder; 8-bearing crankshaft; 160bhp at 3,500rpm (180bhp with single-port block).

The glory that was England's—and Bentley's: the invincible 6½ litre Speed Sixes sweeping on to a 1-2 Le Mans victory in 1930—the fifth and last great triumph by the Bentley marque, doomed for extinction the following year

Transmission: Single dry-plate clutch; separate 4-speed gearbox; propellor shaft final drive.
Chassis: Pressed steel side members; semi-elliptic springing front and rear, friction dampers; self-wrapping brakes to all wheels.
Dimensions: Wheelbase, 11ft 8½in or 12ft 8½in; track, 4ft 8in; approx. car weight, 4,700–5,040lb with open bodywork.
Le Mans Cars: As above, but 200bhp at 3,500rpm; wheelbase, 11ft 0in.

The 4½ Litre

Although it inherited the 100 × 140mm bore and stroke of the six-cylinder 6½ litre Bentley, the 4½ litre four-cylinder model introduced in 1927 was virtually an enlarged 3 litre. The fixed head, single overhead camshaft with vertical shaft drive, and four valves per cylinder all remained, but the swept volume of the engine was 4,379cc, giving a vigorous and thoroughly dependable 105bhp at 3,500rpm. With a 10ft 10½in wheelbase, the chassis could accommodate the most luxurious of bodywork, yet the standard "4½" exceeded 90mph without fuss or strain.

As ever, racing assisted its development. The performance of the winning 3½ litre six-cylinder Lorraines highlighted the 3 litre Bentley's power limi-

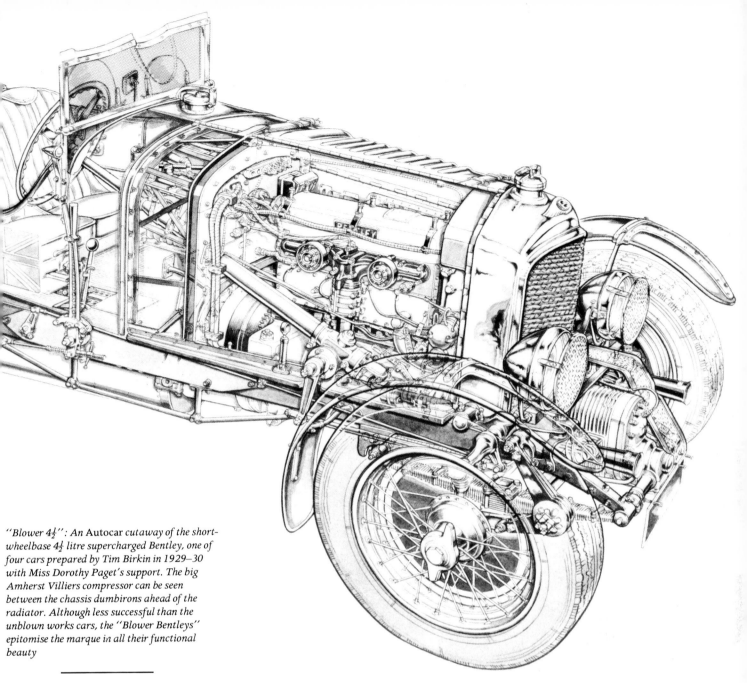

"Blower 4½": An Autocar *cutaway of the short-wheelbase 4½ litre supercharged Bentley, one of four cars prepared by Tim Birkin in 1929–30 with Miss Dorothy Paget's support. The big Amherst Villiers compressor can be seen between the chassis dumbirons ahead of the radiator. Although less successful than the unblown works cars, the "Blower Bentleys" epitomise the marque in all their functional beauty*

tations, but Bentley's own six cylinder, the 6½ litre, was nowhere near ready for racing by 1927. An enlargement of the four cylinder unit was W.O.'s logical solution to the problem, and the first engines were put through in the autumn of 1926, using some 3 litre parts and 6½ litre-type connecting rods. A 3 litre-type chassis, axles and transmission were employed, and a larger radiator and rear fuel tank fitted.

The prototype comfortably led the 1927 Le Mans race for 35 laps, only to be eliminated in the notorious White House crash. After repairs, the same car won a lesser 24 hours race, the Grand Prix de Paris at Montlhéry two months later, and the first production 4½ litre Bentley was shown at Olympia in 1927. Bigger and more imposing than the 3 litre, it had a broader radiator more in proportion with its dimensions, and in handling and road behaviour the 4½

quickly won friends for its flexibility and responsiveness. It could reach 60mph from a standstill in about 15sec, and achieved its maximum of 92mph without stress. At the same time "that bloody thump" which pleased one customer, steam wagon builder E. R. Foden, was inescapable evidence that beneath the long bonnet beat a big "four".

Bentley's racing drivers loved the 4½ litre for its tangible power and inherent stability engendered by what today is known as understeer. For the 1928 Le Mans race, three 4½ litre Bentleys were entered, and as a useful dress rehearsal these ran in the Brooklands Six Hours race a month earlier. Compared with the production model the cars had higher compression, vertical SU carburettors, closer gear ratios and improved braking. The race was run on a class handicap system, and although

the Bentley trio scored 1-2-3 in the unlimited category, and Tim Birkin made the fastest race average, overall victory went to a 1½ litre twin-cam Alfa Romeo—a portent of the future.

At Le Mans they met opposition from another source—the big American 4·9 litre straight-eight Stutz—and only after a tremendous struggle did one 4½ litre Bentley win precariously, its frame cracked and its radiator empty, with the Stutz only eight miles behind in 24 hours. By 1929 the new Bentley Speed Six was ready for racing, but a "4½" placed second to an Alfa Romeo in the first Brooklands Double 12 Hours race. At Le Mans the big new six outpaced all opposition, but three 4½ litre cars completed Bentley's greatest triumph by following home in 2nd, 3rd and 4th places. To cap its achievements, one of the 4½ Le Mans cars stripped of fittings and with a long tail, won the first 500

Colourful combination: Tim Birkin in the 4½ litre Bentley at Le Mans, 1928. In his beloved role of pacemaker, trying to break up the Stutz opposition, Birkin broke a wheel after puncturing. He finally finished 5th, making fastest lap, while another 4½ litre Bentley won

Miles race at Brooklands in October, 1929, averaging 107·32mph.

That long, hard race emphasised the Bentley's *forte*—the reserve strength in chassis and suspension to withstand the cruel repetitive pounding of Brooklands track for over five hours, and of the engine to maintain high revs for seemingly endless laps. Such reserves kept ordinary production Bentleys on the road long after frailer cars of other makes had broken or worn out.

Specification—4½ Litre
Engine: 4 cylinders in line, fixed head; 100 × 140mm, 4,398cc; single shaft-driven ohc operating 4 valves per cylinder; twin carburettors; 2 ML magnetos; 2 plugs per cylinder; 5-bearing crankshaft; 105–110bhp at 3,500rpm.
Transmission: Cone clutch; separate 4-speed gearbox; propellor shaft final drive.
Chassis: Pressed steel side members; semi-elliptic springing front and rear, friction dampers; four-wheel brakes, self-wrapping at front from 1929.
Dimensions: Wheelbase, 10ft 10½in (Standard), 9ft 9½in (Short); track, 4ft 8in; approx. car weight, 3,640lb (Standard), 3,470lb (Short).
Le Mans Cars: As above, but approx. 130bhp at 3,500rpm; wheelbase, 10ft 10½in.

Supercharged Cars—*Standard:* As above, but with Amherst Villiers supercharger; 175bhp at 3,500rpm. Wheelbase, 10ft 10½in or 9ft 9½in.
Le Mans Cars: As above, but 210bhp at 3,500rpm.

The Supercharged 4½ Litre
Although W. O. Bentley was unhappy about it, H. R. S. (Tim) Birkin went ahead with his project to supercharge the 4½ litre Bentley. With financial support from the Hon Dorothy Paget, a special private team was formed, based at Welwyn Garden City, and the engineer Amherst Villiers redesigned the engine to absorb the extra stresses of a huge Villiers finned compressor, installed between the front chassis dumbirons. Twin SU carburettors, and special crankshaft, main and big-end bearings and connecting rods were featured, and an output of over 200bhp was achieved, comparing very well with the circa 125bhp of the unblown Le Mans engine, although driving the blower itself expended 35bhp.

Four cars were laid down, two using the standard 4½ chassis with 10ft 10in wheelbase, and two with 9ft 9½in wheelbase. Birkin's ambitions centred on racing, including the Le Mans 24 Hours for which it was necessary to produce at least 50 examples of the Blower Bentley for sale to customers. Woolf Barnato, who had financed Bentley Motors since 1926, was persuaded by Birkin to

authorise their construction, and W.O. had perforce to accept the situation, while maintaining that the best way to gain more speed was to increase engine size rather than increase its internal stresses.

Although they were very fast, and presented the most purposeful and imposing appearance of any road racing Bentley, the "Blower 4½s" never attained the reliability of the unblown works cars. Both the short-chassis cars entered for Le Mans in 1930 failed, although one set the record lap, and their best performance elsewhere was, ironically, in the French Grand Prix for racing cars, held that year at Pau. Birkin in a "Blower" stripped of wings, lights and other accoutrements finished a strong second to a Bugatti, with a string of Bugattis behind him. A special single-seater Bentley with a blown 4½ litre engine subsequently broke the Brooklands record twice in Birkin's hands.

The fifty production Blower Bentleys were duly manufactured, over half of them having Van den Plas open four-seater bodies, while open two-seater, coupé and Weymann saloon bodywork featured among the rest. About 175bhp was achieved, and these magnificent looking cars proved more reliable than might be expected considering their complications, and surprisingly docile to handle despite their formidable potential. A few examples survive today, and rate as almost priceless rarities.

Stutz Straight 8

American sports cars were a rarity indeed during the 1920s, the US motor industry being chiefly absorbed in quantity production of basic automobiles for world markets. The famous Mercer Raceabout and its great protagonist of pre-1918 days, the Stutz Bearcat, had both disappeared, and while Mercer themselves had wasted away by 1925, that same year brought an unexpected Stutz revival. Harry C. Stutz had left the firm he founded after the First World War, the Indianapolis-based company being taken over by a steel tycoon, Charles Schwab, who in 1925 appointed Frederic E. Moscovics as the new Stutz president.

Moscovics came from the neighbouring Marmon company, where among other things he had projected a new, safe, high-performance car with an eight-cylinder overhead camshaft engine and underslung worm rear drive to secure a low chassis line. Marmon declined to build it, but Schwab gave his new president sanction to produce the car under the Stutz banner, backing him, moreover, with a strong engineering and development team which included the former Métallurgique designer, Paul Bastien from Belgium.

Non-conformist: A refreshing departure from the average quantity-produced American car of the period, the 4·9 litre straight-eight ohc Stutz was formidable enough to challenge the Bentleys at Le Mans. Illustrated is the 1928 chassis with 3-speed gearbox and hydraulic brakes; 4 speeds and twin ohc evolved later

The Stutz "Vertical 8" with "safety chassis" duly appeared at the 1926 New York Auto Show, where its low build and bold specification created a sensation. It had a 4·7 litre in-line, eight-cylinder 16-valve engine designed by chief engineer Charles Greuter, with a single overhead camshaft driven by tensioned double chains, and a statically and dynamically balanced nine-bearing crankshaft, aluminium-alloy connecting rods, and dual ignition with two plugs per cylinder. All this, from the land of iron side-valve "cooking" engines, was highly enterprising, although offset on the first car by a turgid three-speed gearbox and heavy sedan bodywork.

Yet it could top 77mph, was ahead of its time in having hydraulic brakes, (albeit of unusual Timken hydrostatic type employing water and alcohol) and centralised chassis lubrication, while the double-drop frame and low build made the car commendably stable and pleasing to handle. In 1927 Moscovics yielded to temptation and introduced a special four-seater boat-tailed Speedster with a 4·9 litre, 95bhp engine. They called it the Black Hawk, a model which thrust rudely into the AAA stock racing class that year, winning every race bar one, chiefly at the expense of the rival Auburns.

For 1928 the brilliant young driver and engineer Frank Lockhart helped in improving the porting and carburation of the engine, raising output to 115bhp. Stutz put the engine into a new boat-tail two-seater with proper Lockheed

hydraulic brakes and improved aero-dynamics, and confronted Auburn's own boat-tail in the Daytona flying mile sprints, clocking 106·53mph to Auburn's 104·34mph. Then Moscovics challenged Hispano-Suiza to a 24 hours duel at Indianapolis, and lost $25,000 when the Black Hawk broke a valve. Despite this apparent defeat, Charles Weymann, owner of the winning Hispano and creator of the famous Weymann light-weight fabric-on-wood coachwork, was so impressed by the Stutz performance before it broke down that he bought one and took it to Europe to race at Le Mans in June.

His drivers, Bloch and Brisson, were seasoned Le Mans competitors who withstood the Bentley onslaught, took the Stutz down the straights at an impressively quiet 100mph, made full use of its cornering ability, and finished a magnificent second in spite of having three speeds only and a top gear which had to be held in by hand for the last four hours. Brisson then drove the car at Comminges in the French Grand Prix, run that year for sports cars, and took third place, while a British-entered Black Hawk placed third in class in the Ulster TT race, all of which, in a fiercely competitive sphere disputed by Bentley, Mercedes-Benz, Alfa Romeo etc. was stimulatingly un-American at that time.

Having thus burst upon the European sporting scene, Stutz sold quite a few Black Hawks in Europe, the low, elegant American cars vying well with the best European marques on the social sporting

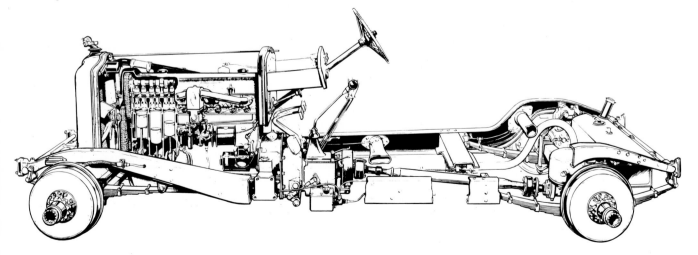

The big, black Stutz of Brisson/Rigal in the early stages of the 1930 Le Mans 24 Hours. With its 5·3 litre twin ohc 32-valve engine this car should have worried the Bentleys, but unluckily was involved in a fire incident, being almost destroyed when the fuel tank exploded

scene. But Le Mans now had Stutz in its grip, and for the 1929 race there were more surprises. Three Stutz were entered this time, a new close-ratio four-speed gearbox had been built, and the single-cam engine was enlarged to 5·3 litres and fitted with a supercharger! The Roots-type blower was fitted between the front dumbirons, a long induction pipe linking it with the carburettor, through which it blew in Mercedes-Benz style; it also followed Mercedes practice in being engaged at will by the driver through a control on the dashboard.

Blower pressure was only 4psi and in tests at Montlhéry before the 24 Hours race its performance proved disappointing. It was decided, accordingly, to run two cars without the blowers, but Brisson and Chiron in the fastest Stutz retained theirs. After an early delay for plugs, Brisson pushed the car hard to keep up with the Bentleys, keeping the supercharger in for long spells. The exhaust pipe became red-hot, and at the next refuel stop some fuel spilled, the car burst into flame, and eventually had to be retired. Only one Stutz survived the 24 hours, struggling home fifth after much plug trouble—a disappointing

result for the Americans.

They tried yet again in 1930. This time the blowers were discarded, but there was a fresh surprise under their big black bonnets—a new twin overhead camshaft head with four valves per cylinder and an exciting 150-plus bhp under the driver's right foot. Two cars ran, but again a fire incident ruined their chances. Brisson's co-driver, Rigal, ran briefly off the road and damaged the exhaust system; he wired it up, but it fell off again at full speed, the car caught fire, the fuel tank exploded, and the Stutz was virtually destroyed. The other car broke its axle, and although Brisson tackled Le Mans yet again in 1931 and 1932 with the Stutz, the factory took little further part in the operation.

They concentrated instead on getting the twin-cam 32-valve DV32 into production in 1931, fitting the race-developed four-speed gearbox, and introducing a special open model with cutaway doors called the Bearcat—a revival of the pre-war name. The new car was guaranteed to attain 100mph in fourth gear, and was supplemented by a shorter, still faster model, the Super Bearcat, with 116in wheelbase. The four-speed gearbox proved to be rather wasted on unappreciative owners who relied on the big straight-eight's ample torque rather than change down. Thus, when seeking a means of cutting costs in bleak 1932, Stutz replaced it with a three-speed synchromesh gearbox.

Alongside the exotic DV32, single-

cam 16-valve models were still offered, both types being available with superb coachwork by the best American *carrossiers* such as Le Baron, Fleetwood and Rollston, and the finest European houses. But the times were sternly against the luxury sporting automobile market, sales dropped alarmingly, and sadly, private car production was finished for Stutz by 1935. Not for another 18 years did another real American sports car appear. And not for another 31 years did another American car improve on the Stutz performance at Le Mans.

Specification

Engine: 8 cylinders in line, detachable head; 82·5 × 114·3mm, 4,888cc (1927–28); 84·5 × 114·3mm, 5,350cc (1929–34); single chain-driven ohc operating 2 valves per cylinder; chain-driven 2 ohc operating 4 valves per cylinder on 1931–34 DV32 models; twin carburettors; dual Delco-Remy coil ignition; 2 plugs per cylinder; 9-bearing crankshaft. *4,888cc unit:* 95bhp at 3,200rpm in 1927, 115bhp at 3,600rpm in 1928. *5,350cc 16 valve unit:* 113bhp at 3,300rpm. *5,350cc 32 valve unit:* 156bhp at 3,900rpm.
Transmission: Multi-plate clutch; 3-speed gearbox in unit with engine (4-speed gearbox from 1929–31); underslung worm final drive.
Chassis: Pressed steel side members; semi-elliptic springs and friction dampers front and rear in 1927, hydraulic dampers from 1928; Timken hydrostatic brakes (1927), Lockheed hydraulic brakes (from late 1927).
Dimensions: Wheelbase, 11ft 2in (two- and four-seater Black Hawk, Bearcat, etc); 9ft 8in (Super Bearcat); front track, 4ft 8½in; rear track, 4ft 10½in.

Mercedes-Benz S models

Speaking, as we are told he did, of "the fastest lorries in Europe", Ettore Bugatti might well have lumped the great white Mercedes-Benz alongside the big green Bentleys. The German *sportwagenen* were just as rugged as their British rivals, and even faster, epitomising the pre-scientific age of heavy, cart-sprung, brute-powered "monsters". The four models that strike such awe in vintage buffs, the S, SS, SSK and SSKL, each progressively more potent and imposing, all sprang from a big 6·2 litre, overhead camshaft six-cylinder touring car, designed in 1924 by Dr Ferdinand Porsche.

Three big white supercharged Mercedes-Benz occupy the front row at the opening meeting at Germany's new Nürburgring in June 1927. Nos. 1 and 2 are the latest 6·8 litre Model S works cars which placed 1-2; No. 3 is an older, privately owned Model K

The car's designation, 24/100/140, recorded its potential with Teutonic thoroughness; 24 for its taxable horse-power; 100 for the bhp without use of the supercharger; 140 for its maximum supercharged output. It was a heavy car, easily able to carry six-seat limousine coachwork, but its supercharged performance made it lamentably under-braked. While striving to remedy this, Porsche at the same time produced a shorter chassis version termed the K (ie *Kurz* or short) or, in Britain, the 33/180, a car which gave distinct promise as a sporting machine.

When Mercedes and Benz combined in July 1926, their chief engineer Dr Porsche obtained permission to further develop a sports car, suitable both to race and to sell. Mercedes were pioneers, of course, in the art of supercharging, and it was their practice to instal the Roots-type blower vertically, ahead of

the engine block, and compress air into single or twin sealed carburettors, rather than "inhale" through them and compress the mixture, as other exponents did. Moreover, the Mercedes blower, which ran at approximately three times engine speed, was not in permanent engagement but was brought into action via a clutch by full depression of the accelerator pedal—when the normally throaty exhaust roar was augmented by a blood-curdling wail, adding to the sheer awe inspired by these legendary Mercs.

While Porsche's *leitmotiv* in developing the big ohc sixes was frankly racing, that of Mercedes-Benz was naturally prestige and sales, and in those hard times they had to keep a tightish financial rein on their chief engineer. The shrewd Porsche foresaw the waning popularity of Grand Prix racing through excessive cost, and the corresponding spread of sports car racing in Europe, which began,

Unique unit: The great single ohc Mercedes-Benz engine designed by Dr. Porsche, in 7·1 litre SS form (38/250 in the UK), showing the vertical Roots-type supercharger which blew through twin Pallas carburettors, and was brought into action by full depression of the accelerator pedal

appositely, in Germany itself. His first step in boosting the K's performance was to increase engine size to 6·8 litres, revise and lower the chassis, improve weight distribution, and fit better brakes.

The resultant Model S had some 180bhp under its vast bonnet, ample for Mercedes-Benz to score outright wins, both in the opening race on the fantastic new Nürburgring circuit in June 1927, and in the subsequent German Grand Prix on the same course. The S was exported to Britain, France and elsewhere as the 36/220 with 11ft 8in wheelbase, a heavy but dramatic-looking car, especially in open four-seater form with long, convex-section mudguards and angled spare wheel on the tail, the big engine providing stirring acceleration with the blower at work, and a maximum speed of around 110mph—with that *noise*!

Porsche next advanced to the SS (or 38/250), opening out the bore to achieve 7·1 litres and over 200bhp *mit kompressor*. The drill for use of this device

was quite rigorous; when engaging it, pressure on the throttle pedal had to be firm to avoid slipping the drive-clutch, while it was not intended to be operative for periods of more than 15 to 20 seconds at a time, chiefly to improve acceleration—which it did with tremendous effect, albeit with alarming fuel consumption. Nor was the *kompressor* to be used on ordinary fuel, a 50-50 benzole mixture being essential to keep internal engine temperatures healthy. The standard blower gave approx. 8psi, but a larger unit, used on the factory racers, raised this to 10psi.

When three SS Mercedes, so equipped, took the first three places in the 1928 German GP at Nürburgring, critics sniffed and commented that a car can always win more easily in its own country. That was answered in the following year, when the great Caracciola took an SS to Northern Ireland for the 1929 Ulster TT and vanquished eight rival Italian Alfa Romeos, five French Bugattis and five home-based Bentleys to score an unforgettable victory on wet roads. By then the Porsche wand had waved again, producing the still more potent SSK, with 17 inches less wheelbase (the K denoting *Kurz* for short again), less weight, still more power and a 126mph maximum. An SSK came an

astonishing third in the sinuous round-the-houses Monaco GP in 1929, beat the Bentleys, Alfas and Bugattis again in the 1930 Irish GP in Phoenix Park, Dublin, and won the 1931 Belgian 24 Hours race.

As a very limited production two-seater sports car, or as a close-coupled drophead coupe, the SSK has been described in fun as "the largest car with the least luggage space", yet it was a magnificent, superbly engineered and vastly covetable machine for the sportsman who knew how to drive it. He needed skill and a deft feel to keep out of trouble and get the best out of his steed, but in reward knew the inexpressible thrill of boundless, very audible power coupled with superb "vintage" road-holding and steering. The SSK was a fitting climax to Dr Porsche's work with Mercedes-Benz, whom he left late in 1928, but the design was further tweaked for racing by his successor.

This was Dr Nibel, who produced the astonishing SSKL (L meaning *Leicht* or light), with copiously drilled short chassis, and the legendary "Elephant" supercharger working at 12psi and giving a ferocious 265bhp or more. Running as a fully-equipped sports car it won Italy's famed Mille Miglia 1000 Miles race in 1931, while stripped for Grand Prix racing it won the Avus,

Eifel and German GPs that same year. No SSKL was ever supplied to a private owner except for racing, but final testimony to its potential came in 1932 when a privately prepared car with special single-seater body won the Avus GP at no less than 120·7mph average, reaching 143mph along the straights.

Specification

Engine: 6 cylinders in line, detachable head; 98 × 150mm, 6,789cc (Model S); 100 × 150mm, 7,069cc (Models SS, SSK, SSKL); wet cylinder liners in light-alloy block; single shaft-driven ohc operating 2 valves per cylinder; Roots-type supercharger engaged at will; twin carburettors; dual ignition by coil and distributor, and magneto; 2 plugs per cylinder; 4-bearing crankshaft; output with blower engaged: 180bhp at 3,000rpm (Model S); 200bhp at 3,000rpm (Model SS); 225bhp at 3,300rpm (SSK); 265+bhp at 3,300rpm (SSKL).

Transmission: Multiple dry-plate clutch; 4-speed gearbox in unit with engine; torque tube final drive.

Chassis: Pressed steel side members; semi-elliptic springing front and rear, hydraulic dampers (friction rear on Model S); four-wheel internal expanding, servo-assisted brakes.

Dimensions: Wheelbase, 11ft 1·8in (S and SS), 9ft 8·1in (SSK and SSKL); track, 4ft 7·7in; approx. dry weight, 4,180lb (S and SS), 3,740lb (SSK), 3,495lb (SSKL).

Above: With its great bonnet occupying almost half of the overall length, this imposing 1928 two-door convertible drophead SS Mercedes-Benz is a Teutonic example of what in modern times is called a 2 + 2

Below: Two vast 7·1 litre Mercedes-Benz thunder down one of the Phoenix Park straights during the 1930 Irish GP, epitomising the "monster" age of sports car racing. Rudolf Caracciola's white SSK No. 3, the race winner, is passing Earl Howe's older SS, No. 2, which finished third

The chain-drive Frazer Nash

Although as different as chalk from cheese, the chain-drive Frazer Nash stands as firm and famous a part of British sports car tradition as the great green vintage Bentleys. It was smaller, lighter, nimbler and cheaper, yet it gave its driver similar inordinate pleasure in fast travel, possessing electrifying acceleration, instantly responsive and ultra-precise steering, and leech-like roadholding. Its production run, too, was little more than that of the Bentley, 15 years to 12 years, although ending less harshly in sheer redundancy.

The "N" of GN, the famous British cyclecar, was Archie Frazer Nash, and when the market for these fiercely energetic, spidery half-breeds faded away, Nash set himself up in a small works on Kingston Hill, Surrey, and in 1924 produced the hand-made Frazer Nash sports car. This used the same GN-type transmission with solid, differential-less rear axle and separate chains, sprockets and dog clutches for each of the three forward speeds—a seemingly crude system which, in fact, was very light, quick-changing, low on power absorption, and very accessible for rapid changes of gear ratio for competition purposes.

After years with fierce, noisy air-cooled twins, however, Nash "went soft" and fitted a 1½ litre water-cooled push-rod overhead valve engine called the Plus-power. Soon, however, he switched to the reliable 69 × 100mm side-valve Anzani unit, conveniently built in the same town. Very responsive to tune, this engine yielded over 50bhp, which in a car scaling a mere 1,512lb all-up weight meant extreme agility and made the 'Nash an instant success in speed events where acceleration and cornering power counted above all.

The chassis, based on the GN "bed-stead" with lean parallel side members, had quarter-elliptic springs all round, reversed at the front and trailing at the rear, while very high-geared rack-and-pinion steering, requiring only three-quarters of a turn lock to lock, accounted for the car's lightning response to the wheel. If lock was somewhat limited, it was second nature for the Frazer Nash specialist to exploit the solid axle and slide the tail! The makers soon widened the front track in any case, achieving that "crab track" for which the chain-drive 'Nash is famous, while bodywork was light and purposeful in aluminium, the transmission countershaft ensuring that any rear seat legroom was nominal only in four-seater models.

A maximum of 70mph, 40mpg and a price of £315 was highly promising in 1925, and a splendid 1-3-5-victory in the Boulogne Light Car GP took the Frazer Nash well out of the ruck of ordinary British sports cars. Being decidedly an individually-built, "bespoke" type of car, few 'Nashes were exactly alike, and with enthusiastic customers asking for extra power and speed, special Boulogne models in two

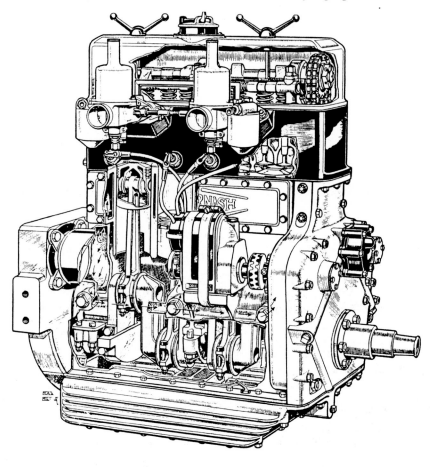

and four-seater forms made their debut, with supercharging giving 85bhp optional. A Cozette blower was used, but it stressed the Anzani side-valve unit cruelly, and few lasted long.

In 1927 Archie Nash sold his car business to the three Aldington brothers, H. J., W. H. and D. A., who re-formed it as AFN Ltd, and transferred it to Isleworth, Middlesex. They continued to build the Boulogne with Anzani engine, made four-speed transmission available from 1928, and soon a new overhead valve engine with identical 69 × 100mm bore and stroke, the Meadows 4ED, replaced the dating Anzani. While 'Nash privateers, known collectively as "the Chain Gang", exploited the exhilarating power-to-weight ratio of their mounts and reaped a rich harvest in British race, hill climb, sprint, trials and rally successes, the cars from Isleworth also ventured into big league races as evidenced by subsequent new models such as the 90mph TT Replica of 1931 and the super-charged Nurburg of 1932.

In general, Frazer Nash nomenclature was confusing, and with Super Sports, Fast Tourer, Interceptor, International, Ulster, Colmore, Exeter, Byfleet, Shelsley and yet other variations on the 1½ litre chain-drive theme, they were clearly very individual sports cars indeed. The Meadows four-cylinder engine was supplemented in 1933 by a 1,657cc six, the Blackburne with twin overhead camshafts, giving smoother but milder performance, while soon a new four, the overhead camshaft Gough specially built for Frazer Nash, largely replaced the Meadows. It responded well to super-charging by a Centric blower, and a single-seater Frazer Nash with a special twin-blown unit broke the Shelsley Walsh hill record in June 1937.

Sadly, the grey financial climate of the 1930s affected sales of so specialised a car, especially when smaller MG Midgets, Singers, etc. could offer sports motoring of a kind at less cost. The last chain-drive Frazer Nash was assembled as late as 1939, but the Aldingtons had seen the light in 1934, when they began selling 1½ and 2 litre six-cylinder BMW cars from Germany as Frazer Nash-BMWs. In the eyes of innumerable 'Nash enthusiasts then and now, however, nothing could replace the solid-axle, chain-driven car from Isleworth for sheer vim and vigour, driver satisfaction and aesthetic appeal. With its radiator set back behind the axle line, the long lean bonnet, the sparse but functional bodywork, wire wheels and big brakes, few rivals looked more the part of the classic British sports car.

Specification

Engine—*Anzani:* 4 cylinders in line, detachable head; 69 × 100mm, 1,496cc; sv; single carburettor; magneto ignition; 4-bearing crankshaft; 38–52bhp at approx. 3,600rpm, or 85bhp with Cozette super-charger.
Meadows: 4 cylinders in line, detachable head; 69 × 100mm, 1,496cc; pushrod ohv; twin carburettors; magneto ignition; 45–55bhp at 4,500rpm.
Blackburne: 6 cylinders in line, detachable head; 57 × 97·9mm, 1,498cc, or 60 × 97·9mm, 1,657cc; 2ohc; twin or triple carburettors; coil ignition; 5-bearing crankshaft; 55–65bhp at 5,000rpm.
Gough: 4 cylinders in line; 69 × 100mm, 1,496cc; single chain-driven ohc; twin SU carburettors; coil and magneto dual ignition; 3-bearing crankshaft; 60–70bhp at 4,500rpm.
Transmission: Dry single-plate clutch; propellor shaft to countershaft; chain-and-sprocket final drive giving 3 forward speeds up to 1927, 4 speeds from 1928.
Chassis: Pressed steel side members; reversed quarter-elliptic front springs; trailing quarter-elliptic rear springs; friction dampers; four-wheel brakes from 1925.
Dimensions: Wheelbase, 8ft 0in (up to 1929), 9ft 0in (from 1929); front track, 4ft; rear track, 3ft 6in.

Left: The 1,496cc 4-cylinder "Gough" engine, with single ohc, twin SU carburettors and 3-bearing crankshaft, built by Frazer Nash to power their chain-drive sports cars from 1934
Below: A pair of 'Nashes in the 1934 Ulster TT race on the Ards circuit outside Belfast. No. 15 is the 6-cylinder Blackburne twin ohc-engined car of the Hon Peter Mitchell-Thompson (later Lord Selsdon), and No. 16 is N. A. Berry's car with 4-cylinder ohc "Gough" engine

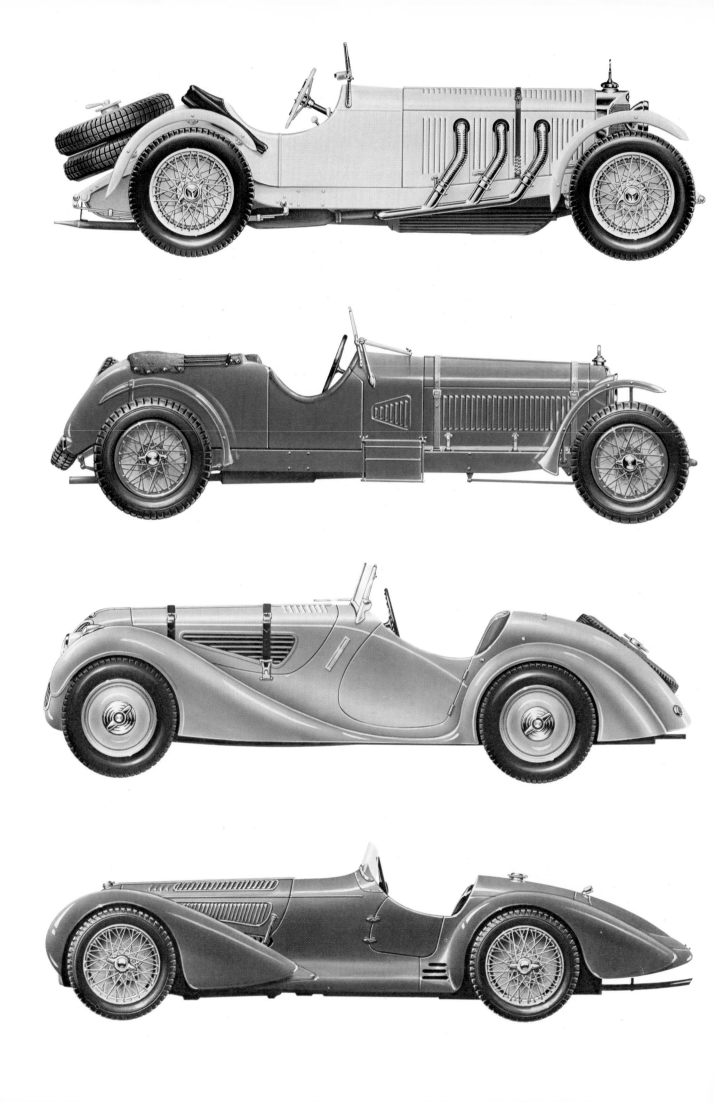

Opposite, top to bottom: *The ever-changing shape: 1928–30 SSK Mercedes-Benz, 7 litres supercharged and "lord" of the "monster" period; 1931–33 Alfa Romeo Tipo 8C 2300—the long-wheelbase Le Mans model, lithe and feline; 1937–39 six-cylinder BMW Type 328 which set new 2 litre sports car standards on road and track; 1938–39 Alfa Romeo 8C 2900B brought* the GP touch to sports cars with its all-independent suspension and design sophistication

Above: *Two examples, 21 years apart, of sporting cars derived from touring designs. The 4 litre side-valve "Prince Henry" Vauxhall of 1912–14 (top), evolved by expedience and ingenuity from the standard touring 3 litre* model. *The 1931–34 2·9 litre Talbot 105 (lower), extensively rallied and raced, sprang from Georges Roesch's brilliant 1·6 litre 14/45 ohv small "six" of 1926*

Talbot 90 and 105

If twin overhead camshafts and super-chargers were a *sine qua non* to most designers seeking high performance in the mid-Vintage years, they were a *bête noire* to Georges Roesch. This meticulous, far-sighted Swiss engineer waged a ruthless war on complication, reciprocating weight, friction and mechanical noise, his main weapons being efficiency, high engine revolutions, high compression and thorough lubrication.

The English firm of Clement Talbot Ltd became part of the Sunbeam-Talbot-Darracq (STD) group after the First World War, and Roesch was given the task in 1925 of reviving the moribund factory at Barlby Road, North Kensington, by designing and producing a new profit-earning car as quickly and cheaply as possible. He answered this daunting commission with the Talbot 14/45, a brilliant long-stroke 1·6 litre six-cylinder touring car featuring pushrod overhead valves operated by needle-thin push-rods and rockers on friction-saving knife-edge pivots, a single carburettor, Delco-Remy coil ignition and thermo-syphon cooling.

Consistent class winner: the 1930 Talbot 90 developed for the Fox & Nicholl racing team used a 2·3 litre six-cylinder pushrod ohv engine in a short Talbot Scout chassis. The engine, fed by a single updraught carburettor, sits low under the lofty bonnet of this inexpensive but effective competition sports car

He deliberately avoided such things as noisy chains, unreliable belts, frail flexible hoses (the radiator was bolted direct to the crankcase), and a flexing chassis in the design. The four-speed gearbox was pressure-lubricated with engine oil 35 years before Issigonis used the system on the Mini, and the clutch withdrawal race, transmission universal ball joint and steering joints had automatic lubrication. Clutch, gearchange, brakes and steering were all above average, while the engine revved fast for 1926 at 4,500rpm, with power in complement, 41bhp being attained on a $5\frac{1}{2}$ to 1 compression ratio in silky silence.

The 14/45 sold as briskly as it performed, which was as well, since the design was rushed into production "blind" before even a prototype was built. Faults manifested themselves but were remedied, power output rose to 46bhp, and by 1928 Roesch was designing a bigger but interchangeable engine to give the car more performance. An enlarged bore and stroke raised capacity to 2,276cc, and with a new, fully counter-balanced, seven-bearing crankshaft a smooth 76bhp at 4,500rpm was realised on a compression ratio of 7:1 and one carburettor. The brakes were improved, centralised chassis lubrication and hydraulic dampers adopted, and the new, more powerful model was destined to appear late in 1929 as the Talbot 75.

Fate now took a hand. For the 1930

season the Surrey firm of Fox & Nicholl sought a new car to contest the 3 litre class in International sports car racing. Chance led them to the Talbot despite its capacity of only 2·3 litres, and Roesch raised the compression ratio to an astonishing 10:1, obtaining a remarkable 85bhp at 4,500rpm for 24 hours on the Barlby Road brake. Installed in the shorter Talbot chassis, that of the newly introduced Scout model with 9ft 3in wheelbase, the first car easily topped 90mph on test, giving the competition model its new type number—the 90.

Three cars were hastily constructed, their lofty build accentuated by their narrow vee-radiators and their white-painted two-seater sports-racing bodies, for a race debut at Brooklands which proved calamitous. In the Double-12 Hours race in May 1930 two of the cars collided, resulting in two deaths, but the shaken team regained their morale and subsequently scored 3-litre class wins in four successive classic races—Le Mans, where two finished third and fourth overall, the Irish GP, the Ulster TT, and the Brooklands 500 Miles race, in which one Talbot with special single-seater body placed fourth overall at over 104mph average—all this from $2\frac{1}{4}$ litre cars of touring origin, and achieved in impressive fussless silence.

Over 200 production examples of the 90 chassis were built between 1930 and 1933, bearing an attractive variety in

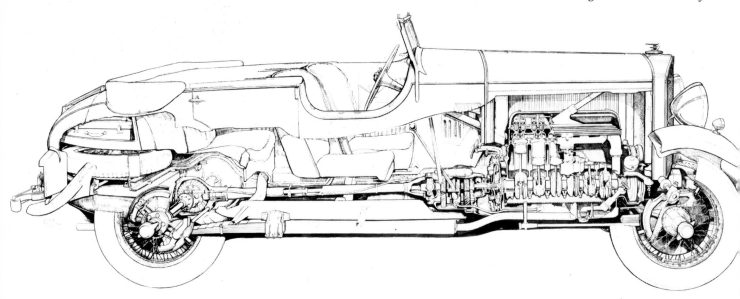

Last outing: Tim Rose-Richards in one of the two 2·9 litre Talbot 105s which contested the 1934 Ulster TT. In this, their very last road race, the cars took 1st and 2nd places in the 2–3 litre class. Four months later the marque was sold out to the Rootes Group

coachwork, including a rakish two-door fabric coupé and the Brooklands Super Speed open two-seater with long Double 12 style sloping tail and wings. In the meantime, anticipating Fox & Nicholl's inevitable request for a full 3 litre Talbot for racing in 1931, Roesch enlarged the unit to 2,969cc, designed a new head with staggered valves, and attained 100bhp at 4,500rpm on a 6·6:1 compression ratio; with a 105mph potential, he called it the 105.

Fitted with 9ft 6in wheelbase chassis, a team of 105s ran in all the major races in 1931 and 1932, looking a little lower, longer and more beautiful than the 90s, especially with their new apple green finish. They considerably enlivened a dull racing period dominated by what Tim Birkin scathingly called "a scuttling kindergarten" of small British cars aided by generous handicapping. The Talbots scored many excellent places—thirds at Le Mans and in the Ulster TT both in

1931 and 1932, seconds in both the 1931 Double 12 and 500 Miles, etc, yet despite their remarkable speeds and reliability, Fate and the handicapping denied them that outright victory which all racing cars and their makers need.

In 1932 the Hon. Brian Lewis even took one to Italy for the Alfa-infested Mille Miglia, finishing a humble 25th after various misfortunes forced him down from 4th place. Talbots also competed in the gruelling Alpine Trial in 1931, 1932 and 1934, finishing each time without loss of marks and winning the Team Prize in the two latter years. A few months later, alas, Fate dealt its cruellest blow. Despite building outstandingly reliable and efficient high-performance cars at reasonable yet profitable prices, Clement Talbot Ltd —the only paying member of the ill-founded STD combine—was sacrificed and sold to Rootes Ltd together with Sunbeam.

At the time of take-over Georges Roesch had a Talbot 110 and kindred 3½ litre Talbot among his projects, the bore of the 105 being opened out to give 3,377cc and 120bhp. The 10ft wheelbase chassis was lowered—a step many felt was long overdue—and some superbly

elegant coachwork was mounted upon it. Production began under the new proprietors, alongside the other models until existing components were used up, in 1937. A year later the combined title Sunbeam-Talbot was applied to a series of Humber and Hillman-based cars; rationalisation had its way, and the name Talbot entered a long sleep.

Specification

Engine—*Model 90:* 6 cylinders in line; 69·5 × 100mm, 2,276cc; pushrod ohv; single carburettor; Delco-Remy coil ignition; 7-bearing crankshaft; 70bhp at 4,500rpm (Competition cars, 93bhp at 4,500rpm). *Model 105:* As above, except 75 × 112mm, 2,960cc; 100bhp at 4,500rpm (Competition cars, 138bhp at 4,800rpm).

Transmission: Single dry-plate clutch; 4-speed gearbox (silent 3rd gearbox on 90 from October 1930, Wilson preselector gearbox on 105 from October 1932); torque tube final drive.

Chassis: Pressed steel side members; semi-elliptic front and rear springs; friction dampers (1929–30), hydraulic dampers thereafter; Perrot-type mechanically-operated brakes (up to 1931), cable operation thereafter.

Dimensions: Wheelbase, 9ft 3in (90, 1929–30); 9ft 6in (90 from October 1930 and all 105s); track, 4ft 7½in.

The 1933 MG Magnette K3 which took British green ahead of Italian red in Italy's greatest road race, the 1,000-miles long Mille Miglia. With 1,087cc Powerplus-supercharged six-cylinder engine and Wilson preselector gearbox, a pair of these Abingdon thoroughbreds defeated two factory supercharged Maseratis and dominated the 1,100cc class

Alfa Romeo 8Cs

Some 40 to 50 years ago it used to be said that "the racing car of today is the sports car of tomorrow". Recoiling from the modern bewinged, mill-wheeled Formula 1 racer, one trusts we will be spared such a fate in the 1980s, but back in the early 1930s the tenet really carried weight, and no marque upheld it better than Alfa Romeo. From Vittorio Jano's P2 Grand Prix design of 1924 was descended the brilliant six-cylinder twin-cam sports Alfas of the late 1920s, and in 1931 the dictates of racing brought forth still more potent successors in a range of supercharged straight-eights designated Tipo 8C 2300.

Although Alfa Romeo also made excellent touring cars and trucks, their heart was unquestionably in racing, needing no spur from *Il Duce* Mussolini, whose habit it was to send their team telegrams commanding them "to win for Italy". But by the end of 1930 it was obvious that Alfa Romeo needed new racing cars; the P2s, although rebuilt, were now seven years old, and Maserati had stolen Portello's thunder with their successful 2½ litre GP cars of 1930. Money was very tight then, and however much Alfas yearned to win back their Grand Prix status, they had to produce a single design versatile enough to power both sports and out-and-out racing cars.

With the success of his six-cylinder sports cars behind him, Ing. Jano was well up to the task, and many design features from the 6C figured in the new design. Using the same 65 × 88mm bore and stroke as the 1750, he added two more cylinders, the blocks being cast in two pairs, separated by a central train of gears driving the supercharger, twin-overhead camshafts, and oil and water pumps. The crankshaft, also divided into two with centres bolted to the primary timing gears, ran in 10 plain bearings for maximum rigidity, while the twin-cam heads, also paired, were cast in light alloy with phosphor bronze valve seats.

The single Alfa-built Roots-type blower, mounted on the right-hand side, received mixture from a forward-mounted Memini carburettor, and delivered it through an imposingly finned inlet manifold, *à la* 1750; this was

but one pleasing feature of an engine of outstanding mechanical beauty, and the rest of the car followed suit. Frame and suspension were conventional, but the low, slender build, wide track and huge four-wheel brakes with aluminium drums filling the wheels, gave an impression of lithe, ruthless efficiency which, enhanced by superb open bodywork from the finest Italian coachbuilders, made the 8C Alfa Romeo in its various forms one of the loveliest of sports cars.

On the brake the new engine yielded an initial unfrenzied 138bhp at 5,000rpm, a higher crankshaft speed than Jano accepted on the earlier sixes. The unit was first fitted into a prototype sports car chassis, and was promptly "blooded" in the 1931 Mille Miglia. Far too new, it could do nothing about Caracciola's tremendous pace in the 7 litre Mercedes-Benz SSKL, but the 8C, representing the new, multi-cylinder, higher-revving, high-efficiency school, had a brilliant career ahead. In racing car form, it failed again at Alessandria, but success came in the Targa Florio, followed smartly by another win in the 10-hour Italian GP at Monza in a new GP chassis. This gained the new racing 2·3 litre Alfa its unofficial sobriquet of "Monza"; it was a car destined to win over a score more major events during the next three seasons.

For Grand Prix events, the Tipo 8C 2300 had a specially short 8ft 8in wheelbase, but the sports versions were built with two wheelbases, the *Corto* (short) at 9ft, and the *Lungo* (long) at 10ft 2in. The first batch of *Lungo* chassis, able to carry open four-seater bodywork, was laid down at Portello in good time for the all-important Le Mans 24 Hours race in June, two of the first going to the British drivers Earl Howe and Tim Birkin. The latter's was collected by his manager, Clive Gallop, and driven over 800 miles from Milan to Holyhead, in time for the Irish GP at Phoenix Park, Dublin, a week before Le Mans. Birkin made the fastest average, won the unlimited class, and only lost the Grand Prix on handicap to an MG Midget through running short of fuel.

For Le Mans, Birkin and Howe shared one Alfa, the pair winning the race after a factory-entered car failed. It marked

the first of four consecutive Le Mans victories for the 2·3 Alfa, which also won the Mille Miglia and Belgian 24 Hours races in 1932 and 1933. Some engines were bored out for racing by the Scuderia Ferrari in 1933 to 2,632cc, one winning yet another Mille Miglia for Alfa Romeo in 1934.

Such successes greatly enhanced the prestige of Jano's beautiful eight-cylinder sports car. As a road machine it was expensive to buy, reliable if carefully maintained, and as mettlesome as any pedigree hunter, hard in ride with short semi-elliptic springs but a whippy frame. It had inherent oversteer, the high-geared steering requiring a discreet "feel" at the wheel; the engine showed remarkable tractability at low speed, but gave electrifying acceleration and a maximum of 115mph and more, achieved in a paeon of enchanting noise compounded by eight potent cylinders, the scream of the blower, and the song of straight-cut gears.

Zagato, Castagna and Touring all adorned these inspiring cars with their *carrozzeria*, perhaps the finest of all being the Zagato Spyder two-seater on the *Corto* chassis, with short, shapely tail embellished with a central spine, angled spare wheel recessed into it, and glorious sweeping wings; a classic sports car indeed!

Specification—8C 2300

Engine: 8 cylinders in line; 65 × 88mm, 2,336cc; 2ohc; Roots-type supercharger; single carburettor; Bosch coil ignition; 10-bearing crankshaft; dry sump lubrication; 142bhp at 5,000rpm (Competition cars, 155–165bhp at 5,200–5,400rpm).
Transmission: Multiple-disc clutch; 4-speed gearbox in unit with engine; torque tube final drive.
Chassis: Pressed steel side members; semi-elliptic springing front and rear, friction dampers; four-wheel mechanical brakes.
Dimensions: Wheelbase, 10ft 2in or 9ft 0in; track, 4ft 6in; approx. chassis weight, 2,184lb (long wheelbase), 2,072lb (short wheelbase).

The 8C 2900

By 1935 the time-honoured semi-elliptic, "cart"-type springing was on its way out in progressive European design

circles. Germany's all-independently sprung Grand Prix cars had pointed the way the previous year, and Alfa Romeo quickly followed suit in 1935 with new GP racing cars having an independent front end by trailing links and coil springs in unit with hydraulic shock absorbers, and an independent rear by transverse leaf spring and swing axles. Having established that their design

worked well in late-1935 races, Alfa Romeo built three new sports cars with similar suspension for the 1936 season.

These cars used 2·9 litre versions of Jano's 8C straight-eight engine, as developed for 1934 Grand Prix racing with twin superchargers on the left-hand side. They ran with lower compression, giving 220bhp at 5,300rpm to the 255bhp of the racers, and the cars had two-seater

Above: *In Bentley's wheeltracks—Tim Birkin leading at Le Mans, 1931—the race he won with Earl Howe in a 2·3 litre straight-eight supercharged Alfa Romeo Tipo 8C 2300. This superb breed of Alfa won the famous French endurance race four years running*

Below: *Milan classic—A cutaway drawing by Robert Roux of the Tipo 8C 2300 Alfa Romeo with which Nuvolari and Sommer won the 1933 Le Mans race. The central timing drives on the twin-cam straight-eight engine, and the Roots-type supercharger can be seen*

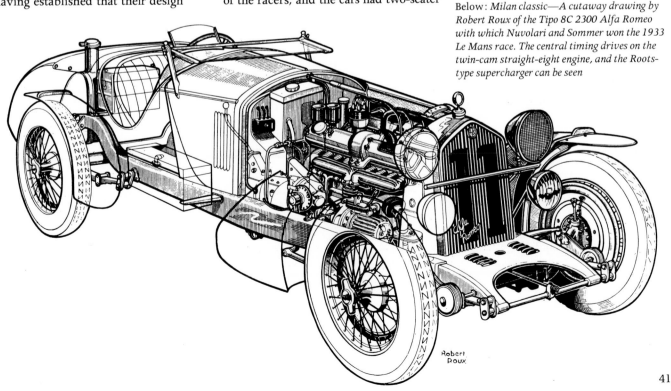

Light in build, aerodynamically efficient in shape, lively in performance, Germany's 2 litre six-cylinder ohv BMW Type 328 was a handsome and highly important sports car, introduced in 1936 and still influencing design after the War. The other "light sports" machine in the picture is a Bucker Jungmeister biplane, a similar type serving more ominously in the 1930s as a standard Luftwaffe training aircraft

bodies with fixed cycle wings, headlights and spare wheels. The Mille Miglia was always a vital "shop window" for Alfa Romeo, and their 1936 display proved to be brilliant, the new cars scooping the first three places. They next cleaned up the Belgian 24 Hours race at Spa, and that winter Portello tooled up for limited production of a new derivative sports model, the 8C 2900B. This was available in *Corto* and *Lungo* wheelbases of 9ft 2¼in and 9ft 10in, and with the blown straight-eight engine giving a mannerly 180bhp, respective speeds were 115 and 106mph.

As usual, these splendid Alfa Romeo chassis attracted the finest bodywork, and in 1937 Carrozzeria Touring produced a most elegant and *avant garde* Spyder two seater with headlights recessed into helmet-type wings, which merged into the body, and a short, shapely tail housing two spare wheels. For Alfa Romeo's 1938 Mille Miglia cars, the Touring concern produced one of the finest looking and most effective sports body designs of any period—the two-seater Spyders built to their new "Superleggera" (super-light) principles employing under-framing of light alloy tubing—on special race-prepared 8C 2900B chassis.

These bolides performed as superbly as they looked, taking the first two

Above: *The Swiss driver Hans Ruesch in his 2·3 litre 8C 2300 "Monza" Alfa Romeo enters a control during the 1934 Mille Miglia—Italy's famous 1,000 miles town to town road race*

Below: *The Italian line. A masterful blend of curves and counter-curves is achieved on this superb 1934 Alfa Romeo 8C 2300 with two-seater coupe bodywork by Castagna—a glorious over-100mph car for pre-war grand touring*

places and then repeating their Belgian 24 Hours victory. Resplendent in blazing Italian red, the Mille Miglia winner was displayed at Earls Court in the 1938 London Motor Show, and was purchased by Hugh Hunter, who raced it extensively during 1939. In a contest at Brooklands to decide "the fastest road car", the Alfa won the first half, but broke its gearbox on the line in the second race, leaving success to a 3½ litre Delahaye. Despite this, there could be little doubt that the Mille Miglia 8C 2900B was Europe's fastest road car of the time, besides being unmatched for sheer purposeful beauty of line.

Specification

Engine: 8 cylinders in line; 68 × 100mm, 2,905cc; 2ohc; twin Roots-type super-chargers; twin carburettors; Vertex magneto ignition; 10-bearing crankshaft; 220bhp at 5,200rpm (Competition cars, 255bhp at 5,300rpm).
Transmission: Multiple-disc clutch; 4-speed gearbox in unit with final drive.
Chassis: Welded box-section side members; independent front suspension by trailing links and coil spring-cum-damper units; independent rear suspension by transverse leaf spring and swing axles; hydraulic and friction dampers; hydraulic brakes.
Dimensions: Wheelbase, 9ft 10in or 9ft 2½in; track, 4ft 4in; approx. car weight, 1,900lb (long wheelbase), 1,790lb (short wheelbase).

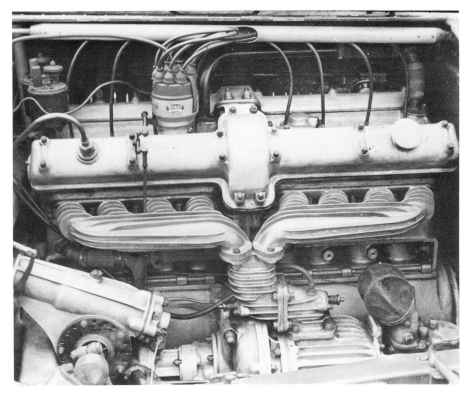

Above: *Art in metal—Alfa Romeo designer Vittorio Jano demanded good looks as well as high performance in his engines; he certainly succeeded with the truly beautiful Tipo 8C 2300 supercharged straight-eight power unit*

Below: *The later eight-cylinder sports Alfa Romeo, the 8C 2900, continued the marque's reputation for extreme aesthetic grace combined with outstanding performance and roadholding. Phil Hill is driving this 1938 Mille Miglia car at Pebble Beach, California, after the Second World War*

"Barchetta": Ferrari began back in 1946 with construction of the first 1½ litre single ohc V12s. Classic among the early models was the Tipo 166 Mille Miglia spyder (above), first produced in 1948 and called the "Barchetta" (or little boat). Carrozzeria Touring styled and built the handsome two-seater bodywork.
"Testa Rossa" (inset): Ten years' progress, and Ferrari are top of the sports car tree. The 250TR single-cam competition 3 litre V12 bodied by Scaglietti won the 1958 World Sports Car Championship. Pictured is Mike Hawthorn at Le Mans that year

MG Magnette K3

Midget, Magna, Magnette . . . MG's creator and "kingpin" Cecil Kimber devised some attractive names for the complex and confusing range of cars turned out at Abingdon-on-Thames in pre-Second World War days. The Midget name, of course survived for decades, but the original of the species was very different to the models of the 1970s. In 1931 in 750cc form it made a resounding impact on the British racing scene when it cleaned up in three major sports cars events at the expense of bigger British and European cars. True, the handicappers helped by under-estimating the calibre of the MG, but when they hardened their hearts against the 750s in 1932 in favour of the 1100cc class, Kimber's thoughts turned also towards that category.

Already in 1932 he had introduced a new small six-cylinder MG, the 1,271cc overhead camshaft Magna, a model of deceptively sporty aspect but mediocre performance, and in 1933 Kimber added a more respectable six to the range. This was the Magnette, sub-typed the K1 in its first form, and a "little Magna" both by implication and by its smaller capacity of 1,087cc, if not for its bigger brakes and wider track. Moreover, unlike the Magna engine with its inlet and exhaust ports all on one side, the Magnette's 57 × 71mm engine had much more potential with a crossflow head, magneto ignition, triple SU carburettors, and the promise of supercharging.

Its *raison d'etre* was obvious, or soon became so; it was MG's new contender in the 1100cc sports and racing class, at that time the joint domain of the British Riley, the French Amilcar and the Italian Maserati. The catalyst which brought it from a catalogue project to a challenger in the metal was the fierce enthusiasm and patriotism of Earl Howe, who badly wanted to see British cars do well in Italy's great 1000 Miles race, the Mille Miglia. His offer to bear part of the costs if MG were to build three cars to challenge in the 1100cc class was accepted by Sir William Morris, proprietor of the company, and with under six months to the race in April 1933, Cecil Kimber embarked immediately

upon the ambitious K3 project.

The engine had a four-bearing crankshaft and was fitted with a Powerplus eccentric-vane type supercharger, giving over 100bhp in early tests compared with around 39bhp from the first unblown Magnette unit. A breakaway from convention was the fitting of a Wilson preselector self-changing four-speed gearbox, for which a neat fore-and-aft change quadrant on top of the gearbox was devised, anticipating modern "automatic" practice. Two prototype cars were quickly built, the first being blooded in the 1933 Monte Carlo Rally—an open car in mid-winter!—where its intrepid drivers finished the course, albeit well down, but won the concluding hill climb.

The other car went out to Italy for tests on the actual Mille Miglia course, calling en route at the Bugatti factory where *le Patron*, Ettore Bugatti himself, opined that the front axle was too weak. Five weeks later the prototype returned to Britain, and much invaluable data relating to gear ratios, brakes, wheel strengths, and other aspects was worked into the three race cars under construction at Abingdon; a hasty reconsideration by MG's stressmen also led to a stiffening-up of the front axle as advised by Bugatti. By dint of prodigious overtime working the cars, resplendent in British racing green, were shipped to Italy in time for practice, giving the Maserati opposition a major shock with their pace.

With expert drivers, two per car, first and second places in the 1100cc class were MG's brilliant reward for so much effort. George Eyston and Count Lurani were the winners, followed by Earl Howe himself and Hugh Hamilton, but the third car, driven by the mercurial Tim Birkin, retired with a broken valve after serving nobly as the pacemaker and breaking up the Italian opposition. Following this magnificent Continental foray MG's versatile new Magnettes, stripped of lights, wings and other impedimenta, proceeded to score several successes as out-and-out racing cars.

Then Italy's greatest racing driver, *Il Maestro* Tazio Nuvolari, was moved to seek an entry in that classic sports car

race, the Ulster TT, with a works K3 Magnette on loan—and he won dramatically from Hamilton's Midget in a striking double for "the Octagon". For 1934 the cars were improved, Marshall Roots-type superchargers replacing the Powerplus, an improved cylinder head was fitted, and the K3 was offered in sports or racing trim with pointed tail for just £795. With wings and lights or without, it made a purposeful picture with the squat MG radiator, its lower left corner "cut out" for the blower induction pipe, its outside exhaust system, and big wire wheels almost filled on the inside with aluminium back-plated brakes.

The K3's second season in sports car racing was less successful. Maseratis were not caught napping a second time in the Mille Miglia, and MG had to rest content with second place. Then at Le Mans, where almost every classic sports car has appeared, a K3 was holding second place behind a blown eight-cylinder Alfa Romeo when a skidding French car put it out in the 10th hour. However, another finished fourth overall and won its class, while a Magnette driven by Enid Riddell placed second

Above: *Carrying the torch—British racing green intruded with startling success on Italian domains when three MG K3 Magnettes entered the 1100cc class of the 1933 Mille Miglia, defeating the Maseratis and Fiats to take 1st and 2nd places. Here are the winners G. E. T. Eyston at the wheel, and Count G. Lurani beside him; behind are Earl Howe and H. C. Hamilton, second home*
Below: *The Mille Miglia K3 laid bare, showing the 1,087cc six-cylinder single ohc supercharged engine, driving through a Wilson preselector gearbox*

overall in the Paris–St Raphael Ladies' Rally, taking the 1100cc prize.

A change of rules excluding superchargers made the K3 redundant for the 1934 Ulster TT, but an unsupercharged NE-type Magnette carried the proud name to another victory. Nineteen years later, of course, it was applied to an MG four-door road saloon of Wolseley origin, but to true Abingdon devotees there is only one *real* Magnette, the blown six-cylinder 1,087cc K3, the most classic of all MGs.

Specification
Engine: 6 cylinders in line; 57 × 71mm, 1,087cc; single ohc operating 2 valves per cylinder; Powerplus vane-type supercharger in 1933, Marshall Roots-type supercharger in 1934; SU carburettor; magneto ignition; 4-bearing crankshaft; 114bhp at 7,000rpm.
Transmission: 4-speed Wilson preselector gearbox; open propellor shaft; bevel final drive.
Chassis: Pressed steel side members, underslung at rear; semi-elliptic leaf springs front and rear, friction dampers; mechanically-operated drum brakes.
Dimensions: Wheelbase, 7ft 10·2in; track, 4ft 0in; approx. dry weight, 2,040lb (1933); 1,990lb (1934).

Aston Martin 1½ litre

Undeniably "they don't build 'em that way anymore", but there was much to be said for the pre-war Aston Martin policy of building *strong*, when it produced such long-lasting cars as their 1½ litre ohc fours, and such impressive competition results. As sports cars they scaled some 2,180lb on the Le Mans or Ulster weighbridge, when an equivalent 1½ litre Lotus of 30 or more years later barely exceeded half that weight. Yet their superb engineering, stimulating performance and beautifully balanced appearance refuted any charge of being ponderous or over-weight. As exemplified by the "International" of 1929–31, the "Le Mans" of 1932–33, or the "Ulster" of 1934–35, these were glorious cars in the classic style, richly redolent of Le Mans and long-distance races in general with their low, purposeful build, tight cycle wings, big headlights, quick-release filler caps, stoneguarding and outside exhausts.

It is fortunate for motoring posterity that such cars existed at all. The Aston Martin concern, founded just before the First World War, only just survived the financial vicissitudes which assailed so many under-capitalised enterprises in the precarious 1920s. When all seemed

---

The low-built and sturdy Aston Martin chassis in 1932 "International" sports road car form, showing the 1½ litre four-cylinder single ohc engine, 4-speed gearbox in unit with remote control gearchange, open propellor shaft, and chassis underslung at the rear.

lost in 1926 the company was reformed at Feltham, Middlesex, its four directors including A. C. Bertelli, an Italian-born engineer who once rode with the great Nazzaro as racing mechanic, and later designed the 1½ litre Enfield-Allday car and the abortive Bertelli sleeve-valve racers.

Despite the shaky times the new company boldly set out to produce a new high-efficiency 1½ litre sports car, the T-type, employing a four-cylinder engine design patented by Bertelli and co-director Renwick. This featured a single overhead camshaft driven by chain with Weller tensioning, and operating inclined valves in wedge-shaped combustion chambers. Bore and stroke were 69·3 × 99mm, giving a capacity of 1,495cc, and the new Aston Martin was announced in September 1927. Chassis and semi-elliptic springing were typically Vintage, and transmission was through a separate four-speed gearbox and torque tube, low build being achieved with the aid of worm final drive.

Large-diameter brakes with Perrot front actuation were fitted, and the steering column was mounted, not on the chassis but higher on the aluminium bulkhead, the set of the steering wheel thus being almost vertical. An open four-seater tourer and a saloon were offered on a 9ft 6in wheelbase, while an open sports three-seater on a shorter chassis was mooted for the near future. These first T-model ohc Aston Martins

proved excessively heavy, and that winter Bertelli waged a war on weight while coping with other problems; his co-directors had withdrawn their support, and he had to find fresh finance and re-float the company.

As an ardent believer in racing, both as the most effective testbed and for publicity, Bertelli laid down two special competition cars on an 8ft 6in wheelbase chassis, underslung at the rear. The engine was given dry sump lubrication, the separate oil tank being installed between the front frame dumbirons ahead of the radiator, duralumin connecting rods, twin carburettors and a central gearchange were fitted, and the steering mounting moved down to the chassis. All this depleted the shallow AM coffers alarmingly, but the marque began a very long association with Le Mans in 1928, where the two cars disappointingly retired.

Bertelli learned some valuable lessons, nonetheless, primarily that the cars were still too heavy, and applied them to a production version, the International 2/4 seater sports. Its neat open bodywork was built by Bertelli's brother Harry in a coachbuilding shop attached to the works, the car cost £598, and AM outdid Bentley Motors' 5-years guarantee by offering first owners one for life! It was a lively car, responsive and pleasant to drive, with an exceptionally flexible engine whisking it up to close on 80mph, remarkable roadholding attributable to the low centre of gravity

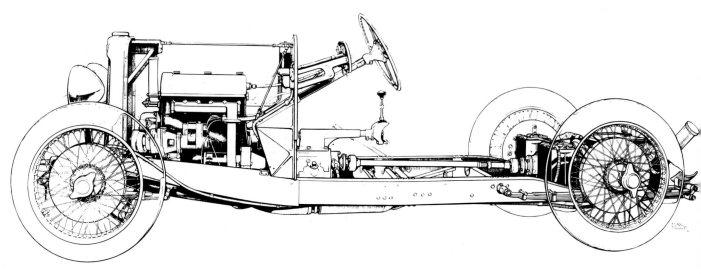

Feltham thoroughbred: One of the purposeful 1935 Le Mans Aston Martins in preparation, with driver Charles Brackenbury and designer/ team manager A. C. Bertelli behind, while journalist Gordon Wilkins examines the cockpit

and careful weight distribution, and extremely powerful brakes. It retained its tune, moreover, and was untemperamental.

Aston Martin speed and stamina became publicly apparent through mounting race successes. They scored class wins in the gruelling Brooklands Double 12 Hours race in 1930 and 1931, and in the 1931 Ulster TT, and one of them was the first "1500" to finish at Le Mans that year, placing 5th overall. Collectively, these feats secured the marque's survival through the depression years, when the International was reissued in somewhat cheaper form with Moss proprietary gearbox in unit with the engine, and bevel final drive.

Sleek, low Le Mans versions with pointed tails were prepared for the 1932 race, scoring AM's biggest success so far with victory in the Rudge-Whitworth Biennial Cup, the pre-war equivalent of the "Index of Performance", plus a class win. From them, in 1933, sprang the popular Le Mans production model with rear "slab" tank and outside exhaust, followed early in 1934 by an even better seller, the Mark II, with new crankshaft, improved head and 73bhp on the brake.

Then came the Ulster (a replica of the 1934 TT cars which captured the team prize), a 100mph sports-racing car of captivating lines, its tail swelling out low down to enclose the horizontal spare wheel. The very special engine gave 80bhp, and this was the car, costing £750 and looking magnificent in *red* rather than British racing green, which spread Aston Martin's fame across Europe with a string of successes. These included their second Rudge Cup at Le Mans, another TT team prize, and class wins in the Mille Miglia and at Pescara, all in 1935, another class "first" at Spa, Belgium, in 1936, and a Bol d'Or 24 Hours race victory as late as 1939. By then

Bertelli, the artist whose *chef d'oeuvre* the Ulster was, had been gone from Feltham for over two years.

Specification

Engine: 4 cylinders in line, detachable head; 69 × 99mm, 1,488cc; single chain-driven ohc; twin carburettors (RAG in 1927, SU thereafter); magneto ignition; 3-bearing crankshaft; dry sump lubrication from 1929; approx. 50bhp at 4,250rpm (1929 T-type); approx. 56bhp at 4,250rpm (1929–32 International); 70bhp at 4,750rpm (1933 Le Mans); 73bhp at 5,200rpm (1934 Le Mans Mk. II); 80bhp at 5,250rpm (1935 Ulster).
Transmission: Single dry-plate clutch; separate 4-speed gearbox, torque tube and worm final drive (1927–1932); 4-speed gearbox in unit with engine, open propellor shaft and spiral-bevel final drive thereafter.
Chassis: Pressed steel side members; semi-elliptic springing front and rear, friction dampers; four-wheel drum brakes, Perrot front actuation (1927–1932), cable operation thereafter.
Dimensions: Wheelbase, 8ft 6in (up to 1934); 8ft 7in (Le Mans Mk. II and Ulster); track, 4ft 4in; approx. car weights, between 2,130 and 2,410lb.

Lagonda 4½ litre

With the demise of the Bentley in 1931, big-engined British sports cars became notably thin on the ground in the early 1930s. The 4½ litre low-chassis Invicta was still on the market although sales were minimal, but September 1933 brought an interesting newcomer, a 4½ litre six from the Lagonda company of Staines, Middlesex. By then the sports car was emerging from the Vintage era, and one might have expected some sophistication in the engine, chassis and suspension, but the new Lagonda was quite unsubtle, revealing little technical advance on the last of the Hendon Bentleys.

Indeed, it lacked their overhead camshaft and four valves per cylinder, for its engine was the 88·5 × 120·6mm, 4,453cc pushrod overhead valve six, of a type built by Henry Meadows Ltd of Wolverhampton since 1928 and was the selfsame unit that powered the 4½ litre Invicta. Its output in Lagonda form, with twin SU carburettors, and a 6:1 compression ratio, was between 110 and 115bhp at a nice steady 3,200rpm, a rotation speed unlikely to trouble the four-bearing crankshaft which had a Lanchester-type vibration damper at the front end, and was statically and dynamically balanced. Dual ignition by BTH magneto and coil, with two plugs per cylinder, featured, and it was a tall, clean, accessible unit with impressive low-speed torque, giving remarkable flexibility without constant resort to the crash-type gears.

Lagondas had built good-looking and generally effective sports cars since 1925, and the 4½ litre was one of their best. They installed the big Meadows engine well back in a sturdy, conventional channel-section chassis with semi-elliptics and dual dampers all round, driving through a separate four-speed gearbox, open propellor shaft and spiral-bevel final drive. The generous 10ft 9in wheelbase permitted a fashionably long bonnet and a choice of graceful, roomy coachwork, bespoke or ready-made, and enhanced by long sweeping wings and the tall and comely slatted radiator.

The standard tourer weighed approx. 3,640lb, which the sturdy Meadows power unit propelled at an unfussed 95mph. Here, then, was a big likeable sporting car, well sprung in the Vintage idiom, excellently braked with servo assistance, and performing without stress. Yet with the magic century so near, someone inevitably wanted a faster one, and somebody else wanted to race it; by chance both wishes were granted almost simultaneously. It happened that the Fox & Nicholl racing stable, some 15 miles from Staines, at Tolworth, Surrey, had lost their Talbots

through the almost criminal demise of that company, and accordingly arranged to prepare and race three special 4½ litre Lagondas in the 1934 Ulster TT.

For expedience, the shorter chassis of the 3½ litre model, with 10ft 3in wheelbase, was used, while the engine gained a strengthened crankshaft and connecting rods and a 7:1 compression ratio, giving about 125bhp. Girling brakes replaced the servo type, and Luvax hydraulic and André Telecontrol dual dampers were fitted. Purposeful open four-seater bodies were built, these having rounded tails, fixed cycle-type wings and a distinctive red finish, the complete cars scaling about 3,080lb.

In the TT race they contributed much drama, the Hon Brian Lewis duelling with Hall's Rolls-type Bentley for second place until a tyre stop forced him back to fourth, while the other two cars

placed fifth and eighth, demonstrating Lagonda stamina. A production edition of the car, called the Rapide or M45R, was announced for 1935 with a choice of bodywork including an elegant open four-seater with convex boot treatment and striking long, swept wings with running boards.

Came 1935, a decisive year for Lagonda, almost bankrupt and near to closing down. But Fox & Nicholl ran two cars at Le Mans in June, and delighted

Its finest hour: The Fox & Nicholl 4½ litre six-cylinder Lagonda of John Hindmarsh/Luis Fontes en route to its historic if lucky win at Le Mans in 1935, breaking the run of Italian successes in the French classic

the British by breaking the Alfa Romeo four-year hold and winning the race outright. With a big end on the way out and oil pressure failing during the last hour, it was a tense, touch-and-go victory, but one which Fox & Nicholl deserved and Lagonda badly needed. It brought fresh finance and a new proprietor, and encouraged the great W. O. Bentley to join the Staines company as Technical Director.

With Lagonda adopting a new one-model policy, Bentley's immediate task was refinement of the 4½ litre. With Meadows' approval he improved the engine, mounted it on rubber, modified the exhaust system and fitted a synchro-mesh gearbox, the resultant LG45 being quieter, smoother and more comfortable, losing something of its hairy, "he-man" character yet contriving to be slightly faster. Some very beautiful luxury coachwork was carried, and if the sporting image diminished somewhat, Fox & Nicholl restored it by putting

three special LG45s to good use in 1936 races.

Their main target was to have been Le Mans, cancelled that year because of strikes, but they scored class wins in both the French GP and the Belgian 24 Hours, were fourth and fifth in the Ulster TT, and third in that notorious car-breaker, the 500 Miles Race at Brooklands. For 1937 Lagonda produced a rather flamboyant Rapide version of the LG45, with higher compression, twin-plated flexible outside exhausts, and flared wings. At a price of £1,050 it was good for 105mph, but was soon super-seded by the Bentley-designed LG6 and the superb V12, both with new chassis having torsion bar independent front suspension and hydraulic brakes, and both taking Lagonda further from the sports category into the luxury car class.

Specification

Engine—*M45R*: Meadows 6 cylinders in line; 88·5 × 120·6mm, 4,453cc; pushrod ohv, 2 per cylinder; twin SU carburettors; dual ignition by coil-and-distributor and BTH magneto; 4 main bearings; approx. 125bhp at 3,200rpm.
LG45R: As above, but with improved head, larger valves, raised compression ratio, etc; approx. 130bhp at 3,600rpm.
Transmission—*M45R*: Single dry-plate clutch; separate 4-speed gearbox (with freewheel, 1934–35); open propellor shaft, spiral-bevel final drive.
LG45R: As above, but gearbox with synchromesh on 2nd, 3rd and 4th speeds.
Chassis: Pressed steel side members; semi-elliptic springing front and rear, Girling-Luvax hydraulic and Andre Telecontrol dual dampers (Luvax only on LG45R); Girling drum brakes.
Dimensions—*M45R*: Wheelbase, 10ft 3in; track, 4ft 10in; approx. car weight, 3,140lb.
LG45R: Wheelbase, 10ft 9in; track, 4ft 9¾in.

Below: *Three big red Lagondas beat Hall's Bentley and the Delahayes off the mark at the start of the 1936 Ulster TT. No. 3 is Earl Howe, No. 2 Pat Fairfield, and No. 1 the Hon Brian Lewis. Fairfield and Howe placed 4th and 5th overall*

Bottom: *Rakish "Rapide"—Heavy flared wings and flexible outside exhaust pipes featured on the 1937 open four-seater sports model on the six-cylinder 4½ litre Lagonda chassis, as improved by W. O. Bentley*

Bugatti Type 57

Almost any sports Bugatti could be rated a classic, but few models by that illustrious marque have stronger claims than the Types 57S, C and SC of the late 1930s, which consolidated their status by winning several major sports car races. Bugatti and motor racing were practically synonymous, of course, and most of the salient features of the Type 57 and derivatives were bred through two decades of competition. Yet despite his affinity for the sport, Ettore Bugatti was notably tardy in heeding its lessons, especially in adopting the twin overhead camshaft system of valve operation which provided efficient hemispherical combustion chambers with angled valves.

He first applied it to the 4·9 litre Type 50 road car of 1930, then to the Types 51 and 54 racing cars of 1931, and by 1933 had got around to modernising the 3·3 litre Type 49, perhaps the best of all touring Bugattis. It was Bugatti's son Jean, more than *le Patron* himself, who was responsible for developing its successor, the Type 57 which, while it retained the 49's bore and stroke of 72 × 100mm (3,257cc), was new in several other important aspects.

Replacing the three vertical valves per cylinder were single inlet and exhaust valves, angled at 90 degrees in a fixed head with central sparking plugs. The gear train driving the two camshafts was at the rear of the engine, with which the four-speed gearbox was in unit. The one-piece crankshaft ran in six plain bearings, the rearmost being between the bottom timing pinion and the flywheel, which housed a single-plate clutch. The chassis with its reversed quarter-elliptics at the rear and semi-elliptics at the front was traditional Bugatti, as was the impeccable workmanship and finish. Rudge wire wheels were standard, and the famous horseshoe radiator had vertical shutters and was of deeper section and less beautiful form than the stark racing types.

Introduced in March 1934, the new model was produced at Molsheim right up to September 1939. The basic Type 57 "normale" was, it should be emphasized, a top-quality touring car in French eyes, albeit its ample power, near-100mph

maximum and high standard of road-holding seemed distinctly sporting to the British. The development of an S (Sport) version was, of course, inevitable. Those ardent English *Bugattistes,* Earl Howe and the Hon. Brian Lewis, were quick to see the Type 57's potential and commissioned two cars with special two-seater light alloy bodywork for the 1935 Ulster TT. Both cars suffered clutch trouble, Lewis having to retire when when lying second, but Howe finished a strong third.

A cleaned-up version of the TT car appeared as the "Compétition" with lowered radiator and bonnet line that same year, and in 1936, when the French grew tired of German cars winning their premier races and switched to sports car rulings, Bugatti, Delahaye and Talbot all came forward to race for France—and against each other. Basing their cars on the Type 57, Bugatti showed extra enterprise in devising special low-drag, all-enveloping stream-lined bodies which paid off handsomely. The engines, forerunners of the Type 57S, had a lighter crankshaft and raised compression, giving over 160bhp, while in the light of Ulster experience, stronger two-plate clutches were fitted.

The first race for the so-called "tank" Bugattis was the 622-mile French Grand Prix, a Molsheim triumph with one T57 winning and the others finishing sixth and 13th. They then took first and second in the Marne GP, and late in the

year a team of three drivers took a "tank" to Montlhéry. They broke several Class C (3 to 5 litres) records including the 24 Hours at 123·93mph, and in 1937 one of the "tanks" won the Le Mans 24 Hour classic—the first French victory since 1926.

In the meantime the Type 57S road model had appeared, having a tuned engine in a lower, shorter chassis, dry sump lubrication, magneto ignition, de Ram hydraulic dampers, and a distinctive vee radiator of subtly pleasing form. It was followed by the 57C and 57SC, the former virtually the 57 with a Roots-type supercharger, gaining an extra 25bhp, improved flexibility and a maximum of 105–110mph. A Type 57C engine was fitted into an improved Bugatti tank for the 1939 Le Mans race; the supercharger allied with the streamlining gave it a potential speed of over 160mph, and the car won Bugatti's second Le Mans victory by over 26 miles.

The ultimate in road performance from the Type 57 was provided by the rare and highly desirable 57SC, a low-chassis 57S with supercharger, capable of 130mph with prodigious acceleration,

Tired of German and Italian victories in their major races, the French switched these to sports car rules in 1936. Here is J-P Wimille in the fully-enveloping streamlined 3·3 litre Bugatti "tank", winning the 1936 French GP at Montlhéry. His co-driver was Raymond Sommer

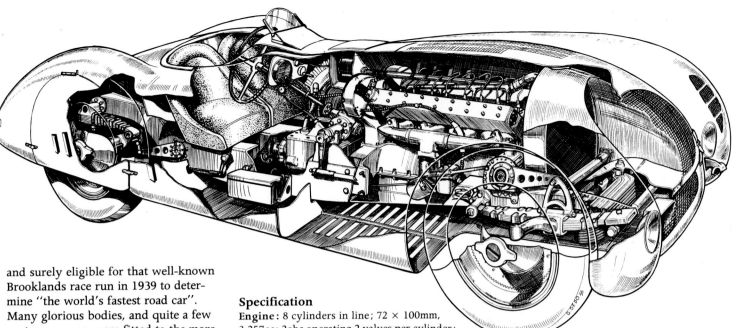

and surely eligible for that well-known Brooklands race run in 1939 to determine "the world's fastest road car". Many glorious bodies, and quite a few grotesque ones, were fitted to the more exotic Type 57 variants, one of the most striking being the Atalante two-door drophead, while a more bizarre interpretation was the Atlantic two-door coupé in electron, with voluptuous curves and an effective rivetted central spine.

Such extravaganzas aside, Molsheim traditionalists may have thought it heresy that Bugatti should adopt rubber engine mountings in 1936, hydraulic brakes in 1938, and telescopic hydraulic dampers in 1939! Such realistic changes could probably be ascribed to Jean Bugatti, whose influence on design at Molsheim grew as the 1930s advanced, but who, most unfortunately, was killed while testing a Bugatti in 1939 when obviously destined to prolong the line of Bugatti automobiles with distinction.

Specification

Engine: 8 cylinders in line; 72 × 100mm, 3,257cc; 2ohc operating 2 valves per cylinder; Stromberg or Bugatti carburettor; dual coil ignition (Types 57 and 57C), Scintilla magneto ignition (Types 57S and 57SC); 6-bearing crankshaft; Roots-type supercharger on Types 57C and 57SC; 135bhp at 4,800rpm (Type 57), 160bhp at 4,800rpm (57C), 170bhp at 5,500rpm (57S), 200bhp at 5,500rpm (57SC).

Transmission: Dry single-plate clutch (57 and 57C), dry two-plate clutch (57S and 57SC); 4-speed gearbox in unit with engine; open propellor shaft; spiral-bevel final drive.

Chassis: Pressed steel side members; semi-elliptic front suspension, reversed $\frac{1}{4}$-elliptic rear suspension; friction dampers (57 and 57C), de Ram hydraulic dampers (57S and 57SC), hydraulic telescopic dampers in 1939; cable-operated drum brakes (up to 1937), Lockheed hydraulic brakes (1938–39).

Dimensions: Wheelbase, 10ft 10in (57 and 57C), 9ft 11·3in (57S and 57SC); track, 4ft 5·1in.

Above: The 1936 "Tank" Bugatti based on the Type 57, as seen by French cutaway artist Gédo. The drawing shows the 3·3 litre straight-eight twin ohc engine of obvious racing derivation, the 4-speed gearbox, and the live rear axle with typical Bugatti reversed quarter-elliptic springs. This car won both the French and Marne GPs in 1936, while an improved version won at Le Mans the following year

Below: Bugatti's second Le Mans victory came in 1939, when Wimille and Veyron drove this supercharged version of the fully streamlined "Tank" to win at a record 86·85mph from a Delage and two British 12 cylinder Lagondas

Delahaye Type 135

One of the bigger surprises in the International sports car world during the "nervy 1930s" was the emergence of the Delahaye from domestic obscurity. If ever a marque seemed to lack the famous "Gallic spark" it was Delahaye, whose typical product up to 1933 was a solid, gloomy, high-built fabric saloon with cart springs and rice pudding performance resembling that of the trucks and fire-fighting vehicles which brought the makers most of their income. It is said that Ettore Bugatti made slighting remarks to Delahaye's chief, Charles Weiffenbach, concerning the excessive weight and slowness of his cars, and certainly they could not have been called "Europe's fastest lorries"! Whatever the spur, in 1933 Delahaye took their first firm steps away from lethargy.

Their liveliest model had a 3·2 litre six-cylinder overhead valve engine which also served in their commercial range, so designer Jean François fitted this into a short 9ft wheelbase chassis with transverse leaf independent front suspension and optional Wilson preselector gearbox, and called it the Super-Luxe. Its high build was no handicap in the 1934 Monte Carlo Rally, wherein works driver Perrot won his class and placed third overall. Some months later a similar chassis with single-seater streamlined body and three-carburettor 112bhp engine broke four world long-distance class C records and 11 international records at Montlhéry, including the 48 hours at 109·54mph and the 10,000km at 104·72mph.

This engine was next put into a light two-seater roadster, which won the touring class of the La Turbie hillclimb, took a coveted Coupe des Alpes in the 1934 Alpine Trial, and in October came home first in the Algerian Touring GP race in North Africa. Records, hillclimbs, rallies, races—*quel surpris*! The

year 1935 served further notice of Delahaye's change of heart. The 3·2 litre 9ft wheelbase car, now justly called the Coupe des Alpes, won three races at Lorraine, Reims and Orléans, won the Paris–St Raphael Ladies' Rally, came fifth at Le Mans, and third on distance in the 24 hours Targa Abruzzo race in Italy, in the heart of Alfa Romeo territory.

Then came the big French decision to switch over to sports car racing in 1936. Delahaye, doubtless fortified by their acquisition of the Delage marque in 1935, decided to participate. A new sporting model with 9ft 8in wheelbase and engine enlarged to 3,557cc appeared at the 1935 Paris Salon as the Type 135, and that winter Delahaye built a batch of 14 lower, lighter, more powerful "Compétition" editions, most of them for private customers. These cars wore shapely light-alloy open two-seater bodies with elegant Gallic curves in radiator, tail and wings, while underneath their French blue *carrosserie* the rugged six-cylinder pushrod ohv engines had triple Solex carburettors, magneto ignition and special oil coolers, and gave about 140bhp at 4,200rpm.

On their debut in the Miramas 3 Hours race early in 1936, the Delahayes

met the fast new 4 litre Talbots, scoring overwhelmingly on reliability by taking the first six places. At Algiers they scored 1-2-3-4, and then they came up against race-bred opposition—a blown Alfa Romeo in the Belgian 24 Hours, relegating them to second and third, and the Bugatti "tank" in the French GP, where they impressed even so by occupying second to fifth places. The French, ever mindful of racing success, studied the production Type 135s at the 1936 Salon with great interest. There were 3·2 and 3·5 litre chassis available in two wheelbases, with two transmission options—a manual four-speed or Cotal electro-magnetic planetary gearbox, in which four activated solenoids acted as clutches for the four speeds.

On such chassis, the cream of French coachbuilders drew on their talents to produce fine, fast *grand routiers*, some gloriously elegant, others spoiled by Continental excesses with curves and counter-curves running riot. The sporting Delahaye 135 gave 130bhp at 3,850rpm, making it a smooth, unfussy performer with a 100mph maximum, precise steering and impeccable road manners.

During the next two seasons, Delahaye competition successes stockpiled. They

Forerunner of the 3½ litre Delahaye Type 135 was the 3·2 litre "Coupe des Alpes" sports two-seater, with one of which Mme Lucy Schell (mother of post-war racing driver Harry Schell) won the 1935 Paris–St Raphael Ladies' Rally. Her husband Laurie won a race at Lorraine that same season with a similar car

won the Monte Carlo Rally, the Rainier Cup sports car race at Monaco, and the Donington 12 Hours race in England during 1937, and the Antwerp GP, Brooklands 3 Hours, and the Le Mans 24 Hours itself in 1938. By 1939 the basically seven-year old design was getting past winning, although R. R. C. Walker's 1936 "Compétition" model driven by A. C. Dobson won the "World's fastest road car" contest at Brooklands after the newer blown straight-eight Mille Miglia Alfa Romeo broke down.

Delahaye had made their point, in any case, and the Type 135 touring and sports models ranked among the foremost French prestige cars. Production was resumed after the War, but the design had dated, while new-style full-width *carrosserie* did not agree with the lissom build of the Delahaye. Nor were the times in favour of expensive luxury cars; the Delahaye-Delage combine did not live beyond 1953, but their Type 135 six remains an outstanding example of the post-Vintage thoroughbred class.

Specification

Engine: 6 cylinders in line; 84 × 107mm, 3,557cc; pushrod-operated ohv, 2 per cylinder; triple Solex carburettors; coil ignition (Scintilla magneto on Compétition models); 4-bearing crankshaft; 130bhp at 3,850rpm (Compétition, 150bhp at 4,200rpm).
Transmission: Single dry-plate clutch;

4-speed manual or Wilson 4-speed pre-selector gearbox up to 1936, Cotal electro-magnetic 4-speed gearbox optional from 1937, all in unit with engine; open propellor shaft; spiral-bevel final drive.
Chassis: Box-section side members; transverse-leaf independent front suspension, semi-elliptic rear springing; friction dampers (up to 1936), Luvax hydraulic and Andre-Hartford friction dampers (from 1937); Bendix servo-mechanical brakes.
Dimensions: Wheelbase, 9ft 8in; front track, 4ft 7in; rear track, 4ft 10in; approx. dry weight, 2,740lb (135 road car); 2,520lb (Compétition).

Above: A pair of Type 135 "Compétition" Delahayes, differing in wing and headlight treatment, but with the same tough 3½ litre six-cylinder engine and chassis with transverse leaf independent front suspension. On the left is an unaltered ex-works car, driver Louis Gérard; on the right is Joseph Paul's car

---

Below: The tough old Delahaye "sixes" gave yeoman service in early post-war racing when new cars were scarce. This example raced by Yves Giraud-Cabantous has a new Grand Prix-style nose, and is winning at San Remo in 1947 from the Italian opposition

Talbot Lago

It seemed unjust, but the only make to survive unscathed when the English-capitalised Sunbeam-Talbot-Darracq combine failed in 1935 was the French Darracq—and to add confusion to the story, this car was called the Talbot in its own country! The whys and wherefores of this minor anomaly in the grand STD confusion need not occupy us here; suffice it that while the British Sunbeam and Talbot marques passed under the Rootes umbrella to endure the fate of rationalisation, Automobiles Talbot in Paris were able to restart with a clean slate.

The new proprietor was Antony F. Lago, an engineer who, like Ettore Bugatti, was Italian-born, French domiciled, and loved motor racing. He had been general manager of the Wilson Self-Changing Gear Co., makers of the famous preselector gearbox until 1933, when he joined STD, becoming works manager of Darracq's old "Perfecta" factory at Suresnes. When the crash came two years later, he managed to round up substantial French capital from accessory makers and other interests, and refloated SA Automobiles Talbot.

Like Bugatti, Lago valued motor racing both as a laboratory and for its prestige benefits, especially when the car being raced was based on production models. With his shareholders' backing, there-fore, he was able to join Bugatti and Delahaye in supporting the French decision to change their Grands Prix into sports car events in 1936. The current Talbot touring car range included a 3 litre six-cylinder model with a 7-bearing crankshaft and Talbot's own patent valve gear, in which a single camshaft in the crankcase operated overhead valves at an included angle of 60 degrees in a hemispherical head, by means of 12 inclined, unequal length pushrods. This engine provided the basis, both of the competition car and the future Talbot-Lago road car.

A distinct parallel with the rival marque Delahaye is noticeable here. Both were virtually moribund with a dull range of cars; both had ohv six-cylinder engines of some potential; both aimed for the same targets—sports car racing and the luxury sporting market. The parallel becomes more remarkable in that both makes had box-section frames with independent front suspension employing a single transverse leaf, and semi-elliptic rear springing; Talbot, however, had an advantage in their superior head design and in engine size, which Lago and his ex-Fiat designer Becchia fixed at 90 × 104mm (3,994cc) for the first competition cars.

Like Delahayes, their debut came in the Miramas 3 Hours in May 1936; two neat pale blue 4 litre Talbots against two works and eight independent Delahayes. One Talbot retired early, the other with half an hour to go when leading, both with broken rockers. Despite considerable speed and expert drivers, the Talbots did not win a single race that season, while like Delahaye they could never quite match the pedigree-bred performance of the Bugattis. The year 1937 brought gratifying atonement; Talbots won the Tunis GP and the Miramas 3 Hours, then placed 1-2-3 in the French GP itself, and 1-2 in the RAC TT at Donington.

The French motor industry and the French public really preened themselves at the 1937 Paris Salon, with at least five distinguished makers—Bugatti, Delage, Delahaye, Hotchkiss and Talbot—all exhibiting *grand routiers* for the delectation of the wealthy. Automobiles Talbot's star contribution was the Lago Spéciale with Wilson self-change gearbox and 4-litre engine giving about 140bhp at 4,100rpm on triple Solex carburettors. Among the striking coachwork on this chassis was a two-seater coupé by Figoni et Falaschi featuring a steeply inclined screen, spatted rear wheels, "spined" tail, and a clean, oval grille recalling the 1936 GP Mercedes-Benz—or anticipating the 1948 Jaguar XK120.

The coming of war ended sports car production at Suresnes for seven years, but by 1947 Lago and his new engineer Marchetti had tooled up to build new Lago Record and Grand Sport models with a 4½ litre, 93 × 110mm version of the pre-war engine in basically pre-war chassis. Then early in 1948 a new Grand Prix racing car was built, its engine having twin camshafts high in the crankcase, operating the inclined ohv through short pushrods in Riley fashion. As single-seaters, these big reliable cars won several major races during the next four seasons through stamina and

Teething troubles spoiled the sleek new 3·9 litre French Talbot's chances in the 1936 French GP; this is Heldé pressing on around Montlhéry before trouble struck. Recompense came in the same race, on the same circuit, a year later, when Talbots took 1st, 2nd, 3rd and 5th places

moderate fuel consumption rather than sheer speed.

Antony Lago then applied the "Today's racing car is tomorrow's sports car" rule literally and converted the monoplace into a two-seater with wings, lights and other essential equipment, the French driver Louis Rosier winning the 1950 Le Mans 24 Hours with it, followed by an older two-seater Talbot in second place. Two years later a similar Talbot-Lago with more advanced enveloping bodywork had a comfortable lead at Le Mans with less than an hour to victory. Unfortunately its driver, Pierre Levegh, was trying to drive the entire 24 hours himself, and sheer fatigue made him miss a gear; a connecting rod let go, and what should have been Talbot's second Le Mans triumph went to Mercedes-Benz.

Like Delahaye, the big sporting Talbot-Lago road cars gave the *carrossiers* splendid opportunities to practise their *metier*, the short wheelbase and big wheels meaning a preponderance of low-built two-seater coupés. Some were of exquisite form and symmetry in the best French manner; others—a few—of grisly aspect with a frenzy of conflicting radii and curlycues, in the worst French manner. But neither the times nor the French taxation system were in sympathy with big-engined, fast, expensive cars, and despite efforts with smaller models, even using other makes of engine, Talbot-Lago could not survive the 1950s, although the Talbot name was revived by the French Peugeot Group shortly after they acquired the European interests of the American Chrysler Corporation.

Specification

Engine—*Lago Spéciale* (1936–1939): 6 cylinders in line; 90 × 104·5mm, 3,994cc; pushrod-operated ohv; twin or triple carburettors; 7-bearing crankshaft; 125 to 140bhp at 4,100rpm according to tune (Competition car, approx. 165bhp). *Lago Record and Grand Sport* (from 1946): As above, except 93 × 110mm, 4,482cc; 165 to 190bhp at 4,200rpm.
Transmission: Wilson 4-speed preselector gearbox; open propellor shaft; spiral-bevel final drive.
Chassis: Box-section side members; independent front suspension by transverse leaf spring; semi-elliptic rear springing; friction dampers (pre-war cars), hydraulic-cum-friction dampers (post-war cars); Bendix cable-operated mechanical brakes (pre-war cars), Lockheed hydraulic brakes (post-war cars).
Dimensions: Wheelbase, 8ft 8in or 9ft 8in; front track, 4ft 8in; rear track, 4ft 10½in; approx. car weight, 3,190lb (open two-seater).

Above: *French curves are practised to excess by the carrossiers* Figoni et Falaschi *on this short-chassis 1939 4 litre Talbot "Lago Spéciale". The enclosed front wheels improved the streamlining at the expense of steering lock*

Left: *Reversion to type, as practised on Louis Rosier's post-war Talbot-Lago GP single-seater, converted to the sports car format from which it descended. The car won Le Mans in 1950*

Below: *Lago's last fling in racing came at Le Mans with this elegant full-width conversion of the Talbot-Lago 4½ litre single-seater Grand Prix car. Pierre Levegh lost Talbot a second 24 Hours victory in 1952 by insisting on driving unrelieved. A similar car won the Casablanca 12 Hours race later that same year*

BMW 328

Although it was called the Alpine Trial, that famous long-distance road event was Europe's toughest rally before the Second World War. It spanned several Alpine countries, lasted five to six days, and took in the most gruelling of mountain passes. In the 1929 event a new "young" make figured among the Coupe des Alpes winners—the German BMW; initials of great renown in the aircraft and motorcycle worlds, but unknown then as a car manufacturer. The car was, in fact, a renamed Dixi-built Austin Seven, the Bayerische Motoren Werke having taken over the Dixi factory at Eisenach and continued production of the Germanised, left-hand drive Austins under licence, as BMWs.

These gave them the entrée they sought into the motor industry, but as makers of aero-engines and a very advanced transverse twin, shaft-drive motorcycle, BMW had far too much talent to rest content with such a bread-and-butter product. Despite the current economic gloom, their chief designer Dr

Fritz Fiedler inaugurated improvements which transformed the little car by 1932, with ohv engine and independent suspension. Two years later they dropped the Seven and moved into the 1·1 and 1½ litre classes with some highly promising small ohv sixes. The 1½ litre unit gave 34bhp in standard form, and was fitted into a short wheelbase tubular chassis with independent front suspension and rack-and-pinion steering. Three such cars ran in the 1934 Alpine Trial and defeated the British Frazer Nash team to win the 1½ litre class.

Much impressed by the agile little German cars, Frazer Nash chief H. J. Aldington took prompt "if you can't beat 'em, join 'em" action and secured UK import rights for BMW cars, thereby introducing the British to new standards of sports car motoring early the following year. Meantime Dr Fiedler had enlarged the engine still further to 65 × 96mm, giving 1,911cc for the Type 319 of 1935, and yet further to 66 × 96mm (1,971cc) for the 326 model

released at the Berlin Show early in 1936. These were advanced designs and from them was derived BMW's most sensational car yet, the Type 328 sports model.

At that stage in the short, violent life of Germany's Third Reich, emphasis was very much on national prestige. Mercedes-Benz and Auto Union carried the banner in Grand Prix spheres, and although BMW had begun a motorcycle racing programme, they now moved into sports car racing as well. Their weapon was the Type 328, which they intended to sell in considerable numbers to private owners, besides operating an official team to contest the International 2 litre class.

Aiming for optimum performance with reliability, Fiedler devised a variation on the Talbot-Lago method of achieving "hemi-head" and angled valve efficiency without resort to overhead camshafts. The pushrods operated one set of inclined valves, while rockers and cross-pushrods actuated the opposite

Below: *Origin of a distinguished species: the 328 sports BMW was evolved from this earlier 1¼ litre 6-cylinder touring BMW which scored a notable class victory in the 1934 Alpine Trial. Very advanced for its time, the chassis had tubular side members, transverse leaf independent front suspension, and rack-and-pinion steering*

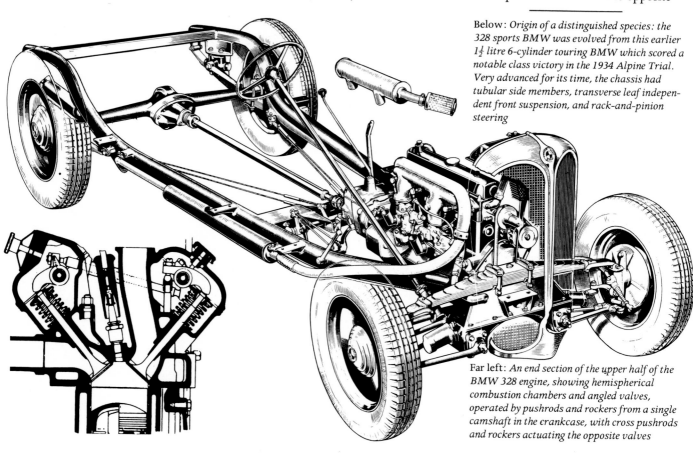

Far left: *An end section of the upper half of the BMW 328 engine, showing hemispherical combustion chambers and angled valves, operated by pushrods and rockers from a single camshaft in the crankcase, with cross pushrods and rockers actuating the opposite valves*

valves. The head was of aluminium, and with three Solex downdraught carburettors above paired vertical inlet ports, 80bhp was attained at 4,500rpm on a $7\frac{1}{2}$:1 compression ratio.

This smooth, potent unit was installed in a light but very rigid welded tubular chassis with 7ft $10\frac{1}{2}$in wheelbase and hydraulic brakes. Delahaye/Talbot style independent front suspension by a single transverse leaf and wishbones was employed, but of lighter interpretation. Rear springing was by semi-elliptics, while direct and precise rack-and-pinion steering was used. Aerodynamically clean and attractive light-alloy two-seater bodywork had integral wings and running boards, recessed headlights and a forward-opening one-piece ''alligator''-type bonnet giving easy engine accessibility. Eighty horsepower with a road weight of under 1,830lb meant a 95mph fully-equipped sports car which could be sold for £695 in Britain. By comparison, the contemporary 2 litre Aston Martin sports two-seater gave 110bhp, weighed 2,580lb, attained 82·8mph and cost £575 with very basic road equipment.

A tuned and modified BMW 328 could easily top 110mph, but although it was raced—and won—extensively, the car was good for more than speed; it was just as suitable for use in a long-distance rally or on a muddy English trials hill as in any race lasting 2 miles or 24 hours, while it could take two people and a modicum of luggage on a long tour or into town for theatre or dinner.

''Bay-em-Vay'' racing successes were innumerable, outstanding among them being their 2-litre class wins in the 1937 Eifelrennen and 1938 Mille Miglia by the British driver A. F. P. Fane, a 1-2-3 class win and team prize in the 1936 Ulster TT, and other class wins in the

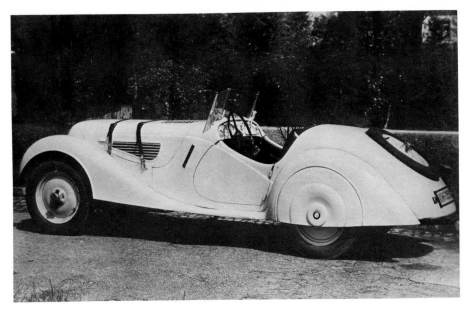

1937 TT, 1938 Antwerp, Spa 24 Hours, Avus and Chimay races, and 1939 Le Mans and Tobruk–Tripoli. At Brooklands in 1937 a 328 averaged 102·2mph for 1 hour on pump fuel, while their biggest win of all came in the 1940 Mille Miglia with a coupé at 103·5mph —a lustrous close to the 328's official career.

After the martial interlude Dr Fiedler's engine lived on a further 15 years or so, under the name of Bristol, the British aircraft concern who revived this brilliant unit for use in their own cars, in the post-war Frazer Nash, and in Cooper, Lister, AC and other prominent British sports and racing cars. As to the lovely little 328 car, the high prices it commands at today's auctions are eloquent of its value to connoisseurs, forty years after its heyday.

Specification

Engine: 6 cylinders in line, aluminium head; 66 × 96mm, 1,971cc; ohv operated by vertical and cross pushrods; triple Solex

Above: *The clean, incisive lines of the Type 328 sports two-seater BMW are apparent in this view. That its performance lived up to its looks and advanced specification was amply borne out by the large number of 2 litre class wins gained by the 328 before and after the war*

Below: *In victory formation, three white works BMW Type 328s driven by Roese, Briem and Heinemann run clean away with the 2 litre class of the 1938 Antwerp GP in Belgium. The cars generally raced with the rear wheel spats removed in the interests of accessibility*

downdraught carburetters; Bosch coil ignition; 4-bearing crankshaft; 80bhp at 4,500rpm.

Transmission: Dry single-plate clutch; 4-speed gearbox (synchromesh on 3rd and 4th) in unit with engine; open propellor shaft; spiral-bevel final drive.

Chassis: Welded steel tubular frame; independent front suspension by transverse leaf spring and wishbones; semi-elliptic rear springs; hydraulic dampers all round; hydraulic brakes.

Dimensions: Wheelbase, 7ft $10\frac{1}{2}$in; front track, 3ft $9\frac{3}{8}$in; rear track, 4ft 0in; approx. car weight, 1,830lb.

Jaguar

The Second World War was over, and barring politics, austerity, problems of labour, supply of materials and a multitude of lesser problems, car designers could look forward to translating at least some of their dream cars into reality. William Lyons of SS Cars Ltd, Coventry, was one who took early practical steps to get his design team working on new post-war models. Mindful of the sinister connotations in the initials SS at that time, he also re-formed the company as Jaguar Cars Ltd in 1945.

Besides being a very shrewd business man, Lyons was a stylist, psychologist and salesman rolled in one. As his pre-war SS range indicated, he knew that most cars sold on appearance, and when planning Jaguar's post-war engines he was insistent that the units should not only *be* right; they had to *look* right too, with the grace and purpose of a racing engine, and preferably with twin overhead camshafts. Some experimental units were built, two twin-cam engines with four and six cylinders code-named XK being favoured, and supply and production circumstances helped the final decision to build the six only.

The XK120 made its debut at Earls Court in 1948, and was the Belle of the Show. It wore captivatingly beautiful two-seater bodywork, styled by Lyons himself, and sweeping incisively back from a neat, simple grille to an unfaired scuttle, raked vee-screen and clean, compact tail. Integral wings swept down

to waist height by the doors, then swelled smoothly over the rear wheels, which had removable spats. All curves blended subtly, and slim bumpers, recessed headlamps and pressed-steel wheels completed an inspired ensemble.

Beneath that beautiful exterior was an arresting mechanical specification, with beauty of a different kind in the 83 × 106mm, 3,442cc six-cylinder engine with seven-bearing crankshaft, alloy head, twin chain-driven overhead camshafts under polished covers, and twin SU carburettors, all as handsome as even Lyons could demand. Engine power of 150bhp at 5,000rpm passed through a four-speed gearbox with synchromesh on all but first gear, and an open propellor shaft to a live, semi-elliptically sprung rear axle, all housed low in a box-section chassis with torsion bar independent front suspension. In the words of one American dealer it was "a knockout", and had there been a Car of the Year award back in 1948, the Jaguar XK120 would surely have won it.

Original plans to build about 200 examples and then concentrate on 100mph twin-cam saloons had to be hastily revised when orders for the XK120 simply flooded in, the bulk of them from the USA, land of the then "almighty dollar", the currency so urgently needed to achieve stability in early post-war Britain. To increase production, Jaguars had to employ steel body pressings instead of the aluminium-on-wood coachwork of the

first cars, and while this meant delays through extra tooling, the ultimate production rate was higher.

In the meantime the first XK120s were creating an International reputation. In May 1949 one was driven at 126·448mph through a measured mile on a Belgian motor road, running with hood and sidescreens erected and on low octane fuel. That publicly justified the car's type number, while a second run with extra aerodynamic aids at 132·59mph made it seem modest. And in August two XK120s finished first and second in the first Silverstone One Hour production car race, these feats helping to establish that Mr Lyons's glorious new car was not "just a pretty face".

It was, indeed, a Jekyll and Hyde car, excellent for touring and tractable at low speeds, although its subdued exhaust burble would break into a dramatic feline snarl when the driver accelerated hard. At a basic £988 it was staggering value, yet it could win major races and rallies, as evidenced by 21 year old "up-and-comer" Stirling Moss when he won the 1950 Dundrod TT in Northern Ireland, and by Ian Appleyard in winning the 1950 Alpine Rally outright. He repeated this success in 1951 with the same car, also winning Holland's Tulip Rally and the RAC's British classic, while the Belgian Johnny Claes won the exceptionally gruelling Liège–Rome–Liège rally in 1951.

XK120s also tackled the Le Mans 24 Hours race as a "probe" in 1950, one car lying an excellent third before retiring, while the other two finished well back, gaining invaluable data and experience that paid off richly in future years. At first the Jaguar's hydraulic drum brakes were not wholly adequate to the performance, but they were improved. The car was in production until 1954, when over 12,000 had been built in three body styles—the open

Two of the greatest: Veteran Italian racing maestro Tazio Nuvolari at the wheel of the XK120 Jaguar he was to race at Silverstone in 1950. Ill health unfortunately prevented him from starting

two-seater, a slightly bulbous fixed-head coupé introduced in 1951, and a drophead coupé the following year.

The Jaguar XK120's successor appeared in October 1954. Called the XK140, its engine now gave 190bhp, and other design improvements included revised weight distribution, stronger front torsion bars, rack and pinion steering and optional overdrive. Something of the XK120's lissom grace was lost in this 3,140lb model, and yet more in its almost portly successor of 1957, the XK150 with 210bhp to compensate for another slight increase in weight. These cars combined more creature comforts with their performance, and the XK150 had disc brakes on all four wheels plus optional Borg-Warner automatic transmission.

An "S" version with even more power—250bhp at 5,500rpm—appeared in 1958, while an optional 3·8 litre engine in 1959 gave 265bhp, so that performance never suffered in the civilising process. The XK150 was, indeed, a remarkably safe, fine-handling GT car with an impressive maximum of well over 130mph, albeit of dating appearance and construction. Its successor was the all-independently sprung E-type.

Specification

Engine—*XK120*: 6 cylinders in line, aluminium head; 83 × 106mm, 3,442cc; 2ohc operating 2 valves per cylinder; twin SU carburettors; coil ignition; 7-bearing crankshaft; 150–160bhp at 5,000rpm.
XK140: As above, except 190bhp at 5,500rpm.
XK150: As above, except 210bhp at 5,500rpm, or 220bhp at 5,500rpm with 87 × 106mm, 3,781cc engine.
Transmission: Single dry-plate clutch; 4-speed gearbox (synchromesh on 2nd, 3rd and 4th); open propellor shaft; hypoid-bevel final drive. Laycock de Normanville overdrive and Borg-Warner automatic transmission optional on XK140 and XK150.
Chassis: Box-section frame, independent front suspension by torsion bars and wishbones; non-independent rear springing by semi-elliptics; telescopic dampers all round; Lockheed hydraulic drum brakes (XK120 and XK140), Dunlop hydraulic disc brakes (XK150).
Dimensions: Wheelbase, 8ft 6in. Track—*XK120*: 4ft 3in (front), 4ft 3½in (rear); *XK140*: 4ft 3½in (front), 4ft 2½in (rear); *XK150*: 4ft 3·6in (front and rear). Approx. dry weight: 2,910lb (XK120); 3,140lb (XK140); 3,160lb (XK150).

The XK120C

Those early XK120 races, culminating in the experimental "dabble" at Le Mans in 1950, whetted Jaguar's appetite for racing. They were as well aware as any marque of the value of competition

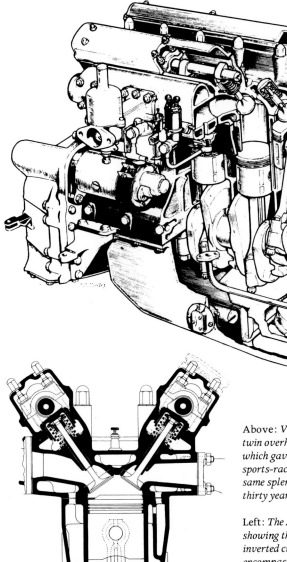

Above: *Versatile unit—The 3½ litre six-cylinder twin overhead camshaft Jaguar XK120 engine, which gave equally good service propelling sports-racing cars or docile luxury saloons. The same splendid basic design serves on today, over thirty years later*

Left: *The Jaguar twin ohc head in section, showing the valves inclined at 70 degrees, with inverted cup of "barrel" type tappets encompassing the valve springs*

success in publicity and sales, but there was an extra factor which interested British manufacturers in those restrictive days—more dollar sales meant a bigger quota of steel! Moreover, Le Mans was the season's most prestigious race by far, and on its post-war revival in 1949 had been won by an Italian Ferrari. In 1950 it went to a French Talbot, so for 1951 William Lyons felt it desirable that a British Jaguar should win it.

The new Le Mans Jaguar was a close secret until the eve of the race, although work began eight months earlier, the aim being not merely a potential Le Mans winner but a sports-racing car for limited production. As many parts of the standard XK120 were to be used as possible, but more speed, less weight, better handling and better brakes were needed. The car was designated the XK120C (for Competition) or more loosely the C-type, and although it seemed the shape of the XK120 two-seater could scarcely be improved upon, somehow Lyons and his team managed it on the

C, a breathtakingly handsome and highly effective machine.

The engine was the 3,442cc XK120 unit with "catalogue" tuning including raised compression ratio, improved porting, bigger valves, modified cams and timing, larger carburettors, lightened flywheel and a special crankshaft damper, all resulting in 210bhp at 5,800rpm on the brake, using 85 octane fuel. A basically standard synchromesh gearbox and rear axle were employed, but radical changes featured in the chassis and rear suspension. The C-type being expressly for racing, just one shallow door sufficed, enabling Jaguar to use a new tubular "space" frame with a deep one-piece bulkhead forming the scuttle. A multiplicity of small-diameter tubes, all carefully stressed in relation to each other and welded together, formed a series of triangulations giving great strength both longitudinally and laterally without excess weight.

The frame ended ahead of the rear axle line, the lower tubular cross member housing a single transverse torsion bar

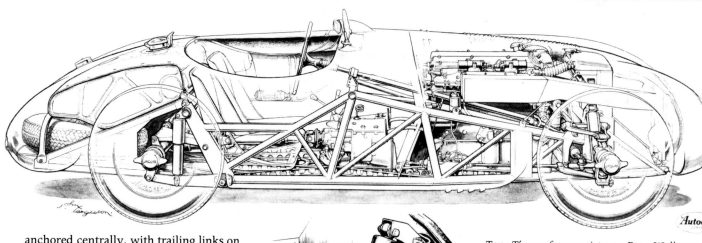

anchored centrally, with trailing links on each side supporting the rear axle. To serve both as the upper link and to provide lateral location, a sturdy A-bracket was mounted to the right, thus resisting the lift and spin encountered with a live axle under hard acceleration. While not independent, this system was a light yet sturdy compromise, excellent for the fast, smooth Le Mans circuit, if less so on twisty, more bumpy courses. The rear upper cross member of the main frame acted as top mount for the hydraulic telescopic dampers, and supported a rearward extension carrying the tail, the 40-gallon fuel tank, and spare wheel.

Lockheed hydraulic self-adjusting drum brakes, two-leading shoe at the front, rack-and-pinion steering and Dunlop knock-off wire wheels with alloy rims featured. All these "mechanicals" were shrouded within a low-drag body of masterly concept, the simple, shapely radiator grille and flush headlights merging smoothly into a sleek,

Top: *T'was a famous victory—Peter Walker at Le Mans in the shapely XK120C with which he and Peter Whitehead won the 24 Hours contest in 1951. This was the first of five Jaguar wins in the world's greatest endurance race*
Above: *Through-view of the Jaguar XK120C in its first form, showing the tubular space frame and non-independent rear axle, suspended by a single transverse torsion bar, radius arms and an A-bracket*
Left: *The power to stop, and to keep on stopping from Le Mans velocities took Jaguar performance above that of the opposition in 1953, when they employed Dunlop disc brakes*

rounded, enveloping body shell of sheer purposeful beauty, enhanced by its British racing green finish. The first car was only completed two months before the race, and the other two with a fortnight to go. As is well known, the XK120C driven by the "two Peters", Whitehead and Walker, won the race while the other cars retired, one after setting a new lap record at 105·2mph. Team manager "Lofty" England, later Jaguar's

managing director, estimated that this fine victory cost the company no more than £15,000.

An exaggerated estimate of the new Mercedes-Benz 300SL's performance cost Jaguar an almost certain repeat victory in 1952. At short notice they extended the nose and tail of the C-types, and all three overheated and retired—an ironic reversal of the tenet "If it looks right, it is right"; the 1952

Le Mans Jaguars (nicknamed "the Boilers") looked wrong, and were! But the firm made no mistakes in 1953, the year they introduced disc brakes to Le Mans. These were a joint Dunlop–Girling product, advantages over drums including their anti-fade and cool-running properties, and Jaguar's sustained superior braking undoubtedly clinched their 1-2-4 victory. Other aids were improved engine output with triple Weber double-choke carburettors, use of an aircraft-type "bag" tank for fuel, and lighter space frames giving an overall car weight of about 2,070lb.

Although XK120Cs won several lesser races elsewhere, including two French 12 hour races at Reims and Hyères in 1953, and did well in American events in private hands, Le Mans was always the makers' primary target, and while building and supplying over 40 production C-types with drum brakes to private owners, they were already engaged in designing their successor, the D-type, for the 1954 race.

Specification—XK120C
Engine: 6 cylinders in line, aluminium head; 83 × 106mm, 3,442cc; 2ohc operating 2 valves per cylinder; twin SU horizontal carburettors (triple Weber double-choke instruments on 1953 works cars); coil ignition; 7-bearing crankshaft; 200bhp at 5,800rpm (80 octane fuel), 210bhp (85 octane fuel), 220bhp (1953 works cars).
Transmission: Single dry-plate clutch; 4-speed gearbox (synchromesh on 2nd 3rd and 4th); open propellor shaft; hypoid-bevel final drive.
Chassis: Triangulated, welded tubular "space" frame with stressed bulkheads and channel-steel base members; independent front suspension by torsion bars and wishbones; non-independent rear axle with single transverse torsion bar, radius arms and offset A-bracket; telescopic hydraulic

dampers all round; Lockheed hydraulic drum brakes on production XK120C and works cars up to 1952, Dunlop disc brakes on works cars, 1953.
Dimensions: Wheelbase, 8ft 0in; track, 4ft 3in; approx. dry weight, 2,070lb.

The D-Type
In this second metamorphosis of XK120 parts and up-to-the-minute thinking, the Jaguar design team contrived yet again to produce the finest-looking sports-racing car of the day. Aircraft technique was applied this time, with a stressed skin, magnesium alloy monocoque centre section, and tubular subframes fore and aft to support the engine and rear axle respectively. The overall body section was elliptical with the radiator air intake a small, simple oval; the driver had a wrap-around screen and a head fairing which merged into a detachable, vertical stabilising fin, and the rear wheels were partly shrouded.

Beneath the svelte exterior, which was primarily the work of aerodynamicist Malcolm Sayer, the engine was developed to give some 245 horsepower at just under 6,000rpm. Larger inlet valves, more cam overlap, and improved inlet manifolding all helped, while an 8 degree incline, plus dry sump lubrication with shallow engine pan and an oil cooler in the nose intake, permitted the squeezing of the long-stroke 3,442cc twin-cam six into a car with a scuttle height of only 2ft 7½in. Also contributing to the low line was an adaptation of the abortive 1952 cooling system ("out of evil cometh good"), with separate header tank behind the radiator proper.

The suspension and braking remained much as on the C-type, but an all-synchromesh four-speed gearbox was

now employed, and Dunlop peg-drive perforated alloy disc wheels broke a long-standing tradition of wire wheels on sports-racing cars. With a wheelbase of only 7ft 6in, the D-type was remarkably compact, extremely effective aerodynamically with approximately 175mph available on a 2·8:1 Le Mans final-drive ratio and incidentally productive of the most superb and awe-inspiring "six cylinder" bark of any Jaguar.

To complete the story, the D-type should have won at Le Mans in 1954, but in fact a formidable 4·9 litre 12 cylinder Ferrari intruded, and Jaguar took a fighting second place. However, D-types won the race in 1955, 1956 and 1957, and thus the car justified itself admirably. It was also built for sale to privileged private customers. Because of high cost in manufacture and repair, the stressed skin magnesium-alloy central "tub" was discarded in 1955 in favour of a non-stressed light-alloy structure.

The 1955 works D-types acquired longer noses and full wrap-around screens which improved the aerodynamics and the drivers' comfort at Le Mans speeds. Engine output was again appreciably increased, and in 1956 experiments began with Lucas fuel injection. However, Jaguar officially withdrew from sports car racing that year, D-types thereafter being raced by private teams such as the famous Scottish

The immortal D-type: Smaller, lighter and faster than the Jaguar XK120C, the 1954 3·4 litre D narrowly missed another Le Mans victory that year. The stressed skin monocoque centre section carried tubular front and rear sub-frames; the impressive low-drag bodywork was the work of Malcolm Sayer

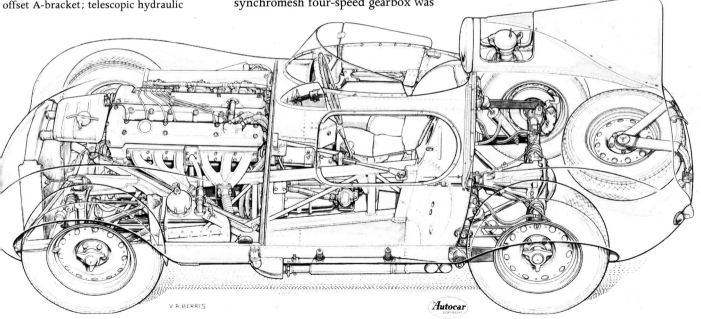

V.R.BERRIS   *Autocar*

In shape, performance, sound and spectacle the Jaguar D-type was every inch a classic sports-racing car. Here the valiant Mike Hawthorn battles with Fangio in one of the rival 300SLR Mercedes-Benz at the tragic Le Mans of 1955

Ecurie Ecosse which scored the last two Le Mans wins for Jaguar. Some engines were enlarged to 3·8 litres (3,781cc) and, apart from Le Mans, numerous wins were achieved all over the world.

With the change in race rules to a 3 litre top capacity limit in 1958, a short-stroke 2,986cc engine was built, but met little success. Some "customer" D-types were refined for use on the road, and early in 1957 a batch of 16 special cars were put through the works, with the designation XKSS. These had deep, full-width screens, more civilised upholstery, a passenger door, bumpers, more comprehensive lighting and other refinements. They lacked the characteristic Jaguar good looks, however, being short and "chunky", but with a potential of over 160mph maximum they were among the fastest road cars ever manufactured. A serious fire at the Jaguar factory in February 1957 ended the short career of this rare model.

Specification—D-Type
Engine: 6 cylinders in line, aluminium head; 83 × 106mm, 3,442cc; 2ohc operating 2 valves per cylinder; triple Weber double-choke carburettors; dry sump lubrication; oil cooler; coil ignition; 245 to 277bhp at 5,500–6,000rpm according to tune, fuel, compression, etc.

Transmission: Triple-plate Borg & Beck hydraulic clutch; 4-speed all-synchromesh gearbox; open propellor shaft; hypoid-bevel final drive.

Chassis: Central monocoque structure with welded fore-and-aft subframes (1954); as above but with bolted engine subframe from 1955; independent front suspension by torsion bars and wishbones; non-independent rear axle with single transverse torsion bar, radius arms and offset A-bracket; telescopic hydraulic dampers all round; Dunlop disc brakes.

Dimensions: Wheelbase, 7ft 6·6in; front track, 4ft 2in; rear track, 4ft 0in; approx. dry weight, 1,900lb.

The E-Type
Although designed as a successor to the XK150 road car, the Jaguar E-type owed its concept almost entirely to the D. It made a sensational debut at the 1961 Geneva Show, but a 3 litre forerunner with fuel injection and independent rear suspension had appeared at Le Mans in 1960, entered by Briggs Cunningham of the USA, and the design was originally mooted for racing in 1956. The new production car had a 3·8 litre six-cylinder unit giving 265bhp at 5,500rpm, and construction followed D-type precedents in featuring a steel monocoque body shell with a forward engine sub-frame built up of square-section tubing, and a separate sub-frame supporting the final drive and independent rear suspension unit. This employed transverse swinging links, radius arms and double

coil springs with coaxial telescopic dampers on each side, fixed-length half shafts passing between.

The front suspension was of established Jaguar type, and servo-assisted Dunlop disc brakes were fitted all round, outboard at the front and in-board at the rear. On an 8ft wheelbase, two-seater convertible and fastback closed bodywork was available, presenting the customary Jaguar litheness on a 150mph car of fantastic value at under £2,200. In 1965 engine capacity was raised to 4,235cc, and an all-synchromesh gearbox fitted. A 2 plus 2 coupé with mini-rear seat and 9in longer wheelbase followed. The lovely low roofline of the original E-type suffered somewhat in the interest of headroom, while automatic transmission and power steering became optional, highlighting the refinement of sports cars since pre-war days. Indeed, despite its electrifying performance the E-type rated as a GT model rather than a sports car.

In 1971, 10 years after its introduction, the E-type advanced to a 12 cylinder engine as the Series 3. Jaguar's long-awaited V12 engine was a 5,343cc 60-degree, ultra short-stroke unit with single overhead camshaft to each block, bowl-in-piston combustion chambers, four carburettors on vertical inlet ports, and 272bhp at 5,850rpm, delivered in a glorious smooth rush of near-silent power. The longer 8ft 9in wheelbase was standardised, and disc wheels and

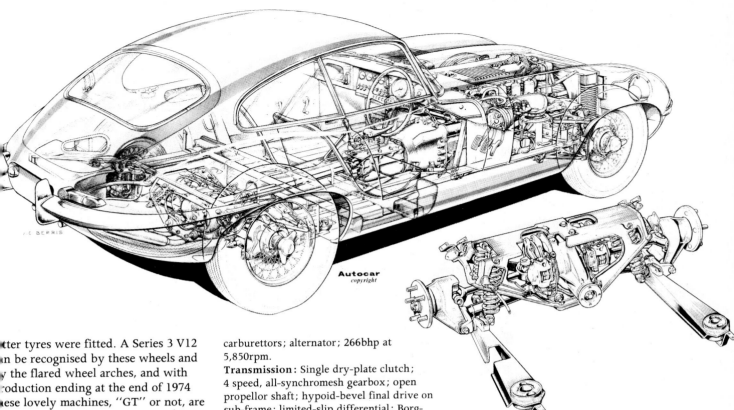

Autocar
copyright

...tter tyres were fitted. A Series 3 V12 ...n be recognised by these wheels and ...y the flared wheel arches, and with ...roduction ending at the end of 1974 ...ese lovely machines, "GT" or not, are ...ready joining the ranks of coveted ...assic sports cars.

...ecification—E-Type

...gine—*Series 1:* 6 cylinders in line, ...uminium head; 87 × 106mm, 3,781cc; 2ohc ...erating 2 valves per cylinder; twin SU ...rburettors; coil ignition; 7-bearing crank- ...aft;265bhp at 5,500rpm.
...ries 2: As above, except 92 × 106mm, ...235cc; 265bhp at 5,400rpm.
...ries 3: 12 cylinders in 60° vee, aluminium ...eads; 90 × 70mm, 5,343cc; ohc (each bank) ...erating 2 valves per cylinder; four SU

carburettors; alternator; 266bhp at 5,850rpm.
Transmission: Single dry-plate clutch; 4 speed, all-synchromesh gearbox; open propellor shaft; hypoid-bevel final drive on sub-frame; limited-slip differential; Borg-Warner automatic transmission optional.
Chassis: Steel monocoque body section with fore-and-aft tubular sub-frames; independent front suspension by torsion bars and wish-bones; independent rear suspension by double-coil springs each side, with fixed-length drive shafts, lower wishbones and radius arms; telescopic hydraulic dampers all round; hydraulic servo-assisted disc brakes.
Dimensions: Wheelbase, 8ft 0in; track, 4ft 2in (2 + 2 and Series 3: wheelbase, 8ft 9in; front track, 4ft 6·3in, rear track, 4ft 5·3in); approx. dry weight, 2,460lb (Series 1), 3,020lb (2 + 2), 3,230lb (Series 3).

Top: *Jaguar's glorious E-type road car in its comely early form as a two-seater coupé with 3·8 litre engine; such cars, once almost commonplace on our roads, are now rare and eagerly sought after*
Above: *Details of the highly effective independent rear suspension of the E-type Jaguar, with twin coil springs on each side and inboard disc brakes*
Below: *This 3·8 litre alloy-bodied E-type of Briggs Cunningham/Bob Grossman placed 9th at Le Mans, 1963, after losing its brakes and requiring a frontal rebuild*

Frazer Nash 2 litre

It was a strange twist of fate that the BMW, which began as a British Austin 7 in the 1920s and became a vigorous example of Teutonic effectiveness in the 1930s, should reappear in the 1940s wearing the decidedly British name of Bristol—new to the automobile world but as famous as BMW in aircraft circles. The link was AFN Ltd, the Aldington brothers' company which had marketed the sporting German sixes as Frazer Nash-BMWs before the Second World War. The 2 litre Type 328 was too good to waste, and with BMW themselves in no fit state to revive it, AFN reached agreement with the Bristol Aeroplane Company whereby both would manufacture variations on the BMW theme in Britain, with Bristol producing the engines. A special *coup* by the Aldingtons was to engineer the release from

prison of BMW's designer, Dr Fritz Fiedler, to join in the enterprise.

As it first appeared in the Bristol 400 coupé of 1946, the Bristol-built BMW engine differed little in design from the German original, retaining the 66 × 96mm bore and stroke and, of course, the famous vertical-cum-cross pushrod valve gear. Frazer Nash announced a new sports car using this engine in higher-performance form the same year, but none was forthcoming until the 1948 London Show, when the "High Speed" competition two-seater was placed on view. Externally this was stark and traditional, with fixed cycle wings, a spacious cockpit with cutaway sides, a rounded tail covering the spare wheel, and an outside exhaust system which in action emitted a memorable snarl.

Beneath these very English externals was a BMW-style welded frame with $5\frac{1}{2}$in diameter tubular side members and 5in cross members. At the front was independent suspension by an upper transverse leaf spring and lower wishbones, *à la* 328, while at the rear the frame kicked up to end above the live rear axle, suspended on 326-type longitudinal torsion bars in preference to the pre-war 328's semi-elliptics. A central, fabricated A-bracket provided lateral location and took driving and brake torque, its fore ends hinged on a cross member, its apex to the differential housing.

The 328's excellent rack-and-pinion steering was used, and the wheelbase was only 8ft long. The 2 litre, triple-carburettor engine had an $8\frac{1}{2}$:1 compression ratio and a gross output of 120bhp at 5,500rpm; it was set well back in the chassis, driving via a four-speed Borg-Warner gearbox and very short, jointed propellor shaft to the rear axle. The sparse bodywork was aluminium-panelled on a veritable cat's cradle of welded small-diameter tubes, dry weight of the car was only about 1,510lb. An unpretentious, functional, honest sports-racer, it looked and acted the part supremely.

Its potential became evident in the first post-war Le Mans 24 Hours in 1949, when the amateur Norman Culpan and H. J. Aldington drove the former's car to a splendid third place behind a Ferrari and a Delage. The name "High Speed" was promptly ditched in favour of "Le Mans Replica", and as such the model did very well in sports car racing during the next few seasons. Bypassing the countless class wins in British sprints, hillclimbs and shorter races, 2 litre 'Nash feats included the Enna and Targa Florio road race victories by the Italian Franco Cortese in 1951, Stirling Moss' British Empire Trophy win at Douglas, IoM the same

Earning its name: The 2 litre six-cylinder Bristol-engined Frazer Nash "High Speed" competition two-seater which took third place at Le Mans in 1949 driven by N. Culpan and H. J. Aldington, thereafter becoming the "Le Mans"

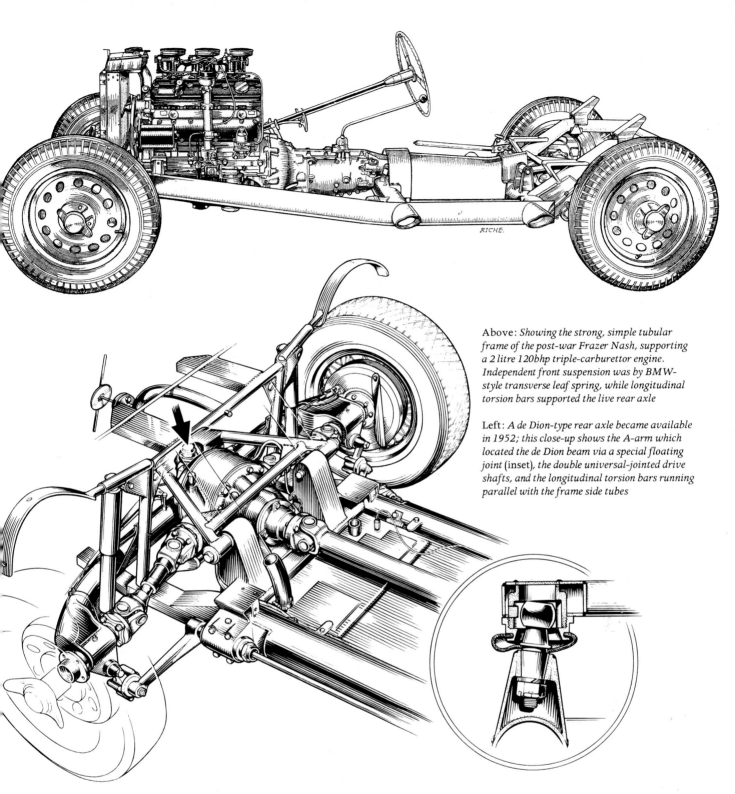

Above: *Showing the strong, simple tubular frame of the post-war Frazer Nash, supporting a 2 litre 120bhp triple-carburettor engine. Independent front suspension was by BMW-style transverse leaf spring, while longitudinal torsion bars supported the live rear axle*

Left: *A de Dion-type rear axle became available in 1952; this close-up shows the A-arm which located the de Dion beam via a special floating joint (inset), the double universal-jointed drive shafts, and the longitudinal torsion bars running parallel with the frame side tubes*

year, and the first place by two American drivers in the 1952 Sebring 12 Hours race in Florida.

Some 60 Le Mans Replicas were built, while a Mark II version, lighter by 100lb and with wire wheels, more power and less frontal area appeared in 1952. This model was available with a de Dion rear axle, also a feature of the "Sebring" of 1953, another wire-wheeled lightweight despite full-width bodywork marred by an ill-shaped radiator intake. Quite the most beautiful post-war Frazer Nash aesthetically was the white-painted "Mille Miglia" two

seater with integral wings and clean styling anticipating that of the MGA. Sadly, the 1950s marked the end of such individual and hence expensive sports cars, and AFN Ltd turned their attention to importing—not modern German-built BMWs as one might have expected but Porsches, which keep them very busy indeed.

Specification
Engine: 6 cylinders in line, aluminium head; 66 × 96mm, 1,971cc; two overhead valves per cylinder, operated by vertical and cross pushrods; triple Solex downdraught

carburettors (SU initially); coil ignition; 4-bearing crankshaft; 110–120bhp at 5,250–5,500rpm.
Transmission: Single dry-plate clutch; 4-speed gearbox (synchromesh on 2nd, 3rd and 4th) in unit with engine; open propellor shaft; spiral-bevel final drive.
Chassis: Welded tubular side members, tubular cross bracing; independent front suspension by transverse leaf spring and wishbones; non-independent rear axle, suspended by longitudinal torsion bars and A-bracket; piston-type hydraulic dampers all round; hydraulic drum brakes.
Dimensions: Wheelbase, 8ft 0in; track, 4ft 0in; approx. dry weight, 1,510lb.

Ferrari front-engined V12s

This book could be filled entirely with Ferraris, for every road car the illustrious Italian marque ever made ranks as a classic sports car, from the first 1½ litre V12 of 1947 to the latest Boxer flat-12 over 30 years later. Enzo Ferrari loved twelve cylinders, from the time he saw the First World War Packard Twin Six staff cars used by the American forces in Europe, while he was very closely associated with the configuration when running the Alfa Romeo racing team in the late 1930s. There have been four, six and eight-cylindered Ferraris as well, of course, but the name will always be associated with the thrilling howl, rising to a potent shriek, of a dozen busy cylinders in a high-efficiency engine built with sheer power and speed as its prior objectives.

Ferrari cars are also inseparable from racing, through their creator's life-long love for it, and this has given them their unique pedigree. Virtually every one of their extensive *Tipi* has been raced somewhere, some time, and almost every design advance in a Ferrari has resulted through racing experience. Certainly in their earlier years one felt that the road cars built and sold to sustain the business of Automobili Ferrari were almost incidental to their racing programme. Later on, commercial motives perforce hardened, and production for lucrative markets was properly planned, yet this endearing Latin leaning towards motor racing through the years has made Ferrari cars what they are—the most exciting in the world.

Excluding the two 1½ litre straight-8 Vettura 815s built for the 1940 Mille Miglia when Ferrari was bound by agreement with Alfa Romeo not to put his name to a car, the first Ferrari to bear the name was the 1,496cc 60 degree V12 built in 1946–47 at his Maranello works some 12 miles south of Modena. This engine, the first *dodici cilindri*, measured

55 × 52·5mm, and had single overhead camshafts to each block, a 7-plain bearing crankshaft, hairpin valve springs, twin magnetos and three Weber carburettors. Its designer was G. Colombo, the ex-Alfa Romeo engineer responsible for the Type 158 supercharged straight-8 racing car. His V12 was the ancestor of all Ferrari twelves, an attractively compact short-stroke big-bore unit offering maximum piston area and 6,000rpm. Its initial 72bhp seemed almost timid but its potential was vast, with supercharging for Grand Prix racing an early priority.

The chassis in which this engine made its debut followed the then current Continental thinking with its oval tubular frame with X bracing, transverse lower leaf independent front suspension, and semi-elliptic back end with live axle. A five-speed gearbox without synchromesh was employed, and with much development work ahead, 1947 was a year of trial and test for Colombo, Ferrari and his engine specialists Lampredi and Bazzi. The unique song of a Ferrari V12 first rang out in anger in a minor race at Piacenza in May, 1947, when Franco Cortese, who had driven for Ferrari since 1932, only lost the lead with two laps to go through a fuel pump defect.

Excluding unreliability, the new cars met surprisingly strong opposition from compatriot Cisitalias, Fiat-Stanguellinis and Maseratis, and apart from minor national wins real success did not attend the V12s until October. By then the 125 had grown into the 1,903cc Type 159, giving a healthier 125bhp at 7,000rpm, and in the 312-mile Turin GP, the single Ferrari driven by the Frenchman Raymond Sommer fought off very

With full-width enveloping body in light alloy by Carrozzeria Touring, the 1½ litre Tipo 125 Ferrari looked a striking car for 1947 from both front and rear aspects, and swiftly lived up to its appearance by its performances in racing

fame was furthered by one particular body option, the captivating full-width Mille Miglia open two-seater built by Touring and nicknamed the *Barchetta* or "little boat".

In 1949 Colombo left Ferrari, and Aurelio Lampredi was appointed chief designer. Having made the 166 engine work effectively he turned to new racing units, producing highly effective un-supercharged Formula 1 and 2 designs, and also laid down a bewildering succession of larger-engined sports models, with equally bewildering type numbers based on the capacity of one cylinder. They included the 2·3 litre Tipo 195, the 2·5 litre 212, 2·7 litre 225, 4·1 litre 340 America, 2·9 litre Europa, and 4·5 litre 375 America. All these were road cars, the mildest of them ideal for fast "grand touring", the wildest scarcely needing more than racing numbers to plunge straight into competition.

Evolution of some types, like the big 375s, came directly through racing. In the Formula 1 battle with Alfa Romeo in 1950–51, Lampredi had developed a big 4½ litre unsupercharged V12, the Tipo 375/F1, and the same basic unit later served in Ferrari sports-racing cars and also in high-speed road models. By 1954 it had grown to a formidable 4·9 litres as the 375 Plus, and this was the engine Ferrari used to beat Jaguar at Le Mans, and also to win the Pan-American Road Race in Mexico that year. The same basic 340bhp unit subsequently powered some fierce, long-legged 160 plus mph 24-plug road coupés and open spyders called the 410 Superamerica, for those competent to handle them.

Such machines, produced in small numbers and basking in the glory of countless competition wins, were very expensive, yet they were the company's profit-makers. Virtually every Italian coachbuilding concern of repute— Vignale, Touring, Zagato, Allemano, Bertone, Stabilimenti Farina, Pininfarina, Ghia, and others had built bodies on

strong Maserati, Alfa Romeo, Talbot, Delahaye and Delage opposition to win by three miles. "I sat down and wept" said Enzo Ferrari, but logic quickly over-rode emotion and a full 2 litre sports Ferrari went into production as the Tipo 166.

This small red bomb took the new marque right to the forefront. In 1948 alone it won three racing classics—the Targa Florio, Mille Miglia and Paris 12 Hours, and in 1949 it took four more— the Targa Florio and Mille Miglia again, plus Le Mans itself and the Belgian 24 Hours, both won by Luigi Chinetti. A 166 was the first Ferrari to reach the United States, where Briggs Cunningham and others raced it successfully, and its

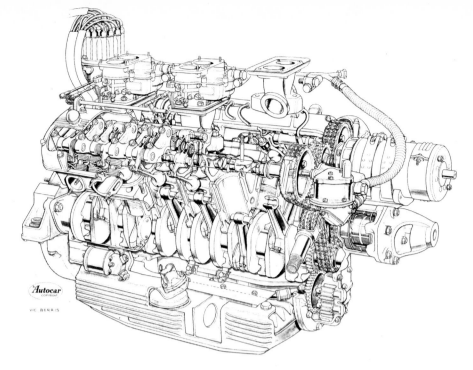

The classic concept: The 60 degree V12 Ferrari 250GT engine, a design of Colombo origin detailed by Lampredi and further developed by Chiti. Measuring 73 × 58·8mm (2,953cc), its power rose from 200bhp in 1954 to 250bhp by 1960. Characteristics include detachable alloy heads, single chain-driven ohc to each cylinder bank, hairpin valve springs and triple carburettors

Ferrari chassis, but by 1954 there were signs of rationalisation. Ferrari and Pininfarina reached a joint agreement, and thereafter the latter produced most of Ferrari's coachwork, a proportion of it being sub-contracted to Scaglietti.

Variations on the Ferrari performance theme were legion; four speeds or five, one, two, three or even six carburettors, single or twin choke, magneto or coil ignition, one plug or two per cylinder. . . Yet despite the high performance, apparent complexity and busy mien of the Colombo/Lampredi V12s, they were remarkably strong, comparatively low-stressed, and possessed impressive reliability. This was given further emphasis when, in 1956, there was a marked rise in popularity of the Gran Turismo (GT) class of racing. This came much closer to genuine production sports car racing than the events disputed by the Mercedes-Benz 300SLR, Jaguar D-type and "near-GP" Ferraris which had made up the World Sports Car Championship; the terrible Mercedes crash at Le Mans in 1955 forced attention still further on the GT class.

The basis of Ferrari's GT challenge was the 250GT Europa with 2,953cc 12-cylinder engine, first introduced in 1953 as a closed *Berlinetta*, ie coupé. This stimulating if rather solid road car was rebodied more sparsely by Pininfarina and raced in light, short wheelbase form with enormous success during the next six seasons. GT Ferraris won the gruelling 3000-mile Tour de France six years running from 1956 to 1961, and dominated GT racing wherever it was staged, in France, Italy, Germany, Britain, Belgium, USA, and elsewhere.

The year 1962 brought a new 3 litre Manufacturers' GT Championship, and an improved Ferrari, the 250GTO, to contest it. The "O" signified *Omologato* or "homologated", as required by the race ruling FIA, and while this was a frank competition machine of ultra-lightweight construction and some

Great moment: The Ferrari mechanics relax at last and bask in the public acclaim as the Phil Hill/Olivier Gendebien 4 litre 330LM parades after its 1962 Le Mans victory

290bhp, it still remained a roadgoing sports car of exhilarating potential. The 250GTO scooped the GT pool again for Ferrari in 1962, 1963 and 1964, despite opposition first from the lightweight E-Type Jaguar and then from the Shelby American Cobras. It also raised Maranello's Tour de France score to 9 consecutive wins, but in 1965 Ferrari concentrated on Formula 1 and prototype sports car racing, and abandoned the GT class after a brilliant decade.

If the GTO's day was done, the memory of this fantastic dual-purpose Ferrari, so electrifying yet tractable on the road, so brilliant in a race, lingers on today, when the model is very hard 'currency'' indeed. Nor did its going mean the end of the front-engined V12 road Ferrari by any means. The *Berlinetta Lusso* was a more refined and very desirable street successor to the stark GTO; the 4 litre 330GT 2 + 2 of 1964 paid lip service to fashion with four headlights (but they were back to two a year later), and serious technical improvements came on the 275GT of 1965, with a rear-mounted five-speed all-synchromesh gearbox, independent rear suspension by coil springs and A-arms, and cast-alloy wheels, soon to replace the traditional Borrani wire-type on all Maranello's road cars.

America was, of course, an immensely important market for Ferrari, and hence US safety and exhaust emission regula-tions had to be taken very seriously. The first compliant model was the new 365GT in 2 + 2 form, introduced late in 1968, with a 4·4 litre engine, limited-slip differential, all-independent suspension with hydro-pneumatic self-levelling, and such un-Ferrari features as power steering and air conditioning—a luxury Ferrari indeed, but still able to propel its passengers at a safe if heady 150mph.

Then came the 365GTB/4, a gloriously

Above: *A full stop to Mille Miglia race history came in 1957, when Taruffi won in this Ferrari 335S with 4ohc 4,023cc V12 engine, on his 13th drive in the Italian road race. De Portago's fatal crash in another 335S, costing 12 lives, ended the Mille Miglia as a race*
Below: *The Ferrari 250TR, 1958 Le Mans winner driven by Gendebien and Phil Hill, had a Testa Rossa competition version of the 250GT engine, with revised heads, "hot" cams and six twin-choke Weber carburettors. It won the 1958 Sports Car Championship for Ferrari*

Tipo 375 America

Engine: 12 cylinders in 60° vee, detachable alloy heads; 84 × 68mm, 4,522cc; single ohc to each bank, chain-driven, operating 2 inclined valves per cylinder; hairpin valve springs; triple twin-choke Weber carburettors; twin magneto ignition; 300bhp at 6,000rpm.

Transmission: Multiple dry-plate clutch; 4-speed all-synchromesh gearbox in unit with final drive; open propellor shaft, hypoid-bevel final drive.

Chassis: Welded oval tubular side members, cross-braced; independent front suspension by lower transverse leaf spring and upper wishbones; non-independent rear suspension by semi-elliptics; hydraulic dampers all round; hydraulic drum brakes.

Dimensions: Wheelbase, 9ft 2·7in; front track, 4ft 2in; rear track, 4ft 3in; approx. dry weight, 2,200lb.

250GT Berlinetta

Engine: 12 cylinders in 60° vee, detachable alloy heads; 73 × 58·8mm, 2,953cc; single ohc to each bank, chain-driven, operating 2 inclined valves per cylinder; three twin-choke Weber carburettors; twin coil ignition; 7-bearing crankshaft; 260bhp at 7,000rpm.

Transmission: Twin dry-plate clutch; 4-speed all-synchromesh gearbox in unit with engine; open propellor shaft; hypoid-bevel final drive.

Chassis: Welded oval tubular side members, tubular cross-bracing; independent front suspension by coil springs and wishbones; non-independent rear suspension by semi-elliptics; hydraulic dampers all round; hydraulic disc brakes.

Dimensions: Wheelbase, 7ft 10·5in; front track, 4ft 5·3in; rear track, 4ft 5·1in; approx. dry weight, 2,400lb.

365GTB/4 Daytona

Engine: 12 cylinders in 60° vee, detachable alloy heads; 81 × 71mm, 4,390cc; 2ohc to each bank, operating 2ohv per cylinder; six twin-choke Weber carburettors; 7-bearing crankshaft; 352bhp at 7,500rpm.

Transmission: Single dry-plate clutch; torque tube drive to 5-speed, all-synchromesh gearbox in unit with final drive; limited-slip differential.

Chassis: Welded multi-tubular frame; independent suspension all round by coil springs and wishbones; hydraulic telescopic dampers; servo-assisted hydraulic disc brakes.

Dimensions: Wheelbase, 7ft 10in; front track, 4ft 8·5in; rear track, 4ft 8in; approx. dry weight, 2,645lb.

sleek *Berlinetta* better known as the Daytona, with a 4·4 litre, four-cam, six-carburettor 352bhp engine and over 170mph beneath the driver's right foot. Its four headlights lived under a full-width bevelled plastic cover merging with the bonnet, and Pininfarina's lines, faithfully interpreted by Scaglietti, were quite breathtakingly perfect. Here was a typical "iron hand in velvet glove" Ferrari of the late 1960s, refined and well-mannered, awesomely fast and a glorious climax to the long, illustrious line of front-engined 12-cylinder Ferraris. It reigned for six years, from 1969 to 1974, then gave way to the mid-engined flat-12 Berlinetta Boxer, a more progressive new generation *dodici cilindri* with all the rich Ferrari character in its specification.

Specification—Tipo 166

Engine: 12 cylinders in 60° vee, detachable alloy heads; 60 × 58·8mm, 1,995cc; single ohc to each bank, chain-driven, operating 2 inclined valves per cylinder; hairpin valve springs; triple Weber carburettors; twin magneto ignition; 7-bearing crankshaft; 140bhp at 6,600rpm (MM), 150bhp at 7,000rpm (SC).

Transmission: Single dry-plate clutch; 5-speed non-synchromesh gearbox in unit with engine.

Chassis: Welded oval tubular frame with X-bracing; independent front suspension by lower transverse leaf spring and upper wishbones; non-independent rear suspension by semi-elliptics; hydraulic dampers all round; hydraulic drum brakes.

Dimensions—MM: Wheelbase, 7ft 2·6in; front track, 4ft 1·8in; rear track, 4ft 1·2in. *SC:* Wheelbase, 7ft 11½in; front track, 4ft 2in; rear track, 3ft 11·4in.

Cunningham

The United States was lucky to have a man so patriotic, so wealthy, and so dedicated to motor racing as Briggs Swift Cunningham. One wonders if they deserved him, for although he tried extremely hard to win the Le Mans 24 Hours race for America, the US automobile industry, apart from Chrysler, did little to help him. It was easy to shrug and declare, "He could afford it", but such determination was rare in rich men and could well have been further exploited. In the end he gave up, his hard-won experience neglected, yet his Le Mans aims became those of the Ford Motor Company 10 years later, and whereas he with his private team failed, they with their corporate might at last succeeded.

Cunningham was plunged into the sports car *milieu* after the Second World War, when Allards, MGs, Healey Silverstones and Jaguar XK120s were exported in quantity by war-impoverished Britain to the 'States in exchange for vitally needed dollars. Italy, too, sent exciting sports cars across the Atlantic, and Briggs Cunningham bought the very first Ferrari to reach US shores, a 2 litre V12 spider, in 1948. The revival of the Le

Mans 24 Hour classic in 1949 further fired him with enthusiasm, and he and New York car importer Phil Walters decided to contest the 1950 race with two privately purchased Cadillacs, one bearing a grotesque American-built open body.

They finished 10th and 11th, gaining invaluable experience, and for 1951 Cunningham resolved to build his own cars and run an all-American team at Le

Right: *C-2R—The 1951 competition Cunningham, seen at the Watkins Glen GP, was big, portly and powerful; 5·4 litres took the three cars to pleasing 1st, 2nd and 4th places*

Below: *C-4R—The 1952 car had more graceful, lissom lines, and weighed over 1,000lb less than its predecessor. One finished 4th at Le Mans, winning its class*

Mans. A plant was opened at West Palm Beach, Florida, a small staff of experts assembled, and design and construction was started. Like so many American competition cars, the Cunninghams began by being too large and heavy.

Below: *The Chrysler "Firepower" V8 engine used in the Cunningham had hemispherical heads with inclined ohv operated by pushrods from a single central camshaft. With a bore and stroke of 96·8 × 92·1mm, the engine was "oversquare"; it put out around 300bhp*

Bottom: *The special Cunningham C-4R with coupé body built to Prof Kamm's aerodynamic principles, which competed at Le Mans in 1952*

The engine used was a beefy Chrysler Firepower hemi-head V8 of 5·5 litres, reworked to give around 240bhp instead of the standard 180. It was mated up to a Cadillac three-speed gearbox and installed in a tubular chassis with de Dion-type rear axle and independent front suspension by wishbones and coil springs.

Designated the C-2R and painted in America's racing colours, blue and white, it emerged an aggressive-looking open two-seater, somewhat resembling an oversize Ferrari *barchetta* but without its lithe grace—and with considerably more avoirdupois, the car weighing about 3,360lb unladen, or 3,810lb with 55 gallons of fuel plus tools aboard! Yet the C-2R was good for almost 150mph down the straights at Le Mans, and held the road well. After prodigious efforts to prepare three cars, two retirements and one 18th place (after lying second for 6 hours) was poor reward, but the Cunningham team applied the lessons they learned to improve the cars for 1952.

Meantime the first of the obligatory 25 road cars which the Le Mans entry rules required to be built was laid down at West Palm Beach. Called the C-3, it followed 1951 Le Mans basic layout, but was fitted with a Chrysler rigid rear axle and a German ZF four-speed gearbox with semi-automatic change, and wore handsome GT coupé coachwork designed by Michelotti and built by Vignale of

Turin. The model retailed at $10,000, while a convertible was also made at $11,000—yet even at such prices these rare and elegant cars scarcely returned a worthwhile profit.

The 1952 Le Mans cars, type numbered C-4R, showed evidence of considerable "banting"; they were 5in shorter in wheelbase, 4in narrower, and almost 1,100lb lighter. Chryslers had raised the Firepower's output to around 300bhp, and a new five-speed ZF gearbox was fitted. The de Dion rear axle gave way to a rigid-type with coil springs, an apparent retrogression which in truth was common-sense on the smooth Le Mans course. New magnesium-alloy quick-release wheels and finned, ventilated A1-fin drum brakes featured, and the blue and white trio looked superbly professional, backed by the impressive Cunningham entourage at Le Mans, including a huge travelling workshop, tender wagons, mobile field kitchen and several cars.

One of the C-4Rs was fitted with aero-dynamic coupé coachwork embodying the principles of the German specialist Professor Kamm, but this suffered valve trouble in the race, as did one of the open cars. However, Briggs Cunningham himself and Bill Spear in the remaining car finished a fine fourth and first in class, Cunningham revealing his physical stamina by driving 20 of the 24 hours. Back in the 'States the cars gained several race wins, notably at Elkhart

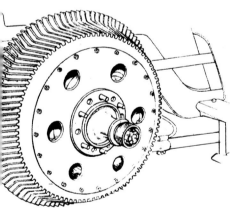

Top: *They nicknamed it "the Shark", but the Cunningham with revised bodywork for 1953 was officially the C-5R. Driven by Fitch and Walters it proved fastest of all cars through the Le Mans flying kilometre at 154·4mph*

Above: *Le Mans is always hard on brakes, especially on big, heavy cars. Those on the 1953 Cunninghams were fitted with special radially-finned drums to improve cooling*

Lake, Turner airfield and Thompson raceway, and early in 1953 one scored the marque's greatest success, first place in the Sebring 12 Hours race.

A C-4R also placed third in the 1953 Reims 12 Hours, winning its class, but at Le Mans was eclipsed by the newer C-5R with rigid front axle. This car took third place behind two disc-braked Jaguars, while C-4Rs were seventh and tenth, marking a full team finish. Yet again the cars wound up their season with several home wins, and if by 1954 the gallant C-4Rs were growing old, their rousing third and fifth places, plus another class win at Le Mans further underlined their speed and stamina. One also won the Watkins Glen GP that Fall, making a pleasing swansong for a fine American competition car.

The company was closed the following year, even Briggs Cunningham at last finding pursuit of a Le Mans victory too expensive. "I don't understand why one of the Detroit companies doesn't jump in, but they apparently won't, and that's that", he observed sadly. He still contested the great French race, running Jaguars, Corvettes and Maseratis, besides opening a magnificent motor museum at Costa Mesa, California. There several surviving Cunninghams, both sports-racing and GT models, can today be examined—big blue-and-white cars, eloquent of a great American sportsman's valiant efforts to fulfil an ambition.

Specification

Engine: Chrysler 8 cylinders in 90° vee; 96·8 × 92·1mm, 5,424·7cc; 2ohv per cylinder, operated by pushrods; four Zenith carburettors; Autolite coil ignition; 300bhp at 5,200rpm.

Transmission: Single dry-plate clutch, 5-speed ZF synchromesh gearbox (3-speed Cadillac box also tried) in unit with engine; open propellor shaft.

Chassis: Welded tubular frame; independent front suspension by coil springs and wishbones; non-independent rear axle with coil springing; Oriflow hydraulic dampers all round; cast magnesium-alloy wheels; hydraulic drum brakes with peripheral cooling fins.

Dimensions: Wheelbase 8ft 4in; track, 4ft 6in; approx. dry weight, 2,510lb.

Aston Martin sixes

If "Aston Martin" equates with "classic sports cars", how much more so when, after the Second World War, it came to be combined with another pedigree marque, Lagonda, and inherited the fruits of chief designer W. O. Bentley's genius? When David Brown of the famous Huddersfield gear-cutting and tractor manufacturing companies acquired the two makes in 1947, and based the new combine, Aston Martin Lagonda Ltd, at the old Aston Martin factory at Feltham in Middlesex, he lost no time in instilling fresh competitive spirit into it. He believed ardently in racing as a developer of design, and was fully aware of the pre-war AM achievements, particularly at Le Mans, which to him stood out as the ultimate test and demonstration of a sports car's capabilities. Through his enthusiasm and determination, therefore, the famous Le Mans "regulars" from Feltham found themselves back on the Sarthe when the unique *Vingt-Quatre Heures* was revived in 1949.

The new generation Le Mans Astons differed from the old Bertelli strain. The three works cars which ran all had full-width coupé bodies of strikingly beautiful shape. Their frames were welded up from square-section tubing, with coil springing all round, independent at the front. Two had four-cylinder 2 litre pushrod ohv engines, and the third a 2·6 litre six-cylinder twin ohc Lagonda unit, designed by W. O. Bentley and "inherited" by Feltham. Fortune was not with them; one of the fours crashed when lying third, and the other took eighth place, while the six, although promisingly fast, lost its coolant early

through a plumbing defect and was out of the race after 50 miles.

But the 2·6 litre six-cylinder car finished third overall in the subsequent Belgian 24 Hours at Spa, behind a Ferrari and a Delage, and David Brown decided to concentrate on this design, both for racing and as a new production model, the pushrod four being dropped. W. O. Bentley's design, as intended for the post-war 2½ litre Lagonda saloon,

Right: *Le Mans was almost a spiritual home for Aston Martin. In 1951 DB2 coupés finished 3rd, 5th and 7th, taking 1-2-3 in class*
Below: *Exceptionally handsome externally, the Aston Martin DB2 was equally impressive beneath its stressed skin bodywork. The W. O. Bentley-designed 2·6 litre six cylinder twin ohc engine gave 107bhp in production form, or over 120bhp when prepared for racing*

Right: *Reg Parnell takes the lead in the 2·9 litre Aston Martin DB3S, heading Stirling Moss's XK120C Jaguar in the 1953 British Empire Trophy race at Douglas, IoM—one of five British events won that season by the DB3S*
Lower: *Peter Collins leading the 1955 Goodwood Nine Hours race in his 2·9 litre DB3S. Electrical troubles spoiled his run, but another DB3S won, driven by Peter Walker and Denis Poore*

was a thoroughly modern 78 × 90mm, 2,580cc unit giving 105bhp at 5,000rpm. It featured a sturdy four-bearing crankshaft, an aluminium head with chain-driven twin overhead camshafts, operating the valves directly through inverted piston-type tappets, wet cylinder liners, and twin SU carburettors.

For competition use, engine output was boosted to 123bhp for 1950, a season in which the comely coupés from Feltham raced in Italy, France and Britain with increasing success. Fourth at Monza and fifth in the Mille Miglia against the home-based Ferraris, Alfas, Maseratis and Oscas was impressive; a 2–3 litre class victory at Le Mans plus fifth and sixth places overall was a heartening replay of pre-war Rudge Cup successes; while a 3 litre class win in the Dundrod TT in Northern Ireland was a useful prelude to introduction of the new road model, the DB2. With its engine in more docile 107bhp form this earned just acclaim as a thoroughly up-to-date two-seater closed sports car, with a purity of body line equalling the best from any Continental *carrossier*, and the performance to back it up.

Beneath its Tickford-built stressed skin bodywork, a notably rigid multi-tube chassis had independent front suspension by trailing links and coil springs, and a live, coil-sprung rear axle with parallel radius arms and a Panhard rod for lateral location. Unladen weight was approximately 2,520lb, and the DB2 had a maximum speed of 110mph (117mph with higher-compression Vantage engine) combined with cat-like roadholding, impeccable road manners and outstanding external and internal finish. From it descended a long, distinguished line of six-cylinder Aston Martin road models, ranging from the DB2/4, DB Mk. III, DB4 and DB4 GT to the DB5, DB6 Volante and DBS, and an equally outstanding succession of sports-racing cars.

Praiseworthy DB2 race performances in 1951 included class wins in the Mille Miglia (''che vettura bellissima'' enthused *Tutto-sport*), and at Le Mans, where one scored third place overall, while a new open car, the DB3, made a promising début in the Dundrod TT,

lying second before retiring. This car had 140bhp behind its ugly ''portcullis'' radiator grille, a five-speed gearbox, a new tubular frame with torsion bar springing front and rear, and a de Dion rear axle with inboard drum brakes. Professor Eberan von Eberhorst, formerly of Auto Union and ERA, was chief designer and the DB3 gained the David Brown team their first outright long-distance race victory in the 1952 Goodwood Nine Hours.

Early the following year a DB3 with 2·9 litre engine fitted took an impressive second to the big Cunningham in the 1953 Sebring 12 Hours in the USA, besides garnering class wins elsewhere. Its successor, the DB3S, was still more successful. The original Bentley-

designed six-cylinder engine had been fortified considerably, the bore and stroke were now 83 × 90mm (2,922cc), and with triple Weber twin-choke carburettors a healthy 180bhp at 5,500rpm was delivered. The five speeds and inboard rear brakes of the DB3 gave way to a four-speed close-ratio gearbox with needle-roller bearings, and outboard brakes on a modified de Dion rear end, while *in toto* the car was shorter, lighter, better looking, aero-dynamically cleaner and faster.

The DB3S won first time out at Charterhall, Scotland; won again in the Isle of Man and at Silverstone; it scored AM's second Goodwood Nine Hours victory, and won them their first TT at Dundrod. The one race it did not win,

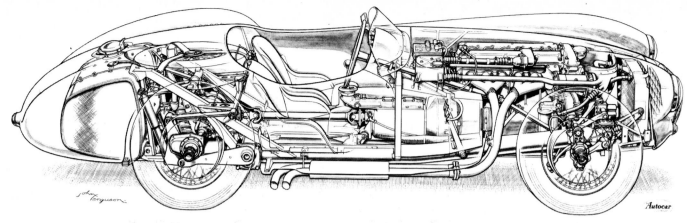

but which was fast becoming "Patron" David Brown's No. 1 target, was Le Mans, where all three cars retired. And during the ensuing three seasons Silverstone, Oulton Park, Aintree, Spa and Goodwood all saw the graceful metallescent green cars take the winner's flag, although Le Mans remained the annual frustration.

In 1954 four DB3Ss, one with supercharged engine, two with alloy heads and twin ignition, and all now fitted with disc brakes, turned out on the Sarthe for the great 24 hours race. Not one Aston finished, two crashing and two retiring. 1955 was better, with Peter Collins and Paul Frère coming second, and in 1956 Collins was again second, this time sharing a car with Stirling Moss. But it was not enough for the Patron. In 1957 a radically redesigned car, the DBR1/300, raised his hopes for that elusive first place at Le Mans. Based on a 2½ litre prototype, the DBR1/250 of 1956, it had an all-alloy block and crankcase with new type bearings, 12-plug alloy head, helical gear drive for the camshafts, dry sump lubrication, triple Weber carburettors and 250bhp at 6,300rpm at the business end.

Reverting to five speeds, a new transverse, constant-mesh gearbox was built in unit with the de Dion rear axle, suspended on lateral torsion bars, while

similar torsion bars with trailing links featured at the front. The chassis, too, was new, being of welded space-type built up of small diameter tubes; the wheelbase was 3in longer than the DB3S at 7ft 6in, but dry weight was down by 175lb. In all, the DBR1 was a very fine car—and it needed to be, for it had to face opposition from 4·1 litre V12 Ferraris, 4·5 litre V8 Maseratis and 3·8 litre six-cylinder Jaguars.

With Le Mans ever in mind, one Aston was given a larger engine of 3·7 litres and sundry other "mods", but was out before half-distance, as was one of the 3 litre cars. The other came 11th in a typical run of Feltham's Le Mans "luck". Things were better elsewhere, new team member Tony Brooks winning two sports car races at Spa, Belgium, and also the very exacting Nürburgring 1000km race in Germany, where he and his relief driver Noel Cunningham-Reid defeated full teams from Ferrari, Maserati and Jaguar.

The 1958 season was still more heartening, David Brown's lovely green cars with their fierce "six cylinder" bark proving aggressively competitive wherever they raced. Stirling Moss kicked off by winning the British Empire Trophy race at Oulton Park with a 3·9 litre-engined DBR2, while in 3 litre cars he led both the Sebring 12 Hours and the Targa Florio before being forced out

with transmission trouble. It was Moss again at Nürburgring, Jack Brabham co-driving, when they won the 1000km from four factory Ferraris, and Moss yet again in the TT at Goodwood, where he led a rousing 1-2-3 Aston Martin victory.

Le Mans, however, brought retirement for all three works Aston Martins, and only Peter and Graham Whitehead in their older private DB3S—the very car which finished second in 1955—saved Feltham's face by scoring yet another second, 13 laps behind the winning Ferrari. Aston Martin had now tackled Le Mans ten years running without outright success, the DBR1 design was beginning to date, and they had a new Formula 1 car as an extra priority. David Brown accordingly decided it was now or never, and that the sports car team should concentrate on the French classic, and not worry about the 1959 World Sports Car Championship, which included four other races.

A single DBR1 went to Sebring but failed, the Targa Florio was missed altogether, and with the Nürburgring 1000km only 10 days before Le Mans the Patron decided to give that a miss too. However, Stirling Moss persuaded him to enter a spare car, the original 1956 prototype, and with Jack Fairman as relief-driver for eight of the 44 laps he won outright, scoring an AM hat-trick at the 'Ring and breaking the

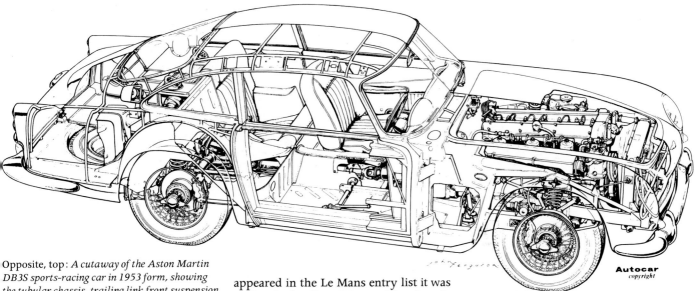

Opposite, top: A cutaway of the Aston Martin DB3S sports-racing car in 1953 form, showing the tubular chassis, trailing link front suspension by torsion bars, and de Dion rear axle. Disc brakes were adopted the following year

Opposite, below: Ambition achieved. 1959 brought Aston Martin and David Brown their long-deferred Le Mans victory. Here is the winning DBR1/300, driven by Salvadori/Shelby. Trintignant/Frère were second in a similar car

Above: Aston Martin's staple products in the 1960s were their big six-cylinder sports coupés which inherited much racing "know-how". This cutaway is of the 4 litre 282bhp DB5 four-seater introduced in 1964

sports car lap record 16 times.

Then came Le Mans, a devastating race in which Aston's team manager John Wyer sent Moss out to set the pace, The ploy worked excellently, every works Ferrari and every Porsche in the race retiring, plus Moss himself, but the resultant 1-2 victory by Salvadori/Shelby and Trintignant/Frère brought a big smile of satisfaction to David Brown's face. Finally, the TT race at Goodwood brought drama with the Moss/Salvadori car catching fire during refuelling. The fantastic Moss took over another DBR1 and shared an exciting victory with Shelby and Fairman. With Porsche second and Ferrari third and fifth, Aston Martin thus scored a double 1959 triumph, winning the World Sports Car Championship by two points from Ferrari and three points from Porsche, becoming the first and so far only British make of car to win the title.

His great ambition achieved, David (later Sir David) Brown withdrew from sports car racing, but the gallant DBR1s were raced in private hands for two more seasons. Nor could a concern so dedicated as Aston Martin keep away from racing, least of all Le Mans. The DB4 GT Zagato, a very fast GT coupé with a 3·7 litre 314bhp engine and body by the Italian Zagato company, was successfully raced in British GT events so when, in 1962, Aston Martin re-

appeared in the Le Mans entry list it was with a sleek 4 litre GT coupé developed from the Zagato and termed Project 212. Its 96 × 92mm oversquare 3,996cc engine with triple Weber carburettors gave 345bhp at 6,000rpm which, with the slippery body shape, made it an over-170mph car.

Astons reverted to type for Le Mans, however, and success eluded the 212 in the 1962 race, and its successor, the 215, in 1963. But the full 4 litre engine in milder, triple SU form giving 282bhp, appeared in the DB5 road car from 1964. Two years later came the DB6, a slightly lengthened version seating four adults with some restriction, while a Vantage-tune engine put out 325bhp, making the Aston Martin one of the fastest road cars of its time, capable of over 150mph with every refinement.

Its price in Britain was fractionally under £5,000, and even at that then high figure it was being built at a loss. The DB6 Mk. II, Volante drophead and DBS four-seater were the last of the beloved Aston sixes, being supplemented and finally replaced by the equally loved 5·4 litre V8s. Financial troubles hit the firm hard in 1972, when Sir David Brown withdrew, and the new proprietors began a long, hard fight back to stability. Today, thankfully, the Aston Martin lives on, a magnificent British sporting thoroughbred with a unique pedigree of racing successes —successes which sustained its name and reputation during the years of crisis.

Specification
DB2

Engine: 6 cylinders in line; 78 × 90mm, 2,580cc; 2ohv per cylinder, operated by twin ohc; twin SU carburettors (road car), coil ignition; 4-bearing crankshaft; 105bhp at 5,000rpm, Racing car with triple Weber carburettors, etc. 123bhp at 5,000rpm.
Transmission: Single dry-plate clutch; 4-speed gearbox (synchromesh on 2nd, 3rd and 4th) in unit with engine; open propellor shaft to hypoid-bevel final drive.

Chassis: Welded multi-tube frame; independent front suspension by coil springs and trailing arms with anti-roll bar; non-independent rear suspension by coil springs and twin trailing arms with Panhard rod; hydraulic dampers all round; hydraulic drum brakes.
Dimensions: Wheelbase, 8ft 3in; track, 4ft 6in; approx. dry weight, 2,520lb (road car); 2,296lb (racing car).

DB3 and DB3S

Engine: 6 cylinders in line; 78 × 90mm, 2,580cc (DB3); 83 × 90mm, 2,922cc (DB3S); 2ohv per cylinder operated by twin ohc; triple Weber carburettors (twin-choke on DB3S), coil ignition; 140bhp at 5,200rpm (DB3); 180bhp at 5,500rpm (DB3S).
Transmission: Single dry-plate clutch; 5-speed gearbox on DB3, 4-speed on DB3S, in unit with engine; open propellor shaft; de Dion rear axle with hypoid-bevel final drive on DB3; spiral-bevel on DB3S.
Chassis: Tubular side members; independent front suspension by trailing links and transverse torsion bars; de Dion rear suspension by transverse torsion bars; hydraulic dampers all round; hydraulic drum brakes, inboard rear on DB3; disc brakes on DB3S from 1954.
Dimensions: Wheelbase, 7ft 9in (DB3); 7ft 3in (DB3S); track, 4ft 1in; approx. dry weight, 2,180lb (DB3); 1,940lb (DB3S).

DBR1/300

Engine: 6 cylinders in line; 83 × 90mm, 2,992cc; 2ohv per cylinder, operated by twin ohc; triple Weber twin-choke carburettors; dual coil ignition, 2 plugs per cylinder; 4-bearing crankshaft; 250bhp at 6300rpm.
Transmission: Single dry-plate clutch; open propellor shaft to 5-speed transverse gearbox in unit with final drive; de Dion type rear axle; ZF limited slip differential.
Chassis: Tubular space frame; independent front suspension by trailing links and trans-verse torsion bars; de Dion rear axle, transverse torsion bar suspension; hydraulic dampers all round; Girling hydraulic disc brakes.
Dimensions: Wheelbase, 7ft 6in; track, 4ft 5in; approx. dry weight, 1,760lb.

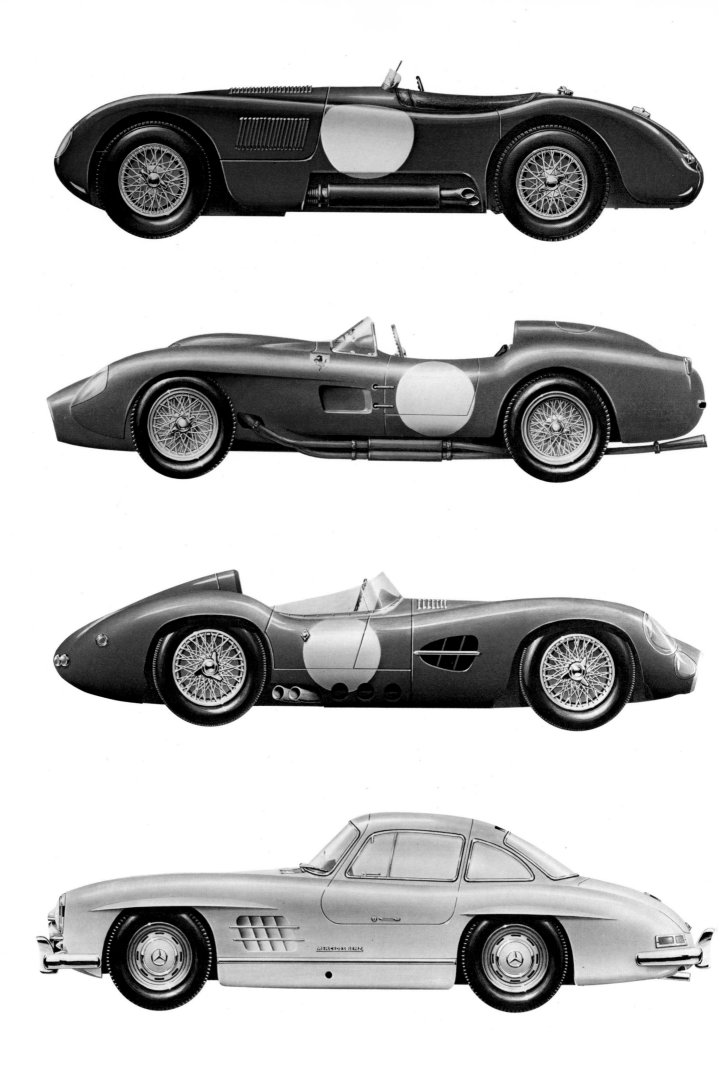

Opposite, top to bottom: *With engines at the front—an International parade of sports car winners, featuring: the 3½ litre six-cylinder Jaguar XK120C, first at Le Mans in 1951 and 1953; Ferrari's 3 litre 12 cylinder 250TR, World Sports Car Championship winner in 1958, 1960 and 1961; Britain's 3 litre six-cylinder Aston Martin DBR1, World Sports Car Champion in* 1959; and Germany's 3 litre six-cylinder Mercedes-Benz 300SL "gullwing" coupé, victor at Le Mans and elsewhere in 1952, depicted here in production road form

Above: *The Marathon de la Route, run over 3,000 miles of the most gruelling roads from Belgium to Bulgaria and back, was ever a yard-stick for sheer meritorious performance. Seen in action are the 1964 victors, Rauno Aaltonen and Tony Ambrose, in their 3 litre Austin-Healey 3000—the virtually indestructible "Big Healey"*

Mercedes-Benz 300SL and 300SLR

Few manufacturers supported motor racing more wholeheartedly than Mercedes-Benz, and their directorate surely found the rehabilitation period after the Second World War profoundly frustrating. Their recovery since 1945, when the Unterturkheim plants were mere heaps of rubble and twisted iron, is a story in itself, yet by 1951 they were able to rebuild their famous 1939 12-cylinder Grand Prix cars and race them again. However, two disappointing performances in Argentina against more modern Ferraris persuaded them that the blown V12s' racing days were done, and their role thereafter became that of demonstrators.

Yet the Mercedes will to race was strong, and while resolving to resume Grand Prix racing with the new Formula 1 in 1954, they turned meantime to sports car racing—"just opening a little window on the motor racing scene", as technical director Fritz Nallinger said almost apologetically. The decision was made a week before Jaguar's magnificent 1951 win at Le Mans with the XK120C developed from production parts. The moral was obvious, and designer Uhlenhaut turned to his own Type 300, "flagship" of the Mercedes line. This was a luxury six-cylinder saloon with tubular chassis, swing rear axles and an 85 × 88mm, 2,996cc engine delivering a velvety 115bhp at 4,600rpm on low compression and low octane fuel. Yet it propelled the 3,700lb 300 at close on 100mph, and from its 7-bearing crankshaft to the unusual aluminium slant head and single overhead camshaft operating staggered parallel valves, this engine promised well.

A 300S version with high-compression triple-carburettor, 150bhp engine and shorter wheelbase appeared at the 1951 Paris Salon, making only mild impact amongst more exotic cars, but the subsequent 300SL or *Sport Leicht* descendant, was to jolt the motor sporting world severely. Type 300 coil spring independent front suspension and rear swing axles were both united with an ingenious new multi-tube welded space frame, notably light yet rigid. Cloaking the entire structure was a superbly clean and effective aero-

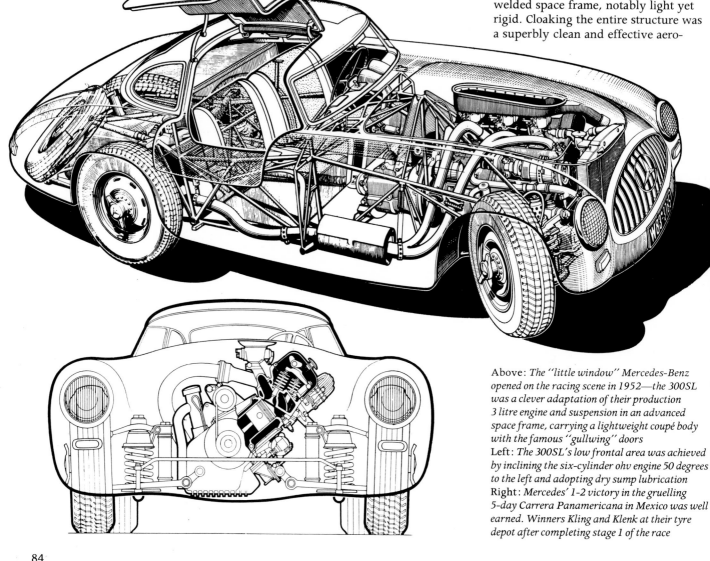

Above: *The "little window" Mercedes-Benz opened on the racing scene in 1952—the 300SL was a clever adaptation of their production 3 litre engine and suspension in an advanced space frame, carrying a lightweight coupé body with the famous "gullwing" doors*
Left: *The 300SL's low frontal area was achieved by inclining the six-cylinder ohv engine 50 degrees to the left and adopting dry sump lubrication*
Right: *Mercedes' 1-2 victory in the gruelling 5-day Carrera Panamericana in Mexico was well earned. Winners Kling and Klenk at their tyre depot after completing stage 1 of the race*

dynamic coupé body, in which the frame side rails were left undisturbed by using specially formed doors, hinged downwards from the centre of the roof—the famous Mercedes gullwing treatment which ensured maximum frame rigidity while complying with FIA regulations, albeit demanding extra agility from the driver.

Further enterprise featured in the engine installation. Now giving 171bhp at 5,200rpm with triple downdraught Solex carburettors, the unit was slanted at 50 degrees from horizontal to provide a low bonnet line, and equipped with dry sump lubrication. Simple nose treatment with an oval GP-like grille and modest overall height kept frontal area impressively low, and quick-release pressed-steel wheels with alloy rims, and wide-drum two-leading-shoe brakes were employed, the dry weight with the 300's heavy cast-iron engine and gearbox coming out at slightly over 1,900lb. Doubts were cast on the efficacy of the rear swing axles for high speed work, with their tendency to "tuck under" when cornering fast, while the engine output was below that of several rivals. Reliance, however, was placed in superior aerodynamics and team knowhow.

There remained, moreover, that intangible "moral ascendancy" possessed by Mercedes-Benz with its unique racing reputation. The fact that "Mercs were back" put their rivals on edge in their very first race, Italy's famous Mille Miglia. Three sleek silver 300SLs ran; one finished second, one fourth and one crashed, a single 2·7 litre 12-cylinder Ferrari on its home ground denying them first place. Yet their speed and near-victory paid off handsomely in subsequent races. At Berne in Switzerland their presence caused the favourite in his factory-loaned 4·1 litre Ferrari to break his transmission on the start line—and Mercedes-Benz finished 1-2-3.

At Le Mans reports of their prodigious speeds in the Mille Miglia "panicked" Jaguars into revising the XK120C cooling and streamlining, precipitating their early retirement. With Aston Martin and Ferrari also out, only an older 4½ litre Talbot stood between the 300SLs and victory; then it broke a connecting rod one hour before the finish, probably through the fatigue of driver Levegh, who was trying to complete the entire 24 hours himself—and Mercedes sailed home 1-2 to a prestigious victory.

At Nürburgring before the home crowd four 300SLs with coupé tops removed sat in formation behind a fleet Gordini, waiting for it to break—then moved in to a 1-2-3-4 demonstration win. Their last race was much tougher—the five-day, 1923-mile Pan-American Road Race in Mexico, with Ferrari, Talbot, Lancia, Gordini and Porsche all present. The Mercedes outpaced some, outlasted others, and despite a buzzard through one screen at 135mph, a dog through another radiator at 125mph, and flying treads at over 150mph, they came through to another 1-2 victory.

The factory 300SL team raced no more after 1952, but the car was put into limited production as a high-performance road model. This was unveiled early in 1954, more refined, more handsome, and with an important engine innovation—Bosch direct fuel injection in place of carburettors. Complex to build, it was costly to buy, but demand by connoisseurs was unexpectedly high, and a total of 3,250 300SLs were produced between 1954 and 1962—"gullwing" coupés up to 1956, and open roadsters with normal side doors thereafter. New low-pivot swing axles were introduced in 1957 to improve handling, and disc brakes featured in 1961–62. That sophisticated slant six engine gave 219bhp at 5,800rpm and a maximum speed of over 150mph, compelling respect, both from the driver and

certainly from his opponents in competition. Many major European rallies and race class wins fell to this brilliant car, rated today as one of the "peak" classic sports cars of the 1950s.

Specification—300SL

Engine: 6 cylinders in line, angled at 50°; 85 × 88mm, 2,996cc; ohc operating 2 valves per cylinder; triple Solex downdraught carburettors; magneto ignition (Bosch coil ignition on production models); 7-bearing crankshaft; 171bhp at 5,200rpm (219bhp at 5,800rpm on production models).
Transmission: Single dry-plate clutch; 4-speed all-synchromesh gearbox in unit with engine; open propellor shaft; hypoid-bevel final drive.
Chassis: Welded tubular space frame; independent front suspension by coil springs and wishbones; swing rear axles with coil springs; telescopic hydraulic dampers all round; hydraulic drum brakes to 1960 (servo-assistance on production models); disc brakes, 1961–62.
Dimensions: Wheelbase, 7ft 10½in; front track, 4ft 6½in (4ft 7in from 1957); rear track, 4ft 9in; approx. dry weight, 1,920lb (competition car); 2,560lb (production car).

The 300SLR

If the Mercedes-Benz 300SL seemed complex in design, what of the 300SLR with its eight cylinders, 10-bearing crankshaft, desmodromic valves, fuel injection, inboard front and rear brakes and, in two races, an air brake as well? Yet it was probably the easier car to develop to race-worthiness, since it derived directly from the W196 Formula 1 Grand Prix single-seater, using basically the same engine enlarged to 3 litres, the same transmission and suspension, and broadly the same space frame. Thus development of the basic design had virtually been completed in 1954 by the W196 when winning four Grands Prix, and only sheer lack of time postponed the 300SLR's appearance until 1955.

Whereas the 2½ litre F1 engine measured 76 × 68·8mm, the 300SLR had a larger bore and stroke, making it "square" at 78 × 78mm (2,982cc). The straight-8 unit was built up in two blocks of four cylinders, with the timing gear train in the centre, as on the pre-war Alfa Romeos. While making up the new cylinder blocks, Mercedes departed from their traditional sheet steel fabrications and had them cast in aluminium alloy. The bores were then chromium-plated to a depth of 0·008in and finished by honing, this process proving very durable. Other variations included a different firing order, wider valve angles, improved porting and provision of the generator and starter motor essential to sports-racing cars.

GTs with a difference: The International Gran Turismo class of racing proved a happy hunting ground for Ferrari's pedigree front-engined V12 berlinettas (above). The 250GT here took second place in the 1961 TT at Goodwood in Mike Parkes' hands; a similar car won the race, driven by Stirling Moss

(Right): A raucous intruder on Ferrari's GT domains in 1964–65 was Carroll Shelby's AC-based Cobra with big 4·7 litre Ford V8 engine. This one, shared by Bon Bondurant and Phil Hill, is grappling with the endless twists and turns of the unique Piccolo Madonie circuit in the 1964 Targa Florio. It retired with suspension

trouble, but another Cobra won the over 3 litre GT class; the following year Shelby's cars won the GT Championship outright

The rest of the engine specification sounds alarmingly complicated, as indeed it was, save to the ultra-efficient Daimler-Benz organisation with its ruthless philosophy of adopting the right solution irrespective of cost and complexity, backed by the resources and reputation for doing it. Twin overhead camshafts operated two valves per cylinder, but in place of return springs these were opened and closed by a positive desmodromic system of cams and rockers. Bosch direct fuel injection, demanding a high-precision fuel pump, was employed, and the built-up crankshaft ran in 10 roller bearings, with a power take-off from the centre to a subshaft, and thence via propellor shaft to a ZF five-speed gearbox in unit with the final drive.

Peak engine output on alcohol was a thought-provoking 340bhp at 7,700rpm, and revs could safely be taken up to 8,000; race output on less potent fuels varied between 276 and 300bhp according to the course. The power unit was slanted even further on the 300SLR, at 33 degrees from horizontal, and the low-nosed full-width bodywork, made in Electron alloy with left-hand drive, inherited much from the older 300SL, although a planned coupé was never raced. Longitudinal torsion bars served front and rear as the suspension medium, and the rear swing axles were located by two curved arms pivoted below the differential casing to provide a low roll centre. The wheelbase and track were identical with those of the longer wheel-base Formula 1 car, and big self-adjusting brakes with wide turbo-finned drums were mounted inboard to reduce unsprung weight.

The air brake, a large hydraulically-controlled flap over the tail, first tried three years earlier on a 300SL, proved very effective at Le Mans and in Sweden, not only in retardation from high speeds, but also in imparting a useful downforce on the car when cornering, thereby inadvertently anticipating the modern ''wing''. The main object was to save the drum brakes in long, fast races, at a time when discs were available only to British cars. Windows were cut for rearward vision, and the flap was operated by the driver through a lever on the scuttle.

But for malign circumstance, the 300SLR's record of success would almost certainly have been higher than in fact it was. Mercedes-Benz' aim was to contest the 1955 World Sports Car Championship, and this they won in glorious fashion despite missing the two opening rounds. Availing themselves of

the finest driving talent, including Fangio, Moss and Peter Collins, they finished first and second in the Mille Miglia, first, second and third in the TT at Dundrod, and first, second and fourth in the Targa Florio, the latter contested at short notice in a final bid for the Championship title. The cars also won the Eifel GP at Nürburgring and the Swedish GP, but their greatest victory could well have been at Le Mans where, instead, they became the unfortunate instrument of fate in the world's worst motor racing disaster.

In a sporting gesture, Mercedes invited Pierre Levegh, the driver who lost the 1952 Le Mans race to the 300SLs during the 23rd hour, to drive one of the 300SLRs in the 1955 race. It was the ill-starred Frenchman who contacted a slewing Austin-Healey when passing at around 150mph, his car hitting

Top: Moss and navigator Jenkinson on the starting ramp, about to set off on their record-shattering Mille Miglia victory with the 300SLR in 1955
Above: Peter Collins was recruited to co-drive with Stirling Moss in the 1955 Targa Florio
Opposite, top: Stirling Moss's 300SLR, bearing honoured wounds, winning the 1955 Dundrod TT

a bank and disintegrating, parts flying into the packed enclosure opposite the pits. Levegh and 81 spectators were killed, and Daimler-Benz withdrew their remaining cars while they were holding first and third positions.

At the close of 1955, having proved their supremacy both in Formula 1 and sports car racing by winning both Championships, Mercedes-Benz somewhat precipitately announced their total withdrawal from racing. They said ''for several years'', but the awe-inspiring silver cars from Unterturkheim have not raced since.

Specification—300SLR

Engine: 8 cylinders in line; 78 × 78mm, 2,982cc; 2 valves per cylinder, desmodromically operated by twin ohc and rockers; Bosch direct fuel injection; Bosch magneto dual ignition, 2 plugs per cylinder; 10-roller bearing crankshaft; 276 to 300bhp at 7,500rpm.

Transmission: Single dry-plate clutch; divided open propellor shaft to 5-speed gearbox (synchromesh on 2nd, 3rd, 4th and 5th) in unit with final drive.

Chassis: Welded multi-tube space frame; independent front suspension by double wishbones and longitudinal torsion bars; independent low-pivot rear swing axles, with longitudinal torsion bars; telescopic hydraulic dampers all round; hydraulic servo-assisted, turbo-cooled inboard drum brakes front and rear, plus air brake for fast circuits.

Dimensions: Wheelbase, 7ft 9¾in; front track, 4ft 2·33in; rear track, 4ft 6·33in; approx. dry weight, 1,830lb.

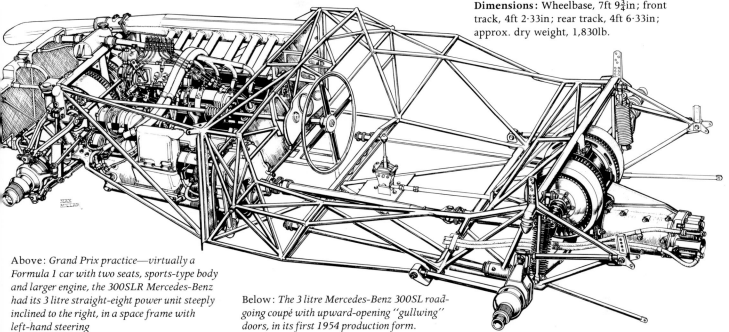

Above: *Grand Prix practice—virtually a Formula 1 car with two seats, sports-type body and larger engine, the 300SLR Mercedes-Benz had its 3 litre straight-eight power unit steeply inclined to the right, in a space frame with left-hand steering*

Below: *The 3 litre Mercedes-Benz 300SL road-going coupé with upward-opening "gullwing" doors, in its first 1954 production form.*

America's challenge: Ferrari's domination of
Le Mans was threatened in 1964 by the first US
Ford expedition to the Sarthe battleground with
their 4·7 litre V8-engined GT40s. All three cars
retired from their first 24 Hours, No. 12 in this
busy pits scene (above), driven by Richard
Attwood and Jo Schlesser, being destroyed by
fire when a split fuel pipe played over the red-hot
rear brake discs

Further pressure on European defenders came
from the Texan Chaparral, with 5·4 litre
Chevrolet V8 engine, automatic transmission,
and a sophisticated chassis. A single 2D coupé
came to Europe in 1966, winning the
Nürburgring 1000km with amazing ease driven
by Phil Hill and Jo Bonnier. Seen at Le Mans here
(right), the same car and drivers had wretched
luck when a flat battery forced them out during
the night

Lancia D24 and Stratos

It has been said that Lancia never made a bad car, and to this could well be added—they never made an uninteresting one either. Their designs have almost always been enterprisingly different, if not in their very earliest days then certainly from 1915, when Vincenzo Lancia registered his first patent for a narrow-angle vee engine. He applied this after the First World War to the monobloc V4 Lambda, that uniquely advanced design with unitary chassis-body structure, independent front suspension, hydraulic dampers and four wheel brakes—all in 1922. Other famous Lancias followed, among them the 1929 V8 Dilambda, the 1932 V4 Augusta, the unitary-bodied, all-independent V4 Aprilia of 1937 and the V6 Aurelia of 1950.

Curiously, while Lancia was a famous pioneer racing driver, Lancia cars had never been raced by the firm, but with his death in 1937, and control passing after the war to his son Gianni, a big change came. The Aurelia began as an advanced saloon designed, significantly, by Vittorio Jano of Fiat and Alfa Romeo fame. It had a compact 1,750cc 60 degree pushrod ohv V6 engine in an all-independently sprung chassis with inboard rear brakes, and as is the way with Italian cars, its liveliness and excellent roadholding simply begged to be exploited in competition.

"We need to push our name—it won't cost much to build a faster model," Gianni Lancia urged his reluctant co-directors. He had his way, and the resultant B20 Aurelia GT, a pretty fast-back styled by Pininfarina in 2 and 2½ litre forms, carried the famous name to many striking GT successes in 1951–1954, two Le Mans class wins and three major rallies included. Having tasted success, Lancia plunged deeper into racing, and from the Aurelia sprang another V6 of much greater potency—the *Competizione* 3 litre designed to challenge Ferrari, Alfa Romeo and Maserati in sports car racing.

While following the Aurelia's basic four-bearing engine layout with staggered cylinders, the new engine was both stronger and larger at 86 × 85mm (2,962cc), with chain-driven twin overhead camshafts to each cylinder bank instead of pushrods, and hemispherical heads. Initial output was 217bhp at 6,800rpm, rising to about 245 bhp, and the unit was installed in a space frame of welded small-diameter tubing. The all-independent suspension by transverse leaf springs and trailing links was "pure Jano" from pre-war Alfa Romeo days; the four-speed gearbox was in unit with rear axle, and the brakes, unusually, were mounted inboard at the front as well as the back, with shafts connecting them to the wheels.

Pininfarina built the functional coupé bodies, and an unusual feature was the driver-controlled adjustment of the rear friction shock absorbers by levers and small chains hanging from the roof, resulting in the team men calling these Lancias the "chain jobs". Known officially as the D20, four cars made their debut in the 1953 Mille Miglia, one of them finishing third. This was encouraging, while first place in their second race, the Targa Florio, was intoxicating. Ambitiously, Scuderia Lancia supercharged the D20 engines for the Le Mans 24 hour classic, but all their cars retired.

After this fiasco the blowers were removed and lighter open bodies fitted, the resultant D23 winning the Lisbon GP in Portugal while, back in Turin, lessons learned were applied to the more powerful D24. This had a 3·3 litre 265bhp engine, de Dion-type rear axle, a slightly longer wheelbase and cleaner bodywork, making it faster and more manageable. Even so, the team suffered the anti-climax of total failure in the Monza GP and the Nürburgring 1000km. Compensation came in the Pan-American Road Race, when Scuderia Lancia crossed the Atlantic, motored down to Mexico, and scored a 1-2-3 triumph.

Fired by even greater enthusiasm, Gianni Lancia now embarked on a very costly Grand Prix programme for 1954 as well as racing the sports cars. Engine trouble at the 11th hour cost them a Sebring victory early in the season, but Ascari's Mille Miglia triumph marked the high spot of the D24's career. It also won the Targa Florio again, the Circuit of Sicily and the Oporto GP, but Lancia lost the World Sports Car Championship to Ferrari when their latest cars, the 3·8 litre D25s with outboard brakes, failed in the decisive round, the Dundrod TT.

Apart from a national event at Syracuse the V6 sports-racing Lancia never raced again. The year 1955 was disastrous for the marque, three exciting but expensive years precipitating a major financial crisis; the GP cars were disposed of to Ferrari, and the family had to cede control to outside capital. "An end to racing and a more businesslike

The lure: Umberto Marzotto winning the GT class in the 1953 Dolomite Cup with his Lancia Aurelia 2500 GT. Such successes in races and rallies led Lancia deeper into motor racing

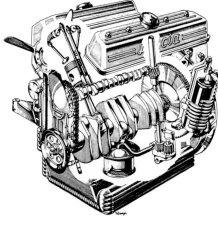

approach to production'' was sternly called for, and Gianni Lancia resigned early in 1956. When the company was able to resume competition, it was in rallying with the immensely successful front-drive V4 twin-cam Fulvia in 1·6 litre HF form.

By 1969, however, Lancia endured further financial traumas, culminating in the famous marque passing under the Fiat wing. After a pause for rehabilitation, it was back in the fray. At the 1970

Turin Show a startling design exercise named the Stratos was shown by Carrozzeria Bertone; an ultra-modern, low-slung, mid-engined ''wedge'' with Fulvia V4 engine set transversely between the driver and the final drive train. It looked a highly improbable Show gimmick but a much more practical Stratos coupé appeared by 1972 with the V4 engine replaced by a very healthy 2·4 litre 65 degree V6 Dino Ferrari engine giving about 190bhp,

driving through a five-speed gearbox.

A fabricated chassis of mixed tube and sheet metal carried fibreglass bodywork, and suspension was independent all round by coils and wishbones. Although ostensibly a production road car, the Stratos was really a competition

Early versions of the Bertone-styled mid-engined Lancia Stratos looked impressively clean and uncluttered before rallying equipment was added to them

Win or lose, no marque supported sports car
racing more consistently than Ferrari of Italy.
Above: A 1963 pit scene at the Targa Florio,
featuring the Belgian Willy Mairesse's 3 litre
V12 rear-engined 250P. The car failed on lap 5,
and Mairesse's last lap effort in another Ferrari
failed to defeat the Porsche challenge by 12 sec
following a spin

Right: The body of the Ferrari 330 P4 rear-
engined Berlinetta admirably balanced
unavoidable frontal area with a low-drag (and
very handsome) form. The Parkes/Scarfiotti car
here finished second to the winning 7 litre Ford
at Le Mans 1967, with a similar Ferrari third

"special" built to further Lancia and Italian prestige. As such it was a splendid *bomba* of exceptional strength, performance and versatility, contesting events ranging from the roughest, toughest cross-country affairs to road rallies and sports car races. The racing versions (occasionally turbocharged) were not a great success, but the factory rally versions, with 270bhp underfoot, or even more (around 280bhp) with 12-valve heads, reaped a rich harvest between 1973 and 1976, including four Monte Carlo rallies, the Tour of Sicily three times, the 1973 Targa Florio, and outright World Rally Championships in 1974 and 1975. Production of this most memorable Lancia ended in 1976 and the factory stopped rallying the Stratos at the end of 1978, although the car continued to gain success in private hands thereafter.

Specification
D23 and D24

Engine: 6 cylinders in 60° vee; 86 × 85mm, 2,962cc (D23) or 88 × 85mm, 3,284cc (D24); 2ohv per cylinder operated by twin ohc on each bank; three Weber twin-choke carburettors; Marelli dual coil ignition, 2 plugs per cylinder; 4-bearing crankshaft; 245bhp at 6,800rpm (D23), 265bhp at 7,000rpm (D24).

Transmission: Open propellor shaft to single dry-plate clutch; 4-speed gearbox in unit with rear drive.

Chassis: Welded tubular space frame; independent suspension front and rear by transverse leaf springs and trailing links on D23; de Dion rear axle on D24; telescopic hydraulic and friction dampers; hydraulic drum brakes, inboard at front and rear.

Dimensions: Wheelbase, 7ft 7·8in (D23), 7ft 9½in (D24); track, 4ft 2·8in; approx. dry weight, 1,570lb (D23); 1,620lb (D24).

Stratos

Engine: 6 cylinders in 65° vee; 92·5 × 60mm, 2,418cc; 2ohv per cylinder operated by twin ohc; triple twin-choke Weber carburettors; dual coil ignition; 4-bearing crankshaft; 190bhp at 7,000rpm (270bhp on team cars). Engine mounted transversely between seats and rear drive.

Transmission: Single dry-plate clutch; 5-speed all-synchromesh gearbox in unit with hypoid-bevel final drive.

Chassis: Fabricated tubular-cum-sheet steel; independent suspension front and rear by coil springs and wishbones, with anti-roll bars; telescopic hydraulic dampers; hydraulic disc brakes.

Dimensions: Wheelbase, 7ft 1¾in; front track, 4ft 8¼in; rear track, 4ft 9½in; approx. dry weight, 2,100lb.

Below: *Cutaway of the Stratos rally car, showing the 2·4 litre Ferrari Dino V6 engine installed transversely ahead of the rear wheels, and driving through a 5-speed transaxle*

Bottom: *A hat trick for Lancia and Sandro Munari (partnered on this occasion by Silvio Maiga) in the 1977 Monte Carlo Rally*

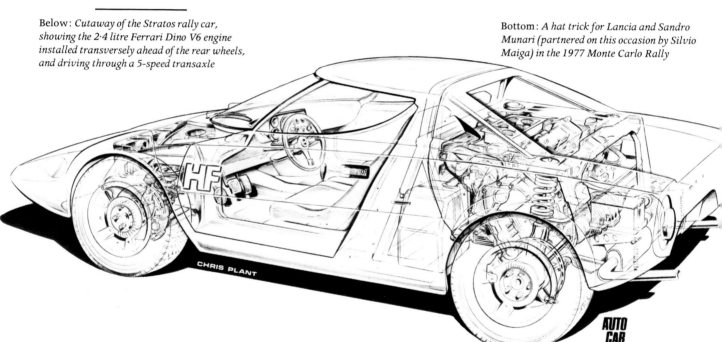

Austin-Healey 3000

Pound sterling for pound avoirdupois, it would be hard to equal the bargain offered by Austin-Healey between 1952 and 1968. Their handsome four-cylinder 2·6 litre 100, capable of over 100mph for a basic £750, developed into the equally good-looking six-cylinder 3000, capable of 120 mph for £762. They went racing, rallying and record-breaking with enormous success, they sold in thousands, and brought great pleasure to a great number of people. Yet it might never have happened, but for a lot of surplus engines at Austin's Longbridge factory, and the imagination of Donald Healey and his son Geoffrey.

The car's beginnings were humble. When production of Austin's somewhat unpredictable A90 Sports was stopped in 1950, many pushrod ohv, twin-

De Luxe 2 + 2: The 3000 Convertible with wind-up windows, one-piece removable top, and two extra seats brought comparative luxury to the "big Healey's" sporting image. This model was in production for eight years, from 1959 to 1967

carburettor 2,660cc engines and gear-boxes intended for it became redundant. Sir Leonard Lord, Austin's dynamic chief, wanted them used up, and Donald Healey, driver/manufacturer and 1931 Monte Carlo Rally winner, found the answer. Knowing sports cars through and through, he had a clear formula in mind for a successful model. It had to be fast, good looking, reliable, easily serviced, and cheap—which was where those A90 engines came in.

Healey and his son Geoffrey quickly laid down a design around the four-cylinder engine and gearbox, giving it a frame underslung at the rear, with box-section side members, coil-and-wishbone independent front suspension, and semi-elliptics at the rear. A floor lever replaced the A90's column gearchange, and clean, shapely two-seater bodywork was built in steel, with a pleasant grille and flush-set headlights. They called it the Healey 100, and although it was squeezed in at short notice on a badly located stand, it attracted unprecedented

public attention at the 1952 Earls Court Motor Show.

Dollar orders poured in, Austins quickly took on full production respon-sibilities, and overnight the car became the Austin-Healey 100. Quantity produc-tion began in 1953 and design refine-ments followed—a four-speed plus overdrive transmission, improved suspension and brakes, and a more powerful, 125mph, disc-braked competi-tion model, the 100S, which finished third at Sebring in 1954, and took class wins there and in the Mille Miglia in 1955. Although fast and undeniably fun, all Austin-Healey fours were some-what crude and cramped, and their engines notably "buzzy", and September 1956 brought a welcome change when the old A90 engine was replaced by the BMC six-cylinder 2,639cc C-series unit.

Apart from having 102bhp compared with the four's 90, the big gain in the new 100-Six was in flexibility and smoothness, while an enlarged cockpit giving 2 + 2 seating, improved hood

In their element: The Finnish rally star Timo Makinen, navigator Mike Wood, and their works Austin-Healey 3000 en route to winning the GT category of the 1963 RAC Rally of Great Britain

and sidescreens, made it a more refined car. In 1959, by which time production had been transferred from Longbridge to the MG works at Abingdon, the C-series engine in six-port "Weslake" form was enlarged to 2,912cc and fitted into a chassis with strengthened transmission and disc front brakes. This was the 3000, which graduated from twin-carburettor 124bhp Mark 1 form to the 1962 triple-carburettor, 132bhp Mark 2, then reverted to twin carburettors in the interests of easy maintenance on the 150bhp Mark 3 from 1964.

A convertible variant of the 2 + 2 was also introduced, its wrap-around windscreen, wind-up windows and one-piece detachable top increasing comfort and also the aerodynamics, unexpectedly raising its maximum to 117mph. Thus the beloved "big Healey" became a well-trimmed and relatively roomy GT car, albeit still with somewhat heavy steering and too little ground clearance. The Mark 3 even had a wood veneer facia and a lockable glove box, and although

the weighty six-cylinder engine meant it was less suitable for racing than the old four, the 3000's power, strength and roadholding made it an outstanding rally car.

After building up a team of top drivers and mechanics, the BMC competitions department at Abingdon managed by Stuart Turner campaigned the 3000 wherever rallies took place between 1959 and 1965. Over 40 class wins were gained in major events, together with some superb outright victories, notably the 1960 Liège–Rome–Liège by the two girls Pat Moss and Ann Wisdom, who also won many Coupes des Dames, the 1961 and 1962 Alpine Rallies by the Morley brothers Don and Erle, the 1964 Austrian Alpine by Paddy Hopkirk, and the 1964 Liège–Sofia–Spa by Rauno Aaltonen.

In the 1965 RAC Rally in Britain, however, Aaltonen's 3000 led most of the way in an epic drive, only to be overtaken on an ice-covered hill by a Mini-Cooper from the same BMC mixed team; this was the writing on the wall for the big, booming Healeys, but they had had a very good run. Only America's Federal safety regulations of 1968 halted their production when structural modifications would have been uneconomic

at that stage of their career. Some 73,000 of all models were built in total, and many survive today, contesting historic sports car events wearing larger tyres than were ever dreamed of in days when they were new.

Specification

Engine: 6 cylinders in line; 83·3 × 89·9mm, 2,912cc; 2ohv per cylinder operated by pushrods; twin SU carburettors (Mks. 1 and 3), triple carburettors (Mk. 2); coil ignition; 4-bearing crankshaft; 124bhp at 4,600rpm (Mk. 1); 132bhp at 4,750rpm (Mk. 2); 150bhp at 5,250rpm.

Transmission: Single dry-plate clutch, 4-speed gearbox (synchromesh on 2nd, 3rd and 4th) in unit with engine, optional overdrive; open propellor shaft; hypoid-bevel final drive.

Chassis: Ladder-type frame with box-section side members; independent front suspension by coil springs and wishbones, with anti-roll bar; non-independent rear suspension by semi-elliptic springs and radius arms; hydraulic dampers all round; hydraulic brakes, Girling disc at front, drum at rear; servo-assistance on Mk. 3, optional on others; Dunlop wire wheels.

Dimensions: Wheelbase, 7ft 7·7in; front track, 4ft 0¾in; rear track, 4ft 2in; approx. dry weight, 2,480lb.

Maserati 300S

"If you really want to live, drive a 250F or 300S at over nine-tenths," wrote Stirling Moss—who should certainly know—in his foreword to the book *Maserati* by Richard Crump and Rob Box. Although the Maserati brothers had nothing to do with those particular cars, having long sold the concern bearing their name, they would have enjoyed that comment by Moss. Like Nicola Romeo, Enzo Ferrari and Ettore Bugatti, they loved racing above all, and to have their cars knowledgeably praised was nectar to the famous *Fratelli* from Bologna.

The new proprietor of Officine Alfieri Maserati SA, the industrialist Comm Adolfo Orsi, was also heavily pro-racing, but tried to leaven his love with commercial common sense. He diversified Maserati activities into manufacturing their famous sparking plugs, machine tools, and other articles on a profitable

Like Mercedes-Benz' 300SLR, the Maserati Tipo 300S introduced in 1955 was a sports-racing edition of their Grand Prix 250F. It won its first 1956 race, the Argentine 1000km, scored again in the Nürburgring 1000km, and also won at Bari, Venezuela, Montlhéry and elsewhere

basis, while his son Omer concentrated on building Maserati sports cars and racing cars for sale to private owners, and ran the factory team largely for prestige purposes.

Success in major races was modest for Maserati at first, but for the 2½ litre Formula 1 introduced in 1954 they built a new, strong, straightforward six-cylinder single-seater, the Tipo 250F, which they sold to successful privateers such as Moss, Salvadori, Bira, etc, and also ran in their own team. With the great Fangio at the wheel the works cars won two Championship GPs in their first season, perhaps encouraging the Orsis to an over-ambitious decision to augment their activities with a sports car racing programme. They took the relatively simple road of enlarging their 250F engine to 3 litres and rebuilding its mixed oval and round-section tubular frame to FIA dimensions, and chose the 1956 World Sports Car Championship as a worthy target.

The result, the 300S, was a fierce but comely *biposto*, bearing full-width "Sport" bodywork but betraying its GP ancestry by its big racing wire wheels, short wheelbase and strident exhaust bark. It was very "250F" under

its Italian-red painted bodyshell, the six-cylinder twin-cam engine sporting three twin-choke Weber carburettors and giving 260bhp to the circa-250 of the smaller GP unit. At the rear end was the same big five-speed transaxle gearbox and de Dion axle, the cross tube located ahead of the axle line. With the transverse leaf spring above and the "sideways on" gearbox behind amidst a lacing of frame tubes, it all looked highly complicated but was, in fact, one of the car's best features, giving excellent roadholding in conjunction with the coil spring front end, good weight distribution and precise steering *à la* 250F.

In all respects it was a strong, relatively simple car which merited less hurried, more thorough preparation than the Maserati racing organisation could give it when also grappling with 1½ and 2 litre sports cars and a Formula 1 team. After some tentative essays in 1955, the 1956 season began splendidly with victory in the Argentine 1000km race by Moss and local driver Menditeguy. Sebring and the Mille Miglia brought no success, but in the Nürburgring 1000km Moss and the 300S did it again, his winning drive being shared by Behra,

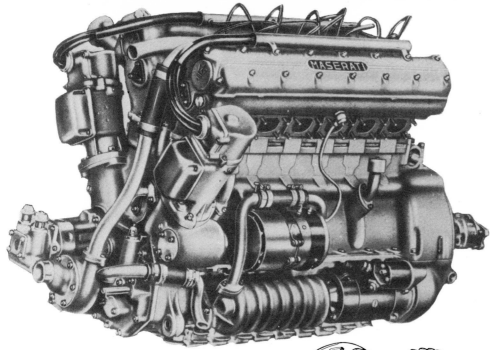

Championship races. Stirling Moss won at Bari, Venezuela, in the Australian TT, and at Nassau, while other 300S drivers won the Paris 1000km and the Coupe du Salon in France and private owners in the USA won several more races. Hopes thus ran high for 1957, but it proved a frustrating season of second places and class "firsts", but only one outright win for the 300S by Fangio in the GP of Cuba. Maserati's Championship challenge was vested in a fierce and very costly 4½ litre four-cam V8 nicknamed "the Bazooka", which won two Championship rounds but again lost the title to Ferrari, and almost broke the company. In a calamitous end-of-season GP at Venezuela all four V8s crashed, two being destroyed by fire, whereupon Comm Orsi ordered Maserati's complete withdrawal from racing.

In 1958 drastic retrenchment took place, wherein the redundant 300S served another useful purpose, for from it was evolved the 3500GT sports car, the first road model ever produced in serious quantities by Maserati in over 30 years. Its 3,485cc engine was a detuned, longer-stroke edition of the 300S, driving through a four-speed ZF gearbox in unit with the engine in place of the expensive transaxle. Vignale, Touring, Frua and other coachbuilders clothed its tubular space frame with suave and tasteful Italian *carrozzeria*, and Maserati joined the ranks of the exotic automobile manufacturers—if they could not beat Ferrari in the World Sports Car Championship, they could bid instead for part of their luxury sports car market.

With careful direction by Adolfo Orsi they did it very effectively, nearly 2,000 3500GTs, along with other models, being built during the next seven years, ensuring the survival of the famous Trident marque into modern times.

Above: The robust heart of the Tipo 300S was its six-cylinder twin ohc dual ignition engine, a 2,991cc variant of the 2½ litre 250F GP unit equipped with lighting and starter gear

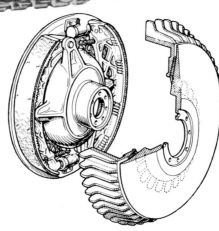

Right: In an effort to combat disc-braked British rivals, Maserati developed these special bi-metal drums with deep cooling fins and hot air outlets

Jean Behra in the still immature Tipo 300S trying to keep up with rival 3 litre cars from Mercedes-Benz and Aston Martin in the 1955 TT race at Dundrod. Eventually he crashed, losing an ear when thrown out on to the road

Schell and Taruffi owing to a quick changeover of cars during the race. Then came the decisive Swedish GP, which proved disastrous for Maserati with all five cars retiring—leaving Ferrari with the laurels and the Championship.

Ironically, the 300S thereafter enjoyed success after success in 1956 non-

Specification
Engine: 6 cylinders in line, detachable alloy head; 84 × 90mm, 2,991cc; 2ohc operating 2ohv per cylinder; triple Weber twin-choke carburettors; twin Marelli magneto ignition, 2 plugs per cylinder; 7-bearing crankshaft; 260bhp at 6,500rpm.
Transmission: Single dry-plate clutch; open propellor shaft to 5-speed transverse gearbox in unit with final drive; limited-slip differential.
Chassis: Welded multi-tubular frame; independent front suspension by coil springs and wishbones; de Dion type rear suspension with transverse leaf spring; hydraulic dampers all round; hydraulic drum brakes.
Dimensions: Wheelbase, 7ft 8·4in; front track, 4ft 4in; rear track, 4ft 2in; approx. dry weight, 1,650lb.

Chevrolet Corvette

Confident Americans in the early 1950s, eyeing the thousands of European sports cars pouring into their country, were wont to say that the US automobile industry was busy enough, mass-producing sedans for the world, "but of course, if they wanted to build sports cars they'd make 'em better than the Europeans." They have never quite managed this, but the Chevrolet Corvette has certainly proved their most successful effort, as indicated by sales so far exceeding 500,000.

The Chevrolet division of General Motors began work on a fibreglass-bodied open two-seater in 1952, using stock parts including a 150bhp six-cylinder engine fitted with three carburettors, an automatic two-speed transmission, and a chassis shortened to Jaguar XK120 wheelbase dimensions. The body wore a toothy grille and stock-pattern curved windshield, and apart from the apparent American inability to avoid needless styling gimmickry, was well proportioned. Chevrolet built 315 Corvettes in 1953, all in white moulded fibreglass with red upholstery, and all were snapped up at prices higher than the GM sales executive desired.

But a truer, less expensive Corvette sports car soon emerged, and by 1955 a V8 engine and manual three-speed gearbox became options. The following year the styling included the famous "scooped" flanks, the hardtop model being a fine example of the art of fibreglass moulding. The rival Ford Thunderbird had now appeared—a sure sign that the Corvette was a success—but Chevrolet countered by acquiring a genuine racing image. Engineer Zora Duntov, late of Porsche and Allard, got to work boosting the 4·3 litre, 265cu in

Corvette, and the result was a new "stock" record at Daytona beach by John Fitch at an average speed of 145·54mph, and a "modified stock" by Duntov himself at 147·3mph.

Then came the sensational news that four "stock" Corvettes were entered for the 1956 Sebring 12 Hours race, ostensibly by a private team but obviously with GM's backing. A fifth Corvette, more special with 5·2 litre engine, and four-speed gearbox, also ran in Fitch's expert hands; it finished ninth overall and won the over-5 litre class, while two

other Corvettes finished further back. Hopes of a Corvette entry at Le Mans were not fulfilled, but private owners began to campaign their cars in American SCCA races, and in 1957 Chevrolet sprang another surprise—the Corvette SS. This GM "research project" masterminded by Zora Duntov was a sports-racing car with tubular space frame, 305bhp 4·64 litre V8 engine with fuel injection, de Dion rear axle, inboard rear brakes, cast-magnesium wheels and magnesium-alloy bodywork!

Both Fangio and Moss tried and

Old and new: The first Chevrolet Corvette (above) as it appeared in 1953, with six-cylinder engine, white moulded fibreglass two-seater bodywork, stock windscreen, 1950s-style radiator grille, and red upholstery. The later Corvette style is seen in the 1977 model (right), its nose jutting forward, and Chevrolet V8 engine in many optional forms beneath that long hood

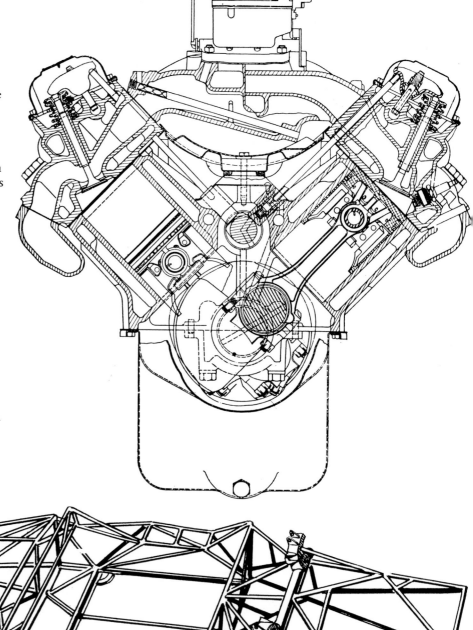

The Chevrolet pushrod overhead valve 90 degree V8 engine which forms the basis of Corvette sports units; strong, effortless and working at relatively leisured pressures, it is both reliable and long-lasting

approved this exciting car during practice at Sebring, but the one example competing, driven by Fitch/Taruffi, retired after 23 laps with a dud coil. Hopes for a Le Mans entry really ran high this time, but the American manufacturers agreed not to take part in racing at that time, and the SS project was killed stone dead. It was not wholly wasted, however, for some of the better features were inherited by the Corvette Sting Ray in the 1960s.

Domestically, Corvettes were beginning to accumulate SCCA class championships which eventually totalled 19, and during 1957 Rochester fuel injection and an excellent four-speed Borg-Warner all-synchromesh gearbox became optional. Engine size went up from 4·3 to 4·5 litres (283cu in), giving a coincidental 283bhp at 6,200 rpm; this was the Corvette in full maturity, a stimulating and responsive sports car capable of terrific acceleration and 125mph maximum, perhaps the most classic of all the breed, and only

requiring better brakes for complete security.

In 1958 the "Fibreglass flier" suffered a tarting up by the stylists, acquiring false power bulges and intakes, four headlights and pointless strips of chrome, but the stout ohv V8 heart continued to beat strongly, competition versions giving 315bhp with aluminium heads by 1960. That year Briggs Cunningham took a Corvette team to Le Mans, one placing eighth, another tenth, confirming the model's stamina and keeping

sales brisk. In 1963 came the sleek Corvette Sting Ray, with an all-new chassis having all-independent springing, optional power steering and a long E-type Jaguar-style nose with retracting headlights.

With sales of well over 20,000 Corvettes per year, GM clearly knew their market, and among innumerable options, automatic transmission, power steering and air conditioning were notably popular, "sporting" or not. At the exotic end, the hottest 425bhp,

For research only: The European-style welded tubular space frame of the Corvette SS sports-racing prototype of 1957—an exciting General Motors project that was regrettably stillborn

7 litre Sting Ray did 0 to 60mph in 5·4sec, and on to 140mph in 17sec, such sizzling performance being controlled by disc brakes, and offset by low speed intractability and a fuel consumption of around 10mpg. In 1968 the stylists got loose again, imparting a brutish look with more front overhang and para-

Above: *In distinguished company—four Chevrolet Corvettes competed at Le Mans in 1960, three entered by Briggs Cunningham and one by the Camoradi team. John Fitch/Bob Grossman in one car took eighth place, being the fifth GT finisher, another was still running, one was eliminated in an accident, and one had engine trouble*

doxically less luggage space, and two years later an even bigger engine, the 7·4 litre (454cu in) 475bhp V8, was offered to offset power loss through emission control equipment.

This unit derived from the famous Chevrolet Porcupine, so-called for its pushrod operated valves angled in two planes to improve head "breathing", and a great NASCAR stock car racing favourite since 1963. An even more potent derivative was a leading force in CanAm racing in America from 1966. The Corvette is still in production today, now over a quarter-century old. Through the years it has grown bigger, heavier and more powerful, relying frankly on sheer horsepower for its performance. Whether President Carter's

pressure on fuel conservation will end its life remains to be seen, but at late '70s prices—it is cheaper than the Triumph TR7 and less than half the price of the Ferrari 308GTB—America's only real sports car is as popular as ever.

Below: *Profile view—in the last decade the Corvette has become a purposeful yet relatively opulent two-place coupé with a wide choice in engine and transmission specifications, and potential maximum speeds approaching 140mph. With a list price of around $9,400 the car is understandably popular*

Le Mans (1976): The 7 litre US IMSA class "Spirit of Le Mans 1976" driven by John and Burt Greenwood and Bernard Darniche. The 660bhp "silhouette" Corvette approached 215mph but its tyres wilted. The lower view reveals the massive rollbar and huge fuel tank

Specification

Engine: (1955 to date): 8 cylinders in 90° vee; 2ohv per cylinder operated by push-rods; several carburettor options; coil ignition; 5-bearing crankshaft. Engine options include fuel injection from 1957 to 1965; road car power outputs range from 195bhp at 5,000rpm (1955 4·3 litre unit) to 475bhp at 6,000rpm (1970 7·4 litre unit).

Transmission: Single dry-plate clutch; gearbox in unit with engine; 3-speed manual change gearbox, 1955–1957; 4 speeds from 1958; automatic 2 or 3-speed transmission optional; open propellor shaft; hypoid-bevel final drive.

Chassis: Box-section side members, boxed cross-bracing; independent front suspension by wishbones and coil springs; non-independent rear suspension by coil springs and torque arms, 1955–1963; independent rear by transverse leaf spring, and lower wishbones 1963 on; telescopic dampers all round; hydraulic drum/disc brake options; power steering optional 1964 on.

Dimensions: Wheelbase, 8ft 6in (1955–63); 8ft 2in (thereafter); front track, 4ft 8·3in; rear track, 4ft 9in; approx. dry weight, 2,450lb.

Maserati Birdcage

If beauty is efficiency, the Maserati "Birdcage" was inefficient; its builders worried not about aesthetics, but about creating an effective sports-racing car as inexpensively and quickly as possible. As a compromise between parts availability, cost and race regulations, however, it was highly ingenious, and deserved more success than it gained. Although Comm Adolfo Orsi's withdrawal of Maserati from all forms of racing at the end of 1957 was "firm and final", somehow it was impossible for a marque born and bred to the sport to keep away from it.

Already in 1958 the competition department was back at work, the important difference being that they were building and preparing cars for paying customers, rather than for Maserati's own team. With one or two Italian amateur drivers seeking new mounts for 2 litre class hill climbing in Europe, and a strongly supported 2 litre sports class in the USA, one of their projects was to build a new car for this category. Designed by their technical chief Giulio Alfieri, with Orsi's strictures to avoid waste ringing in his ears, it departed refreshingly from the *status quo* of competition sports cars.

Inhibited by the cost factor, Alfieri made ample use of redundant 250F and 300S Maserati parts, including the coil spring front suspension and de Dion

back end, uniting them in a most unusual frame. This was of space type, built from a multiplicity of thin steel tubing varying between 1 and 1·5mm (approx. 3/64 and 1/16in) in diameter, with flat pierced strips for gusseting and the lower body panels welded on for extra strength. Every member was in stress, and set so close that an unknown wag likened the frame to a birdcage—and the name stuck, even though the official designation was Tipo 60. In the words of one magazine, "With so much frame there was hardly any space for the space."

Costs of the engine had also been met already. It was the 200S twin-cam four first made in 1956 for an earlier sports-racer and for speed boats. A sturdy 92 × 75mm, 1,993cc unit, it gave 195bhp at 7,800 rpm, and was remodelled with dry sump lubrication so that it could be installed in front at an angle of

45 degrees to secure as low a bonnet line as possible. It drove through a transverse five-speed gearbox of 250F lineage, albeit with magnesium housing, and Girling disc brakes were fitted all round. Minimal bodywork with a very low nose and a cocked-up, stumpy tail covered the "birdcage", and the ultra-light frame and small overall dimensions, with a wheelbase of only 7ft 4in, meant a dry weight of only 1,237lb, promising exceptional performance.

Emerging from official liquidation in April 1959, Maseratis celebrated by sending the Tipo 60 to Rouen, France, for the 2 litre sports car race there in July. Stirling Moss drove it, and simply ran away with the race despite considerable Lotus and Lola opposition. A few weeks later it won the Pontedecimo–Giovi hill climb, driven by Govoni who beat Ferrari's rival 2 litre, the V6 Dino. In the meantime the works had swiftly

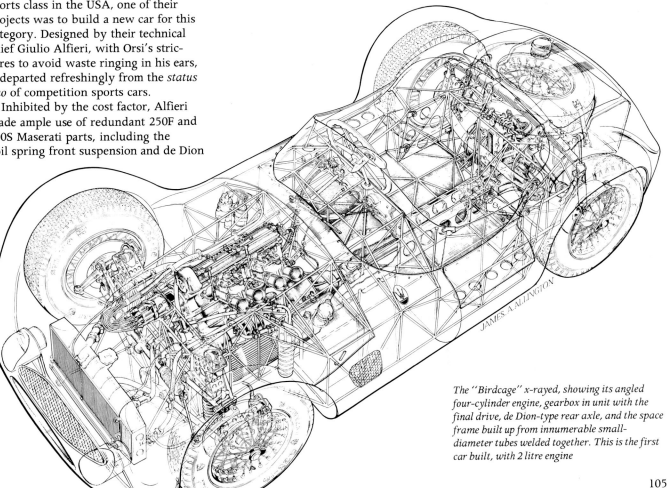

The "Birdcage" x-rayed, showing its angled four-cylinder engine, gearbox in unit with the final drive, de Dion-type rear axle, and the space frame built up from innumerable small-diameter tubes welded together. This is the first car built, with 2 litre engine

developed a 2·8 litre version of the engine to contest the 3 litre class, which in 1960 was to become the top limit in American sports car racing for twin ohc engines.

Such was Maserati's reputation that they had received a dozen orders for these before 1959 was out, and more in subsequent weeks. The cylinders, opened out to their very limit, measured 100 × 92mm (2,890cc), and output at 240bhp was 45hp more than the 60. An oil cooler was fitted, and the unit, again angled at 45 degrees, fitted snugly into the same 7ft 4in chassis. Called the Tipo 61, the car weighed only 33lb more than the 2 litre. The American Lloyd Casner bought three of these for his Team Camoradi (Casner Motor Racing Division) and after one car had shown its paces at Nassau late in 1959, leading only to retire, Stirling Moss drove another to victory in the Cuban GP in Havana.

In the Argentine 1000km, one Birdcage pulled out a lead of nearly 2 minutes over the Ferraris, only to retire with gearbox trouble, a pattern that was to become all too familiar with the very fast but fragile Maserati. At Sebring, Moss and Dan Gurney led by 2 laps when the transmission failed, and in the Targa Florio Maglioli/Vaccarella led by over 4 minutes when a flying stone emptied their fuel tank. But other Type

61s won at Riverside, Laguna Seca and Palm Springs in California, while the combined talents of Moss and Gurney brought victory to the Birdcage at last in a Sports Car Championship race, the Nürburgring 1000km, in Germany. An extra Camoradi "weapon" there was the employment of Piero Taruffi as team manager, and their two cars finished first and fifth in very difficult foggy conditions.

Three Camoradi Type 61s then ran at Le Mans, where the ludicrous new deep windscreen rules imposed by the FIA on sports-racing cars made the Maseratis even uglier, particularly one car which technically complied with its long "screen" extending at a shallow angle right from nose to scuttle. This one made fastest lap in a wet race at over 123mph, but all three cars retired. Apart from US national events, where the 61s scored more wins at Riverside and Elkhart Lake, they did not reappear until 1961, by which time the works had produced a rear-engined version, the hideous and unsuccessful Tipo 63.

As for the 61, despite its high promise it continued an erratic career, its sole European success a repeat of Camoradi's 1960 Nürburgring 1000km victory, the drivers this time being Masten Gregory and *the Patron* himself, Lloyd Casner. In the States a Birdcage won the important Road America 500 Miles race at Elkhart Lake, but 1961 marked the virtual end for the uncomely Maserati. Call it "Birdcage", "Spaghetti special" or Tipo 61, it will long be remembered for stirring up fresh interest and excitement in at least two of the World Sports Car Championship series.

Why the Tipo 60 and 61 got their nickname—a glimpse of the slant-four engine of the 2·9 litre 61, surrounded by frame tubes

Specification

Engine: 4 cylinders in line; engine inclined at 45°; 100 × 92mm, 2,890cc; 2ohc operating 2 valves per cylinder; hairpin valve springs; twin Weber double-choke carburettors; dual coil ignition; 2 plugs per cylinder; 5-bearing crankshaft; 240bhp at 6,800rpm.

Transmission: Multi-plate clutch and open propellor shaft to 5-speed transverse gearbox in unit with rear drive; ZF differential.

Chassis: Welded multiple tubular construction; independent front suspension by coil springs and wishbones with anti-roll bar; coaxial hydraulic telescopic dampers; de Dion-type rear axle with transverse leaf spring; hydraulic telescopic dampers; Girling hydraulic disc brakes.

Dimensions: Wheelbase, 7ft 4in; front track, 4ft 2in; rear track, 4ft 0in; approx. dry weight, 1,260lb.

The 2·9 litre Type 61 Maserati in 1960 Le Mans long-tailed trim, with driver Masten Gregory peering over the Camoradi team's ingenious interpretation of the FIA's ludicrous "deep screen" rule. The "Birdcage" clocked 169·26mph —fastest of all—but did not finish

Ferrari rear-engined V12s

As a traditionalist with 40 years of motor racing behind him, Enzo Ferrari found it hard to switch from the *status quo* of front engines to the *terra incognita* of rear, or strictly mid-location. He authorised it reluctantly in 1960 on a V6 single-seater, and the unexpected success of this car in F2 form encouraged him to adopt the layout on several variations of the V6 Dino sports car in 1962. These in turn performed so well that, despite Ferrari's misgivings about excess weight and resultant "dumb-bell" effect at the rear, a 3 litre V12 engine was experimentally installed in a 2½ litre Dino chassis. The result was so encouraging that a new 3 litre car, designed from the outset for rear engine

---

The flowing grace of the classic Italian sports car has gone, but the pace and stamina of the chunky-looking 3 litre Ferrari 250P gained it many victories. The Surtees/Mairesse car seen here retired from Le Mans 1963, but Scarfiotti/Bandini in another 250P won at 118·1mph

location, was completed late in 1962, emerging for the 1963 prototype sports-racing season as the Type 250P.

A short-tailed, almost stumpy spider with neat integral rollbar behind the cockpit, the 250P won three of the four major long-distance races in the Manufacturers' Championship for Prototypes, including the all-important Le Mans 24 Hours, and took the overall title. The 250P was then promoted to the 275P with 3,285cc engine for 1964, when again it won three races, Le Mans included, and again took the Championship.

Meanwhile a controversial offspring, the 250LM, had appeared. This was basically the 250P with a roof on and, after the first car, a 3·3 litre engine, and was intended to contest the GT class. One hundred examples had to be built for the FIA to grant homologation, but this they declined to do, requiring further evidence that the cars had actually been built, much to Ferrari's

disgust. In 1964, therefore, the 250LM that should have challenged the GT Shelby Cobras had to compete as a prototype. Privately-owned examples nonetheless won several races, including the Le Mans event in 1965, when Masten Gregory and Jochen Rindt in an American-entered 250LM saved Ferrari's face after the works cars—now 330 P2s with 4 litre engines—broke down in the battle with the Fords.

These P2 variants of the 275 and 330 had twin-cam heads, dual ignition, improved chassis, and alloy instead of wire wheels, while the 365 P2 had a 4·4 litre single-cam engine and was intended for private owners. Next came the 1966 330 P3 with fuel injection, wider track, ZF gearbox, and the 1967 330 P4 with three valves per cylinder and all-new Ferrari transmission. These all won races and took the 1967 World Championship, but could not prevent Ford winning at Le Mans in 1966 and 1967. Then the prototype

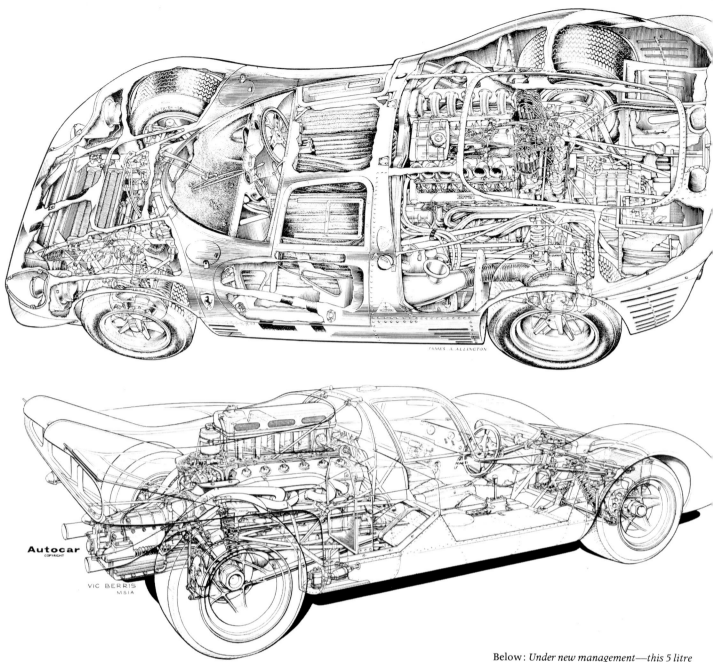

Autocar
COPYRIGHT

VIC BERRIS
MSIA

JAMES A. ALLINGTON

Top: *Power-packed—A cutaway drawing of the 1967 Ferrari 330P4, with 4-cam, 24-plug, 36-valve 4 litre V12 engine. These cars won at Daytona and Monza that year, and finished second at Le Mans behind a 7 litre Ford*

Above: *Group 5—Ferrari's 1970 Type 512S was a 5 litre, 48-valve, 550bhp plus Berlinetta with Lucas fuel injection, able to reach 218mph in fifth gear at Le Mans. It could not hold the Porsches and only won at Sebring that year*

Below: *Under new management—this 5 litre 512M Ferrari, prepared by Roger Penske's Sunoco team and driven by Mark Donohue and David Hobbs, finished third in the 1971 Daytona 24 Hours despite delays. In a field dominated by Porsche 917s it made fastest practice laps both at Daytona and Sebring*

capacity limit was reduced to 3 litres from 1968, Ferrari contesting it somewhat half-heartedly in 1969 with the 312P—virtually a Formula 1 car in enveloping "two-seater" bodywork with long, swept nose and blunt stern. It had a 48-valve 420bhp 2,910cc V12 engine with Lucas fuel injection, and although fast and reliable it could not match the Porsches, and won nothing.

A more powerful car, the handsome Group 5 512S coupé with 4,994cc power unit, followed 312P design closely; one scored in the 1970 Sebring 12 Hours, while an improved version, the 512M, took the Kyalami 9 Hours in South Africa. The 1971 races were used for developing a new car, the 312PB, in good time for the 3 litre sports car formula coming into force in 1972. Once again a GP bolide "in a sports jacket", the 312PB used the Ferrari Formula 1 flat-12 engine, transmission and running

---

Dominant type: The Ferrari 3 litre flat-12 Tipo 312PB, the car which won 10 races out of 10 in the 1972 World Manufacturers' Championship, and two in 1973. Seen here is the Jacky Ickx/Brian Redman car at Le Mans 1973, where they lay 3rd in the final hour but had to retire

gear. It was small and fierce, commanding 445bhp at a vociferous 10,800rpm, and with a choice of top drivers including Ickx, Andretti, Peterson and Redman, the 312P gave Ferrari a golden season in 1972.

In 10 Championship races they scored 10 wins, taking first and second on seven occasions and 1-2-3-4 on another; they stayed away from Le Mans, leaving Matra an open road to victory, but in 1973 Matra in turn felt confident enough to challenge for the Championship, and with Alfa Romeo opposition also stiffening, Ferrari netted only two wins. With Formula 1 occupying them full time, the "Prancing Horse" of Maranello has not been seen since in prototype sports car racing or its modern derivatives, and long-distance racing is very much the poorer without the glorious Italian-red Ferraris blaring out their thrilling multi-cylinder song.

Throughout this period Ferrari's V12 road models remained front-engined. The mid-engine location so superior for racing was grudging when it came to leg and luggage room for two people, and with full order books for the front-engined Daytona there was no point in drastic revision before the 1970s. No Ferrari design or experience is ever

wasted, however. From Formula 1 to prototypes, and from prototypes to GT road cars, the magnificent Ferrari flat-12 four-cam engine appeared in a sensational new mid-engined model, the 365GT/BB, at the 1971 Turin Show.

The BB denoted Berlinetta Boxer, the former meaning "small saloon", the latter being the Continental term for a horizontally opposed engine. Here was a design to challenge the rival Lamborghini as the world's finest super-car—and with matchless racing experience rather than tractor-building as its pedigree. Set low between the seats and rear axle in a low, suave two-door coupé styled by Pininfarina, the BB's 81 × 71mm, 4,390cc engine had six double-choke Weber carburettors and an output of 344bhp at 7,200rpm able to blast it along at 175mph. The all-independently sprung multi-tubular frame was built up from square-section tubes, and transmission was by a five-speed all-synchromesh transverse gearbox in unit with the final drive.

Production began in 1973, the delectable BB replacing the front-engined Daytona which had the same bore and stroke but cylinders in a vee. The six twin-choke Weber carburettors became four triple-choke units, and in 1975 the

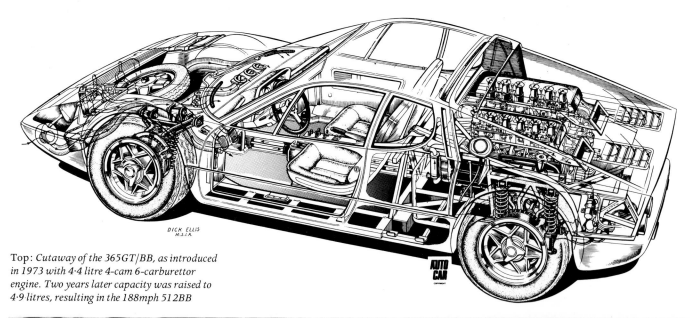

Top: *Cutaway of the 365GT/BB, as introduced in 1973 with 4·4 litre 4-cam 6-carburettor engine. Two years later capacity was raised to 4·9 litres, resulting in the 188mph 512BB*

Above: *Although factory Ferraris no longer appear at Le Mans, private teams still race the products of Maranello. Shown here is a 512BB driven by Andruet/Dini in the 1978 race*

engine was enlarged to 82 × 78mm (4,942cc), adding 16bhp to its already copious horsepower, raising maximum speed to a claimed 188 mph, and giving greater tractability. The larger engine has dry sump lubrication, and other subtle "mods" gilded this formidable Maranello lily—the 512BB—still further. It ranks as an "exotic" car today, a "classic" tomorrow.

Specification
Type 312PB Prototype
Engine: 180° (flat) 12 cylinder; 80 × 49·6mm, 2,992cc; 2ohc to each bank operating 4 valves per cylinder; Lucas fuel injection; Marelli transistorised ignition; 4-bearing crankshaft; 445bhp at 10,800rpm.
Transmission: Single dry-plate clutch, 5-speed gearbox in unit with final drive.
Chassis: Multi-tube semi-monocoque; independent suspension front and rear; coil springs and wishbones at front; coil springs, wishbones and twin radius arms at rear; coaxial hydraulic telescopic dampers; hydraulic disc brakes.
Dimensions: Wheelbase, 7ft 3½in; approx. dry weight, 1,430lb.

Type 512GT/BB (1975 to date)
Engine: 180° 12 cylinder; 82 × 78mm, 4,942cc; 2ohc to each bank operating 2 valves per cylinder; four triple-choke Weber down-draught carburettors; transistorised ignition; 7-bearing crankshaft; 360bhp at 6,200rpm.
Transmission: Single dry-plate clutch; 5-speed all-synchromesh gearbox in unit with final drive.
Chassis: Welded square-section multi-tubular; independent suspension front and rear; front by coil springs and wishbones; rear by double coil springs and wishbones; anti-roll bars; hydraulic telescopic dampers; hydraulic disc brakes.
Dimensions: Wheelbase, 8ft 2·4in; track, 4ft 11in; approx. dry weight, 2,480lb.

Lotus 23

The author was but one of many thousands of people watching the 1962 Nürburgring 1000km race, who was greatly surprised (and delighted) when an impudent little 1½ litre four-cylinder Ford-engined Lotus, designated the 23, jumped into the lead at the Le Mans-type start and completed its first 14·2-mile lap *28 seconds* ahead of the pursuing Porsches and Ferraris—bigger, more powerful cars accustomed to dominating that classic German sports car race. With typical Nürburgring "wet-and-dry" conditions helping, the little Lotus was 101sec ahead by lap 7; after a further circuit its driver, the future World Champion Jim Clark, had increased his lead to over 2 minutes.

It could not last; as the roads dried the Ferraris and Porsches with twice the brake horsepower and more began to catch up. Finally the combination of fading brakes, a gear jumping out, and exhaust fumes escaping from a broken tailpipe proved the Lotus' undoing on lap 11, when a dazed and "woozy" Clark lost control and ended up in a ditch. Seldom had a new competition

---

Clean and simple: The fleet little Lotus 23 sports-racing car in 1962 form, when available with 997, 1,097 or 1,599cc Ford pushrod ohv engines for private owners to buy and race. Its design was based on the 22 Formula Junior single-seater, with full-width, fibreglass-panelled bodywork

model made a more striking International debut, underlining what limited but tractable power in a light, controllable car could do in difficult circumstances.

The Lotus 23 first came into public view at the Racing Car Show at Olympia, London, in January 1962. It was not their first sports-racing car, of course, antecedents designed by the illustrious Colin Chapman including the Mark 6 and 7 clubmen's "kit" cars, the Marks 8, 9, 10, 11, 15 and 17 sports-racers, all front-engined, and the rear-engined Mark 19 or Lotus Monte Carlo, developed from the Type 18 Formula 1 car, and which gained numerous prominent wins in Britain, USA and Canada.

Like the 19, the 23 was the direct descendant of a single-seater, the Formula Junior Lotus which, as the Mark 20, practically swept the FJ board in 1961, and was succeeded a year later by the improved and equally successful 22. Apart from its wider frame and full-width two-seater bodywork and sporting equipment, the 23 was virtually identical mechanically to the 22 which shared the same stand at Olympia. Its chassis comprised a multi-tubular space frame built up from square, rectangular and small-diameter round tubing, with fabricated steel bulkheads. The suspension, always a Lotus strong point, was independent all round, using coil springs and double wishbones at the front, and coil springs with single top link, lower wishbone

and parallel radius arms at the rear. Coaxial telescopic dampers, rack-and-pinion steering and disc brakes featured, and 13in wheels assisted in keeping a low profile.

Coming in that era before aerodynamic efficiency seemed to mean aesthetic offence, the 23 had a clean, simple open body with fibreglass panels, a small intake low in the nose, a shallow, steeply raked screen merging each side into the rear wings, and a short tail. As it ran at Nürburgring in 1962 the engine was a pre-production example of the 1½ litre Ford 116E "Classic" five-bearing unit, fitted with a twin overhead-camshaft alloy head designed for Lotus by Harry Mundy of Jaguar and Coventry Climax fame. The camshafts were driven by roller chain off the front end of the crankshaft, and the inclined valves were operated, Jaguar-fashion, by inverted bucket-type tappets which also enclosed the valve springs.

The inlet manifolds were cast into the head, and carried twin Weber carburettors, and this 1,499cc unit gave an initial 100bhp at 5,900rpm, with more power obviously in reserve pending further development. The first engine to bear the name Lotus, it was destined to power the future Elan road car and also the Lotus-Cortina high-performance saloon, the Nürburgring race being chosen as a suitable long-distance test for the new unit. A special Lotus 23 with smaller 997cc twin-cam Anglia-

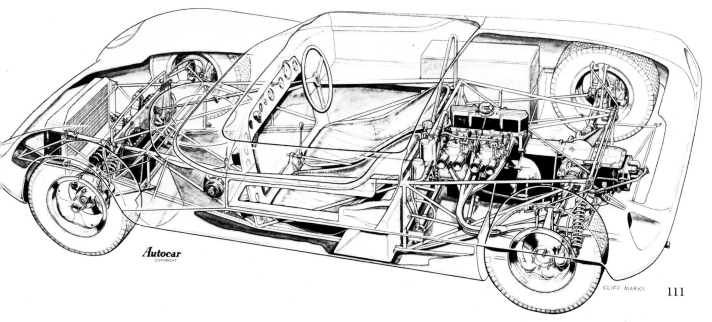

CLIFF MARKS

based engine had also been entered by Lotus for the Le Mans 24 Hours three weeks later, with the lucrative Index of Performance obviously in mind. But this was long-established French territory, and the partisan organisers succeeded in rejecting the little Lotus on sundry technical pretexts.

Subsequent races confirmed that the French had reason to fear the potential of the Lotus 23. In 1962 it became available to private owners with optional 997, 1100 and 1500cc Ford engines modified by Cosworth and other engine specialists, scoring numerous successes on British circuits, while abroad Alan Rees took second place to a Ferrari at Clermont-Ferrand, a 997cc 23 scored a class win in the Paris 1000km, and Jack Brabham won the 2 litre class of the Canadian GP at Mosport.

The year 1963 saw the introduction of the Lotus 23B, with a 1,558cc twin-cam Lotus-Ford power unit and VW-based Hewland five-speed gearbox with limited-slip differential. To withstand the power output of 143bhp (at 6,800 rpm) from the engine, the car was somewhat beefed-up, and given enough twists and turns in the racing circuits, the small, light, nippy 23B became a scourge to bigger, clumsier cars. Victories fell to it on every British circuit

in 1963; Jim Clark won the 102-mile Oulton Park Trophy race, followed by three more 23Bs, and won again at Crystal Palace and in the *Autosport* 3 Hours at Snetterton, while other successful 23B exponents included Mike Beckwith, Tony Hegbourne, Paul Hawkins and Rodney Bloor.

Abroad, Lotus 23Bs won the Japanese and Singapore GPs, and picked up numerous class wins in Sweden, France, Germany, Austria, Italy, United States, and Nassau. In the 226 mile Auvergne Trophy race, Hegbourne placed second to a Ferrari Testa Rossa, and in the Canadian GP Graham Hill in a 23B was beaten only by a 250P Ferrari. While experts such as Clark, Hill, Brabham and others were glad to race the 23B, the car's simple, effective design and responsive handling also made it an excellent "apprentice" car to racing, and among British drivers who made their name with the help of this pretty little Lotus were Robin Widdows, Tony Dean, Alan Rollinson, Mo Nunn and Peter Gethin.

A total of 131 Lotus 23s and 23Bs were built between 1962 and 1966 with engines including Coventry Climax and Alfa Romeo as well as various Fords. In its day the car cost under £2,000 ready to race, but today examples are eagerly

Above, left: *Surprise packet—Jim Clark in the impudent little Lotus 23 with pre-production 1½ litre twin-cam Lotus-Ford engine, well ahead of the Porsche, Ferrari and Aston Martin opposition in the opening rounds of the 1962 Nürburgring 1000km race. He had over 2 minutes' lead by lap 8, but retired three laps later after rocking the sports car establishment*
Above: *A close-up of the 1,558cc Lotus-Ford engine with twin ohc cylinder head designed by Harry Mundy, as fitted to the 1963 Lotus 23B*

sought at three times that figure for historic sports car racing.

Specification
Engine: Rear-mounted Lotus-Ford, 4 cylinders in line; 82·55 × 72·74mm, 1,558cc; 2ohv per cylinder, operated by twin ohc; twin Weber carburettors; 5-bearing crankshaft; 143bhp at 8,000rpm.
Transmission: Single dry-plate clutch; 5-speed all-synchromesh Hewland-VW gearbox, in unit with final drive; limited-slip differential.
Chassis: Multi-tubular space frame; independent front suspension by coil springs and wishbones; independent rear suspension by coil springs and single top link, lower wishbone and parallel radius arms; coaxial telescopic hydraulic dampers front and rear; hydraulic disc brakes.
Dimensions: Wheelbase, 7ft 6in; front track, 4ft 3½in; rear track, 4ft 2in; approx. dry weight, 1,120lb.

AC Shelby Cobra

At the start of the 1960s, the United States was the Cinderella of International sports car racing. The Cunninghams had come and gone, the Scarabs had cleaned up in their own country but did not come to Europe, and Lance Reventlow had turned his interest, and his dollars, to an abortive Grand Prix car. Tall, rugged Carroll Shelby of Texas, Le Mans co-winner in 1959 with an Aston Martin, felt there was a less costly way of winning races and when a heart condition obliged him to give up race driving, he set out to build a new sports-racing car.

High power-to-weight ratio was the key, allied to reliability and simplicity, and it was from the latter that Cunningham and Scarab had tended to stray, even though they used production-based engines. For his car, Shelby considered the Chevrolet engine, then tried the Buick aluminium V8 which became today's Rover unit, but had considerable trouble with a test engine. Then he heard that Ford USA were introducing a compact new ohv V8, the 221cu in, 3·6 litre Fairlane. He contacted them, and to his joy they not only agreed to supply engines

but also put $25,000 into the venture —obviously seeing his project as a potential Corvette killer.

Shelby now needed a chassis—and an estimate on building his own showed it to be uneconomical and time-wasting. So he looked around. He had often seen the neat British AC Aces scooping the 2 litre production car races run by the SCCA (Sports Car Club of America), and admired their simple, effective design and svelte lines. They had all-independent suspension by transverse leaf springs at each end of an H-form, or "ladder", frame with big diameter tubular side members.

The Ace was based on a design by an engineer from Royston, John Tojeiro, who in 1953 built a highly successful 2 litre Bristol-engined car for the racing driver Cliff Davis. Its comely bodywork was modelled closely on Davis' earlier 1½ litre Cooper-MG—and that was modelled equally closely on the lovely little Ferrari Mille Miglia *Barchetta* of 1949, built by Carrozzeria Touring of Turin. Thus, when AC Cars Ltd of Thames Ditton, Surrey, reached agreement with Tojeiro to base their new Ace

on the Tojeiro-Bristol, they too reproduced the bewitching lines of the *Barchetta*!

But all that was in 1953, and by 1962, after several hundred Aces had been produced, AC Cars ran into an engine supply problem. Bristol had decided to drop production of their BMW-based six, so AC arranged to fit the Rudd-prepared 2·6 litre British Ford Zephyr six-cylinder unit. Then out of the blue came an enquiry from Carroll Shelby, asking if they were prepared to fit a 221cu in V8 Ford engine into their chassis. They were, and very soon Shelby (and one of the V8s) was at Thames Ditton, working with AC's engineers and Vin Davidson from Tojeiro to produce what came to be called the Cobra.

When completed it was sent back to the USA and a larger 260cu in, 4,260cc Ford V8 engine installed as standard. With the Ace's shapely body, wheel arches scalloped out to accommodate the big fat Goodyear tyres on disc-braked alloy wheels, the car looked appropriately mean and tough, the deep growl of the 4·2 litre engine making it

Tubes of many diameters made up the frame and body supports for the V8 Ford-powered Shelby Cobra, seen in 1965 US road form with coil spring front suspension and left-hand drive. With 289cu in, 4·7 litre engines, Cobras won the 1965 GT Championship, scoring eight wins out of eleven races

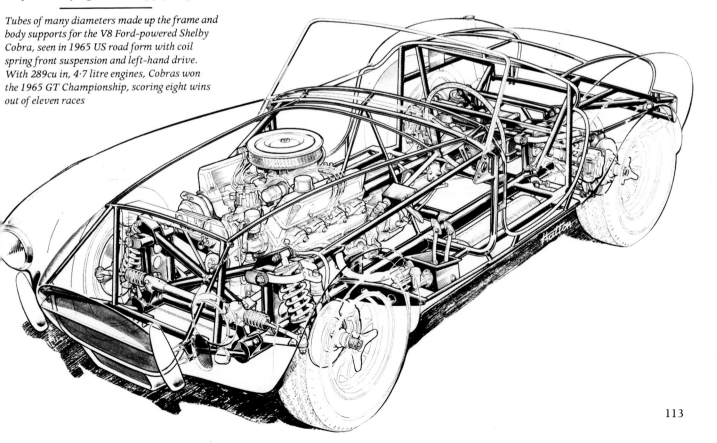

even more "animal". Compared with the 12 cylinder Ferraris it was unsophisticated, but at a USA figure of $5,995 it cost less than half as much, practically equalled their power-to-weight ratio, did 0 to 60mph in less than 5 scarifying seconds, and clocked 153mph almost first time out. Very soon it was battling with the Corvettes—and beating them—in SCCA racing, while AC Cars, with a first order for 100, got down to building the chassis and bodies, these being sent out to Shelby's plant in California to have their engines fitted.

Riverside in January 1963 marked the first of many Cobra home wins, culminating in the first of nine SCCA regional class championships. For 1964, then, Shelby set his sights on the FIA Manufacturers' GT Championship, which was disputed on US and European circuits. The cars were further beefed up to take a bigger "289" 4·7 litre engine which, with four Weber twin-choke carburettors, special cams, and bigger valves put out close to 325bhp. Rack-and-pinion steering was fitted and the front suspension improved, while a clean, wind-cheating Kamm-tailed Cobra coupé, the Daytona, was also built, gaining some 25mph.

GT Champ: The Jack Sears/John Whitmore Shelby Cobra Daytona coupé seen during the 1965 Reims 12 Hours race. It broke down, but the sister car of Bob Bondurant/Jo Schlesser won the GT class, placing 5th overall behind four Ferraris

Then the pale blue Cobras really went racing. They took GT "firsts" at Sebring (placing 1-2-3-5-6 in class and fourth overall), Le Mans (and fourth overall) and the Goodwood TT, plus first in class in the Targa Florio, finishing a close second to Ferrari in the Championship. By then Ford themselves had entered the hurly-burly of International racing, and Shelby and his team became involved with the GT40s as well as running the Cobras. How well they coped is shown by their 1965 record. Of eleven GT Championship races, the big-wheeled, bellowing Cobras won eight, at Daytona, Sebring, Monza, Nürburgring, Oulton Park (the TT), Le Mans, Reims and Enna, in Sicily, easily gaining the Championship title for America.

Back home, privately run Cobras had the SCCA class and US Road Racing Championships all sewn up, and so much success at such reasonable cost brought brisk demand. With lights, hood and sidescreens, "bumperettes" and a few other refinements the road car still looked what it was—a street legalised racer, built to carry two people very very quickly. With Ford themselves now deep in racing, Cobra withdrew from International contention after 1965, but Shelby's big engine/small chassis formula had paid off admirably.

In all, some 1,140 Cobras in 260, 289, 427 and 428 (standard Ford engine) forms were produced between 1962 and 1968. Fiercest of them all was the 7 litre 427 with NASCAR-developed engine giving a "street" 450 bhp or track 490bhp, all in a 2,150lb car! It had a stronger frame and wishbone-and-coil front suspension, but with 0 to 100mph reached in under 9 seconds, and 160mph maximum on the standard rear axle, here was the glorious, frightening epitome of the "hairy" over-engined motor car. US Federal safety laws killed off these exciting front-engined "primitives", but with newer designs overtaking them anyway, their time, sadly, was up.

Specification

Engine: Ford 90° V8; three options: 96·5 × 73mm, 4,261cc (260); 101·6 × 73mm, 4,727cc (289); 107·5 × 96mm, 6,997cc (427); pushrod-operated 2ohv per cylinder; choice of carburettors; coil ignition; 5-bearing crankshaft. Approx. outputs—road models: 164bhp at 4,400rpm (260); 271bhp at 4,400rpm (289); 425bhp at 4,600rpm (427); competition models, 370bhp at 5,200rpm (289).

Transmission: Single dry-plate clutch, 4-speed all-synchromesh gearbox in unit with engine, open propellor shaft to limited slip differential.

Chassis: Tubular side members; independent front and rear suspension by top transverse leaf springs and wishbones; coil springs at front on 427; hydraulic dampers all round; Girling disc brakes; wire wheels (cast-alloy optional).

Dimensions: Wheelbase, 7ft 6in; front track, 4ft 7in; rear track, 4ft 6in; approx. dry weight, 2,100lb (260 and 289); 2,150lb (427).

Ford GT40

When a big manufacturer, world-famed for over half a century of building cheap, reliable, family-carrying motor cars, takes to racing, then success is almost obligatory. First changes in the American Ford company's long established image came in the 1950s, in touring car events and NASCAR stock car racing. Then in 1962 they repudiated the earlier AMA agreement to abstain from racing and plunged into an ambitious sport programme encompassing stock, drag, Indianapolis and GT prototype racing.

The primary target in the latter category was Le Mans, that fascinating, exhausting, most prestigious of races, which no American car had yet succeeded in winning. Since a production-based 4·2 litre pushrod ohv Ford V8 engine had already powered a Lotus monocoque very close to outright victory at Indianapolis in 1963, the same unit should serve well in a sports-racer. This would of course, be mid-engined, and employ all the modern constructional and aerodynamic techniques, with no strictures on expenditure; *carte blanche* to build a Le Mans winner, in effect, with all that that involved in design, computer research, the setting up of specialist staff and workshops, wind tunnel testing, engine development and other aspects of the complex, costly, exciting science of big-time motor racing.

The long arm of coincidence helped speed the Ford operation, when Eric Broadley's small Lola enterprise in Bromley, Kent produced a squat 4·2 litre V8 Ford mid-engined racing coupé early

Above: *Progenitor of the Le Mans-winning Fords was Eric Broadley's mid-engined Lola GT (above), first seen at the London Racing Show in January 1963. It had a 4·3 litre Shelby-tuned Ford V8 engine and monocoque chassis with tubular suspension sub-frames*

Below: *Realisation by Ford in 1964 showed several chassis changes*

Right: *The GT40's first race was the 1964 Nürburgring 1000km, where it revealed promise but also early mechanical frailties*
Centre: *A season's development and a larger 4·7 litre engine brought the GT40 its first race win, the 1965 Daytona 2000km*
Lower: *Fourth Le Mans win for Ford came in 1969, when the J. W. Automotive-entered Mk. 2 driven by Ickx and Oliver beat Porsche by 100 yards*

in 1963. Following GP practice its engine was ahead of the rear axle, and the four-speed Colotti gearbox behind, while the body structure comprised a steel semi-monocoque centre section with welded tubular sub-frames fore and aft. The Lola GT came remarkably close to Ford's own paper concept of a GT proto-type, even to the roof height of 40 inches—a dimension to which the subsequent GT40 owed its type number.

With two Lolas already available for testing, Ford lost no time in enlisting Broadley's services, and he, Roy Lunn, John Wyer the former Aston Martin team manager, and other experts formed the nucleus of a new Ford European operation at Slough, Bucks. With manu-facture divided between the USA and the UK, the first two Ford GT40s were completed in April 1964. The chassis were similar to Lola, but with many constructional differences and sleeker looks. The fore and aft sub-frames were fabricated in sheet steel rather than from tubes, and driver comfort was carefully studied; the doors cut into the roof for easy entry, and the pedals rather than the seat were adjustable for length. Workmanship and engineering through-out were to very high standards, and the cars were remarkably strong. However, somewhat hasty participation in the Le Mans test weekend revealed dire aerodynamic shortcomings on the GT40, and both cars crashed. A "duck-tail" spoiler was added at the rear, greatly improving stability and rear wheel adhesion, after which the GT40 was "blooded" in that gruelling German event, the Nürburgring 1000km race.

The car ran well, lasting 2½ hours when a vital rear suspension weld gave way. Then came the all-important Le Mans, where Ford's challenge on accepted Ferrari territory aroused tremendous interest. Three pugnacious-looking GT40s in Ford blue-and-white faced eight prototype Ferraris, and the race revealed the immaturity of the American interlopers—and their future promise. One led the race but suffered gearbox failure, one caught fire, and the

third lasted 13½ hours and made a 131·29mph record lap before it, too, succumbed to gearbox trouble. "We live and learn", said Henry Ford II philo-sophically.

For 1965 the Texan Carroll Shelby took over the racing of the GT40s, the 4·2 litre engines being replaced by 385bhp 4·7 litre units as used in the Shelby Cobras. Cast-alloy wheels replaced wire type, and the disc brakes, which over-heated badly, were improved. Things began well with a 4·7 GT40 winning its first 1965 race, the Daytona 2000km, while at Sebring one finished second, taking the prototype class. Le Mans, however, brought another fiasco; two Mark 2 cars with

7 litre 485 bhp Ford Galaxie engines had been built by Ford USA and these, plus the 4·7s, now with ZF five-speed gear-boxes, made six Ford runners. Every one had retired by midnight.

The 7 litre Mark 2 had a "going through" for 1966, with improvements in aerodynamics, cooling, weight-saving and chassis, while a digression was the much lighter Model J with epoxy-bonded aircraft-type "chassis" of aluminium honeycomb sandwich and low-drag open bodywork. Early in the year the Mark 2s scored two consecu-tive 1-2-3 victories at Daytona and Sebring, after which came the big one—Le Mans. For Ford's third attempt they mounted a massive eight-car onslaught of Mark 2s, with five GT40s in support. Henry Ford II had the honour of starting a race in which his Mark 2s scored a magnificent 1-2-3 triumph, completely routing the Ferraris.

Having achieved their aim at a cost estimated at over £3,000,000, Ford might well have withdrawn from racing and basked in their new-found prestige, but instead they raced on in 1967. A new closed version of the "sandwich" Model J, the Mark 4, won at Sebring; with its side windows narrowed, and heavy flanks sweeping over the rear wheels, some of the GT40's good looks had gone, but this was a formidable machine, the big 500bhp Galaxie engine providing massive torque without undue strain.

Le Mans 1967 was almost all that Ford could ask, with two Mark 4s in first and fourth places, bracketing two Ferraris. The following day the FIA announced new sports car racing rules for 1968 onwards, limiting Group 4 sports cars to 5 litres and Group 6 prototypes to 3 litres. It is probable that Ford had already decided to withdraw

from European racing after 1967, but the FIA announcement killed the big 7 litre Mark 4s stone dead.

Yet this was far from the end of the story. The Group 4 GT40, updated and refined by John Wyer's Gulf-sponsored JWA team, was raced with remarkable success for the next two seasons. Its successes included the BOAC 500 Miles at Brands Hatch, Monza 1000km, Watkins Glen 6 Hours and Le Mans itself in 1968, culminating in their taking the World Championship of Makes. Nor was that all. 1969 brought the fourth successive Le Mans victory for Ford in the face of Porsche, Ferrari, Matra and Alpine opposition, the brilliant Belgian Jacky Ickx winning by 100 yards after an epic 23rd hour battle with Porsche.

So much success, much of it an unanticipated bonus, made all Ford's early hard work and colossal expenditure doubly worthwhile. And it added further glamour to those very rare and much coveted road-going GT40s built at Slough, giving the owners extra pride in their classic sports car properties.

Specification

Engine: 90° V8; 101·6 × 72·9mm, 4,736cc (GT40); 107·5 × 96·1mm, 6,997cc (Mk. 2 and Mk. 4); pushrod operated 2ohv per cylinder; four twin-choke Weber carburettors (early GT40); twin four-choke Holley carburettors (GT40 from 1967); one four-choke Holley carburettor (Mk. 2); twin four-choke Holley carburettors (Mk. 4); 5-bearing crankshaft; 390bhp at 7,000rpm (GT40); 485bhp at 6,200rpm (Mk. 2); 500bhp at 5,000rpm (Mk. 4).

Transmission:—*GT40:* Multi-dry plate clutch to gearbox in unit with final drive; Colotti 4-speed box (1963–64), then ZF 5-speed all-synchromesh box from 1965. *Mk.2 and Mk.4:* Dry two-plate clutch; Ford 4-speed all-synchromesh gearbox in unit with final drive.

Chassis—*GT40 and Mk.2:* Fabricated steel semi-monocoque with square tube reinforcement and fibreglass unstressed body panels. *Mk.4:* Expanded aluminium honeycomb "sandwich" shell, with unstressed fibreglass body panels. *All types:* Independent suspension all round, front by double wishbones and coil springs; rear by single transverse top link, lower wishbones and twin trailing arms; coaxial hydraulic telescopic dampers; hydraulic disc brakes.

Dimensions: Wheelbase, 7ft 6in; front track, 4ft 6in (GT40); 4ft 9in (Mk.2); 4ft 7in (Mk.4); rear track, 4ft 6in (GT40); 4ft 8in (Mk.2); 4ft 7in (Mk.4); approx. dry weight, 1,835lb (GT40); 2,505lb (Mk.2); 2,205lb (Mk.4).

Left: *The objective—the Dan Gurney/A. J. Foyt Mark 4 winning Le Mans in 1967—Ford's second victory on the Sarthe. The car was considerably larger than the GT40*

Below: *The means—a look inside the successful Mark 4. The composite chassis/body structure used a very light but strong aluminium honeycomb sandwich. The big 7 litre Galaxie-based V8 engine had twin Holley 4-barrel carburettors and drove through a Ford 4-speed gearbox*

Chaparral

Until the early 1960s, American sports-racing cars were largely follow-ons from European practice; they were thus always a year or more behind in development, with the extra handicaps of having to use heavy production-based engines and the American tendency to "build big". Scarab fought against this practice and brought finesse to the craft, but it was the 1963 Chaparral which advanced US design from the imitative to the innovative, and beyond to the radical scientific stage where Europe, instead of teaching, was glad to learn.

The word "chaparral" has two meanings; it is a big, leggy snake-killing bird also called the road runner, and it is the high scrub that grows in the south-western deserts of the USA. As indicated by the trade mark, Texan Jim Hall's car was the snake-killer, symbolic of the region in which he lived. The first Chaparral car was really an updated Scarab or a Troutman-Barnes (highly talented partners, who had earlier been with Lance Reventlow, building the Chevrolet front-engined space-framed car for Jim Hall in 1961).

After six were built and raced successfully, Hall and his partner, Hap Sharp, decided to design and construct a new, rear-engined car, the Chaparral 2, which departed radically from convention in having a semi-monocoque hull of metal-reinforced fibreglass, built up in

two halves and cemented together. It employed several Lotus suspension parts, Cooper steering, a Colotti gearbox, and a Chevrolet 400bhp 5·4 litre V8 engine. It was remarkably light at around 1,200lb dry, and on its début at Riverside in October 1963, Jim Hall outpaced a star field including Lotus, Ferraris, Coopers and Scarabs, opening a half-mile gap before the electrics failed.

But the 2 grew more reliable, and shed its "special" character as more and more parts were made by Chaparral themselves in their Midland, Texas, plant. It also began to lose its clean, smooth looks as Hall experimented with spoilers, air dams, louvres, scoops etc, while the intake tubes for the quadruple twin-choke Weber carburettors stood up like power station smoke stacks. A wealthy but qualified and wholly dedicated engineer, Hall was intent on making the Chaparral a success, and besides his own ingenuity and tenacity he got General Motors to give increasing support as the race wins multiplied.

By the end of 1964 the cars from Texas had seven US wins to their credit, assisted by a surprise feature on a racing car—automatic transmission. This was a GM fitment embodying a hydraulic coupling, initially with two speeds, later three, the driver simply lifting off momentarily and flicking a lever. It worked well and featured on all subse-

quent Chaparrals. In 1965 the team moved sensationally into the "big time" by winning the Sebring 12 Hours race from the new Ford, a Ferrari and another American challenger, the Cobra. Elsewhere in the US they scooped 13 more wins, plus others in Canada and Nassau, encouraging Hall and Sharp to tackle Europe in 1966 with their latest car, the 2D.

This was a coupé, with a fibreglass body, Mercedes-style gullwing doors and rather chunky build. Its stock-based Chevrolet motor and automatic transmission seemed inappropriate to challenge the "local boys" on the murderous, interminable Nürburgring, but to wide surprise and also pleasure to many, Phil Hill and Joakin Bonnier in the Chaparral absolutely "walked" the race despite Ferraris, Porsches, Fords, Cobras, rain and a broken screen wiper. Le Mans in contrast was a pure fiasco, with retirement of a perfectly healthy Chaparral with a flat battery early in the night.

Meantime, Jim Hall was back home, completing two 2E open cars for the

Breaker of tradition: The Chaparral 2D fibreglass coupé of 1966, which came—a single car against a full Ferrari team—to Europe's most difficult circuit, the Nürburgring, and won the 1000km race despite the "handicaps" of a stock-based US motor and 2-speed automatic transmission

Autocar
copyright

VIC BERRIS

Above: *On alien territory—the Chaparral 2F
with 7 litre 575bhp Chevrolet V8 engine and big
wing was just a ''bit too much car'' for the
notorious Targa Florio mountain circuit in
Sicily, but Phil Hill and Hap Sharp had it up to
4th place before retiring*

Below: *The intricacies and ingenuity of Jim
Hall's Chaparral 2F design are exposed in this
cutaway. The semi-monocoque chassis was made
of fibreglass-reinforced plastic, and the dry
weight was remarkably low at 1,750lb*

new CanAm Group 7 prototype class of racing. The 2E had an aluminium monocoque instead of fibreglass, and a revolutionary new fitment—a large aerofoil, fixed on uprights 31in above the tail. This was driver-actuated to exert a downforce on the rear suspension, improving tyre adhesion and roadholding, and its début at Bridgehampton was memorable. Hall made pole position in one car, but non-started when vibration broke the aerofoil, while Phil Hill in the other winged 2E placed fourth. And in their next race, at Laguna Seca, they placed 1-2.

The significance of Hall's innovation was not appreciated immediately, for here was the first wing to be used in actual racing—a device destined to revolutionise Grand Prix design. A clever Swiss, Michael May, had pioneered such a device on his Porsche 550 back in 1956, but did not race it. Chaparral's next surprise was the 1967

Hall's amazing last word in Chaparral sports-racing cars was the 2J of 1970, the highly controversial CanAm "sucker car" with powered fans improving adhesion by drawing the car downward, aided by skirted bodysides. Rival teams forced the outlawing of this pioneer "ground effect" car.

7 litre 2F coupé, with its body made in a PVC foam "sandwich", a system remarkably light but strong. It had radiators amidships, a deep, square and ugly but purposeful rear end, and a CanAm-style wing above. Acceleration with one of Chevrolet's special aluminium "porcupine" engines plus the wing was prodigious, but the 1966 transmission was not strong enough. Disappointingly, a bold European tour taking in six major races brought but one victory, in the Brands Hatch Six Hours, by Phil Hill and Mike Spence.

Jim Hall confined his last surprise to the CanAm class—the controversial "sucker car" called the 2J. This appeared at Watkins Glen in 1970, and amazed and affronted rivals by its bizarre nature and appearance. Its broad, severely square rear end contained two extractor fans driven by a German JLO 50hp twin-cylinder two-stroke engine of snowmobile type. These fans created a partial vacuum, having the effect of drawing the car downward, the bodysides being sealed with flexible transparent thermoplastic skirts. Nicknamed the "vacuum cleaner", or sometimes "the shoebox" for its deplorable lines, the 2J was amazingly effective while it lasted. In four races it took pole

position three times, but fan drive or auxiliary motor troubles spoiled its chances.

Undoubtedly Hall would have got it right, but the "ground effect" Chaparral never raced again; rival teams clamoured that it was unfair, and the FIA banned it. Yet Jim Hall's remarkable prescience was again borne out, for like the wing, ground effect has become a decisive science in today's racing world.

Specification
Engine: Chevrolet 90° V8, mid-located; 102 × 82·6mm, 5,360cc (2D); 108 × 95·3mm, 6,995cc (2F); pushrod ohv; four Weber twin-choke carburettors; coil ignition; 5-bearing crankshaft; 415bhp at 7,000rpm (2D); 575bhp at 7,500rpm (2F).
Transmission: GM automatic with hydraulic torque convertor; 2-speeds, then 3-speeds (2D); 3-speeds (2F).
Chassis: Steel-reinforced fibreglass semi-monocoque chassis-cum-body; independent front suspension by coil springs and wishbones; independent rear suspension by coil springs, transverse top link, reversed lower wishbone and radius arms; hydraulic dampers; hydraulic disc brakes; aerofoil on 2F, strutted to rear hub carriers.
Dimensions: Wheelbase, 7ft 7in; front track, 4ft 7in; rear track, 4ft 10in; approx. dry weight, 1,660lb (2D); 1,750lb (2F).

The four-cylinder Porsches

It takes time for a sports car to qualify as a "classic", and the first Porsche, the Type 356, based on the utilitarian air-cooled flat-four Volkswagen Beetle, seemed inauspicious material. Yet in 1947 it pioneered a principle destined to become common in high-performance sports-racing cars, the mid-engine configuration. It also had torsion bar all-independent suspension and one of the first space frames, when most production sports models still followed pre-war pattern.

The car was built in Gmünd, Austria, conception and design coming largely from Dr Ferry Porsche, son of the illustrious Prof Ferdinand Porsche who designed the "parent" VW. Standard VW front suspension, steering, transmission, brakes and wheels were employed, but the basic 25bhp engine, tweaked to yield an extra 10hp, was turned about-face to drive back via the four-speed gearbox, behind the rear axle line. The mechanism was enclosed by a remarkably clean "dish-cover" open two-seater body in aluminium, designed by the gifted Erwin Komenda.

To gain some vital extra space and simplify design and production on their next car, the Porsches had to revert to the normal VW engine location behind the final drive line – as idealists this could not have pleased them. This, the 356/2, had a welded platform frame carrying a two-door coupé even more attractive than the roadster, its graceful, decisive lines only mildly offset by a certain portliness in the flanks. As to handling, oversteer was a preponderant characteristic with those swing axles and overhanging engine, but like the VW driver, the Porsche man adapted himself to his steed.

Over fifty Type 356/2 models were built in 1949–50, the year the firm moved from Gmünd to Zuffenhausen, near Stuttgart, Germany, and as produc-

tion mounted the basic design was improved and refined, engine performance was increased and the "sporty VW" image faded. Racing was, of course, in Porsche's blood, and without delay Porsches were raced. The first notable success came at Le Mans, when two French *Porschistes* won the 1100cc class in 1951, and then repeated the act in 1952. By such feats, and many others, did Porsche become a much-respected name in world sports car markets.

The faithful flat-four engine was swiftly developed in 1100, 1300 and 1500cc versions, the latter being available for some years with a roller bearing crankshaft and by 1952 was producing 70bhp in "Super" form. The popular open Speedster was introduced in 1954 with a 1·5 litre engine and then with a 1·6 litre unit, an ideal "club racing car" for young competition-minded Americans. The first sports-racing "special" was the 1·5 litre 110bhp Type 550 Spyder, with a 4ohc engine in the ideal position, ahead of the final drive. In 1954 alone this short, shapely open two-seater scored class wins in the 1954 Mille Miglia, Le Mans, Reims 12 Hours, Nürburgring and Carrera Panamericana races, and established Porsche as a leading sports car manufacturer.

The Spyder went into small scale production, and both factory and private

cars garnered many more class successes, including 1-2-3s at Le Mans and in the Dundrod TT in 1955. A new space frame and five-speed gearbox promoted the Spyder to RS (Rennsport) specification for 1956, when one car scored Porsche's first, but far from last outright Targa Florio victory, besides collecting the customary quota of class wins elsewhere. The next stage in racing Porsches was the 1·6 litre RSK, with subtle chassis and suspension changes, and 148bhp to propel a dry weight of 1,150lb.

Variants of this little silver bomb took both 2 litre and 1½ litre class firsts at Le Mans in 1958, and the following year, with new coil-spring rear suspension, a 1500RSK headed a veritable Zuffenhausen grand slam in the Targa Florio, followed by an RS and two Carrera 2s. The latter were fierce little 356A rear-engined coupés with the 1·6 litre four-cam Spyder motor, contesting the GT racing class but also extremely wieldy rally cars, as indicated by their wins in that toughest of road events, the Liège–Rome–Liège, in 1957 and 1959.

In 1960 the FIA changed the sports-racing regulations at very short notice, so the RSK was rejigged as the RS60, with wider space frame, 4in longer wheelbase, smaller wheels and 1·5 or 1·6 litre engines. The type was also available

Forerunner of all Porsches was the advanced 356/1 built at Gmund, Austria, in 1947. Its VW-based flat-four aircooled engine was turned about-face in a space-type frame and located ahead of the rear axle, driving back through a VW 4-speed gearbox

Top: *Four-cam—the J. Claes/P. Stasse Porsche 550 Spyder which won the 1500cc class at Le Mans in 1954. Its 4ohc mid-located engine gave 110bhp and took it to four other class wins that year*

Above: *Forming up for another 1½ litre class win, the Maglioli/Herrmann and von Frankenberg/von Trips Porsche RS1500 coupés run nose to tail at Le Mans in 1956. But No. 24 suffered piston failure, and No. 25 won, placing 5th overall*

———————————

to private owners, and at Sebring, Florida, in 1960 a works RS60 scored an outstanding victory in the 12 Hours for Porsche, with a private entry second. Then came a third Targa Florio win,

with an RS60 fitted with a 1,679cc engine, and the type placed well in other races and won the 1960 European Mountain Championship.

Porsche KG were now getting deep into F2 and F1 single-seater racing, and meantime the rear-engined 356 and 356A production models became the 356B in 1959 with improved transmission and braking, stubbier gear lever, cleaner nose, higher headlights and bumpers, a 2 + 2 body and four varieties of 1,600cc engine. The B graduated to the C in 1963 with still more body comfort, larger rear window and disc brakes; production of this long-lived type with flat-four engine behind

the rear axle finally ended in 1965.

Porsche's last well-known four was the mid-engined 904GTS of 1964–66, a 2 litre, four-cam, five-speed competition coupé with exceptionally low, pleasing lines. It used the old Type 356 wheel and brake assemblies, but departed from Porsche convention in having a box-section ladder-type frame with wishbone-and-coil springing inherited from the racing cars, and disc brakes. It marked Porsche's first use of fibreglass for the bodywork, bonded to the chassis to contribute to torsional stiffness—the bodies, incidentally, being made by the Heinkel aircraft concern. One hundred examples were built to qualify for homologation as a GT car, with engine power options of 155bhp and 180bhp.

Two 904GTS defied form by outlasting faster prototypes and taking the first two places in the 1964 Targa Florio, one of the winning drivers being Colin Davis, son of S. C. H. Davis of Le Mans and Bentley fame. Displaying its versatility, another example took second place in the 1965 Monte Carlo Rally, while the model reaped a harvest of class wins. Thereafter Porsche relied on six, eight and twelve cylinders for their classic sports and competition models.

Specification

Engine: Rear-mounted, air-cooled flat-4; 73·5 × 64mm, 1,086cc; 80 × 64mm, 1,286cc; from 1953—74·5 × 74mm, 1,290cc; 80 × 74mm, 1,488cc; 82·5 × 74mm, 1,582cc; 2ohv per cylinder, pushrod-operated from single central camshaft; twin downdraught carburettors; 3-bearing crankshaft. Power outputs (varying with equipment and tune): 1300, from 44bhp at 4,200rpm to 60bhp at 5,500rpm (Super); 1500, from 55bhp at 4,400rpm to 70bhp at 5,000rpm (Super); 1600, from 60bhp at 4,500rpm to 75bhp at 5,000rpm (Super).

Transmission: Single dry-plate clutch; 4-speed gearbox, all-synchromesh from 1952, in unit with spiral-bevel final drive.
Chassis: Pressed steel platform-type; independent front suspension by parallel trailing links and square laminated transverse torsion bars; rear swing axles with radius arms and square laminated transverse torsion bars; hydraulic telescopic dampers; hydraulic drum brakes.
Dimensions: Wheelbase, 6ft 10¾in; track (up to 1955), 4ft 2¾in (front), 4ft 1¼in (rear); track (after 1955), 4ft 3½in (front), 4ft 2¼in (rear); approx. dry weight, from 1,640 to 1,925lb.

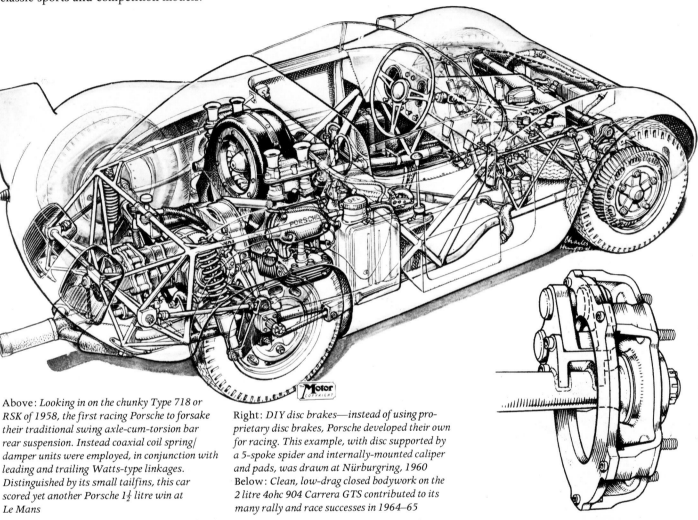

Above: *Looking in on the chunky Type 718 or RSK of 1958, the first racing Porsche to forsake their traditional swing axle-cum-torsion bar rear suspension. Instead coaxial coil spring/damper units were employed, in conjunction with leading and trailing Watts-type linkages. Distinguished by its small tailfins, this car scored yet another Porsche 1½ litre win at Le Mans*

Right: *DIY disc brakes—instead of using proprietary disc brakes, Porsche developed their own for racing. This example, with disc supported by a 5-spoke spider and internally-mounted caliper and pads, was drawn at Nürburgring, 1960*
Below: *Clean, low-drag closed bodywork on the 2 litre 4ohc 904 Carrera GTS contributed to its many rally and race successes in 1964–65*

McLaren M8

The motor racing public are fickle in their outlook on monopolists. A car which enjoys a run of wins through its own merit is first admired, then condemned because it makes racing boring; a consistent winner cannot win! There is no doubt that during their five year reign over CanAm racing in America, defeat was often wished upon the McLaren team if only to vary the *status quo* and have something other than the orange cars take the chequered flag for once. Yet their very pace, efficiency and mastery over the opposition compelled admiration, more so when the sheer simplicity of their "armoury" was appreciated.

The McLaren operation was never big, but its principals, headed by Bruce McLaren, certainly knew what they were about. Bruce was, of course, a New Zealander and a successful Grand Prix driver, whose interests and engineering talent took him into racing car manufacture as well. Besides Formula 1 his attention became focused on the lucrative new US–Canadian CanAm sports-racing car series of races for Group 7, which began in 1966. He contested the inaugural season with a space-framed, Chevrolet-engined car, the McLaren M1B, and finished third on points.

When it was over the little McLaren team, then six strong, found time to analyse the lessons of that first CanAm, and work out a fresh design for 1967. From a consensus of ideas by the effervescent McLaren and Robin Herd the new car, the M6A, was designed around a 5·9 litre cast-iron Chevrolet V8 engine a good, strong, powerful and not too expensive pushrod ohv unit which they equipped with Lucas fuel injection. The car had a compact, simple monocoque chassis built up in aluminium and magnesium sheet, bonded together both by epoxy resin cement and rivets. The engine contributed to an exceptionally rigid structure, a full-width magnesium plate being bolted across its front end, and supporting the rear suspension trailing members in conjunction with two rear frame arms.

The coil spring-and-wishbone suspension was simple, strong and easily set up, with quick-change anti-roll bars, and the Girling disc brakes were outboard in four-spoke cast-magnesium wheels. Goodyear tyres, then new to racing, were worn, the 12½in wide rear tyres seeming vast by 1967 standards. The fibreglass body incorporated a nose radiator, flexible rubber bag fuel tanks in side boxes, and a neat integral rear spoiler. The Chevrolet engines were

Effective simplicity characterised the McLaren design for CanAm class racing. The 427 cu in, 7 litre light alloy Chevrolet V8 engine of the M8A of 1968 shown here served as a stressed member in the monocoque hull. A 4-speed Hewland gearbox and Lucas fuel injection with impressive "power station" intake trumpets featured

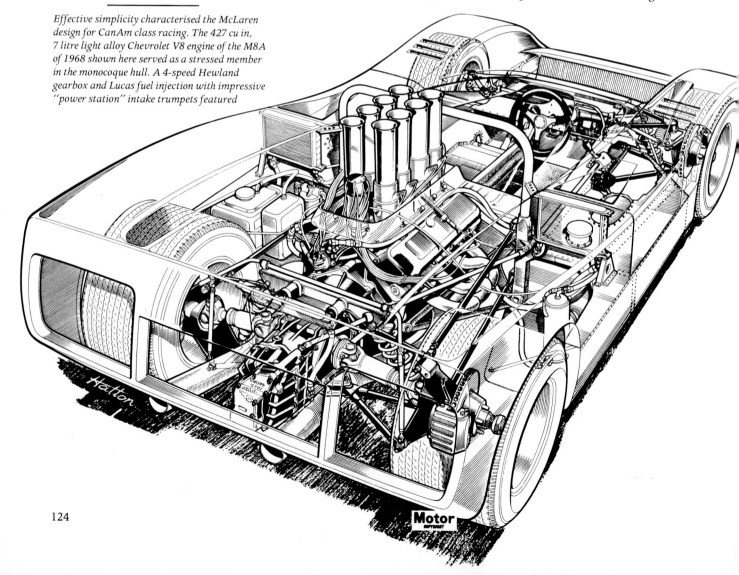

Right: *Kiwis ascendant—McLaren domination at Laguna Seca in 1969, demonstrated by three New Zealanders with Chris Amon leading Bruce McLaren and Denny Hulme in three orange-painted, winged M8Bs. Amon later crashed, but the others finished 1st and 2nd. McLaren cars won all eleven CanAm races that season*

Right, lower: *First American driver to win the CanAm title, in 1971, Peter Revson in the M8F*

specially prepared by "bhp wizard" Gary Knutson, who extracted around 520bhp, while the cars were built at McLaren's new works at Colnbrook, conveniently near London airport. As McLaren sports-racing cars were also to be built for sale by Trojan-Elva at Croydon, the works team painted their own M6As a pleasant orange, which became the accepted McLaren colour.

Another New Zealand driver and friend, Denny Hulme, joined the team that year, he and McLaren confronting their CanAm rivals with invaluable Grand Prix "know how" and first class cars. The six qualifying races took place between September and November, Hulme winning three and McLaren two, the latter also taking two second places to win the Championship on points. Not surprisingly "the Bruce and Denny show" was back in 1968 with the latest edition of the CanAm McLaren, the M8A. This time the more powerful 7 litre aluminium Chevrolet 427 engine with staggered valves was employed, dry sump lubrication being adapted to position it lower. The engine now also served as a stress-bearing part of the monocoque, which with two bulkheads instead of four was appreciably lighter than in 1967. The bigger engine gave some 620bhp at 7,000rpm, the tracks were widened, Lockheed brakes adopted, and the bodywork shortened at the rear and cleaned up.

"Clean up" was also the term for the McLarens' progress through the 1968 series; all six rounds fell to the Kiwi cars, although two races went to private owners when the works cars met trouble, and Hulme emerged the CanAm champion. Seasonal improvements ensued, and with a new high wing on struts linked with the rear suspension, still wider tyres and an extra 5bhp, the M8A became the M8B. This type eclipsed all previous McLaren feats with 100 per cent works success in 1969. Of the eleven qualifying races, Hulme won five and McLaren won six, the latter becoming the champion. That year the team won just over $300,000, besides receiving as much again in sponsorship money from Gulf, Goodyear and Reynolds Aluminum.

McLaren ambitions extended in 1970 to include Indianapolis as well as F1 and CanAm, but the team suffered a shattering blow when Bruce McLaren was killed while testing the newest 7·6 litre CanAm car, the M8D, at Goodwood. Gallantly the company carried on, the Californian Dan Gurney standing in to drive alongside Denny Hulme. Gurney won two races, Hulme six, and new team member Peter Gethin one, a McLaren clean sweep being interrupted by a Porsche win in one race only.

The fifth Group 7 McLaren, the 1971 M8F, had considerably cleaned up bodywork, a 3in longer wheelbase, 17in wide rear wheels in place of the former "16s", improved suspension, and engine sizes ranging between 7·6 and 8·1 litres (giving between 670 and 740bhp), the latter having an all-aluminium block cast by Reynolds. Despite spasmodic challenges from Lola, Ferrari and Porsche rivals, the 1971 CanAm was yet another McLaren benefit. Hulme won three rounds but his new team mate, the American Peter Revson, became champion by winning four.

In five CanAm seasons the orange fliers had won a total of 37 races, a remarkable achievement by any make in any era, but 1972 brought their first major check with the coming of the Penske Porsche flat-12 Type 917s.

McLarens found themselves relegated to mid-field despite a revised design, the M20. This had water radiators moved back alongside the mid-engine instead of in the nose, a nose aerofoil, and 750bhp plus better torque from the engine. But the turbocharged Porsches with around 900bhp could not be denied, and the Kiwi cars were fortunate to win rounds 1, 3 and 6 when the German flat-12s gave trouble. Then, pushed harder, the McLarens began to break and a monopoly was ended. If from the interest factor it was as well, after Porsche's two year rein the CanAm began to fade away; two years later the great Group 7 series was dead.

Specification—McLaren M8A
Engine: Chevrolet 90° V8, mid-located; 108 × 95mm, 6,990cc; 2ohv per cylinder, pushrod-operated; Lucas fuel injection; 5-bearing crankshaft; 620bhp at 7,000rpm (1968).
Transmission: Triple dry-plate clutch; Hewland 4-speed gearbox behind final drive.
Chassis: Rivetted and bonded aluminium monocoque with steel bulkheads; engine forming stressed member; independent front suspension by coil springs and wishbones; independent rear suspension by coil springs and single upper link, reversed lower wishbone and twin radius arms; coaxial hydraulic telescopic dampers; hydraulic disc brakes.
Dimensions: Wheelbase, 7ft 10in; front track, 4ft 9½in; rear track, 4ft 6½in.

Matra 670

The refreshing thing about Matra was that they were so completely new to motor racing. They had no distinguished reputation or pedigree as automobile makers; they were aerospace, rocket and military equipment specialists who joined the car industry almost by chance. Yet when they decided to go motor racing, primarily to publicise their name internationally, they did it with most impressive efficiency, defeated the establishment, and brought France back to the summit in a sport she used to dominate.

The name Matra derives from Mécanique-Aviation-Traction, a firm which made aircraft fuselages and other parts by sub-contract, then switched after the war to guided missiles and other complex devices demanding ultra-accurate manufacture. As they thrived, SA Engins Matra diversified widely, just one sideline being plastics. Among their many customers for these was René Bonnet, the ''B'' in the DB sports car concern and subsequent builder of a Renault-engined sports coupé, the Réné Bonnet Djet. As a friend, Matra's chief Marcel Chassagny had put some money into Bonnet's struggling business, and when more and more was needed to

keep it afloat, Matra were almost obliged to take the outfit over.

Thus, late in 1964, one of France's biggest aerospace enterprises found itself with a car division building Matra Djets. A new Taunus-engined model, the 530, followed, and next their energetic and far-sighted manager Jean-Luc Lagardère had them making a Formula 3 monocoque single-seater. This was extremely well designed and built, and was soon winning races, to the delight of the patriotic French. Next Matra advanced swiftly into 2 litre sports car racing and Formula 2, then Formula 1, with substantial aid from the French Government and the state-owned Elf petroleum company.

When announcing this intoxicating news in Paris early in 1967, Lagardère boldly added that Matra had two ambitions: the 1969 World Championship, and outright victory at Le Mans in 1970 with 100 per cent French cars. He was over-optimistic; a Matra certainly took Jackie Stewart to the 1969 World Championship, but it had a Cosworth-

Ford engine, not a Matra. And it was not until 1972 that they cracked the tough Le Mans nut, although they then atoned by winning it three times in succession and added two World Manufacturers' Championships as well.

To achieve their 100 per cent French victory, Matra had to have an engine. After tentative early sports car dabbles in 1966 and 1967 with 2 litre BRM and 4·7 litre Ford V8 engines, they commissioned a specialist concern, Moteur Moderne, to build and develop an all-new 3 litre V12 unit designed by Georges Martin. This was to serve both in Formula 1 single-seaters and in prototype sports cars and the basic specification, with 60 degree cylinder banks, wet liners, 4ohc, four valves per cylinder and seven-bearing crankshaft, was redolent both of Ferrari and BRM V12 practice. The workmanship, however, was superb, and initial power output encouraging at 385bhp at 9,500rpm. The unit was installed in an ungainly coupé, the Type MS630, on which non-French components included Lucas fuel injec-

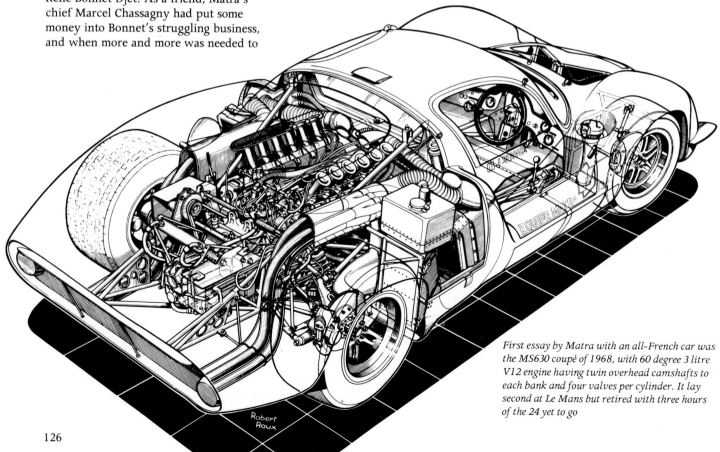

First essay by Matra with an all-French car was the MS630 coupé of 1968, with 60 degree 3 litre V12 engine having twin overhead camshafts to each bank and four valves per cylinder. It lay second at Le Mans but retired with three hours of the 24 yet to go

Above: *The 1971 version of the 3 litre Matra V12, the MS660, failed at Le Mans but won the Paris 1000km race at Montlhéry and dominated the eight-day Tour de France, a combined road and circuit event*

Below: *22 years after Talbot's 1950 victory, 1972 saw French racing blue ascendant again at Le Mans, when G. Hill/Pescarolo and Cevert/ Ganley took the first two places, their Matra-Simca MS670s now giving a reliable 480bhp*

tion, a ZF five-speed gearbox, ATE disc brakes and Goodyear tyres.

So sports car racing gained a thrilling new exhaust note and some French blue to offset the preponderant reds and multi-colours of sponsored rivals. The Type 630 ran extremely well against the 5 litre Porsches and Fords at Le Mans, moving up to second place before retiring in the 21st hour. Matra-Sports learned much from that first

3 litre foray, and in 1969, with pleasing new open bodywork both for the old 630s and new, more powerful 650s, they placed an impressive fourth, fifth and seventh.

A win in the Paris 1000km race rounded off the season, and in 1970 Matra linked up with Chrysler-France, thereby easing their sales problems with the 530 coupé, and boosting their racing effort under the name Matra-Simca.

Nine on the trot: Total success for Matra-Simca came in 1974, when the MS670C with large rear wing, inboard rear brakes and high engine air intake won nine races in a row, in Belgium, Germany, Italy, France (twice), Austria, USA, Britain and South Africa

With cars still further improved, they now felt strong enough to "mix it" with the formidable Porsche, Ferrari and Alfa Romeo opposition, but apart from wins in the non-Championship Argentine and Paris 1000 km races, their season proved disastrous. In four races at Daytona, Sebring, Brands Hatch and Monza their best was fifth place, while at Le Mans all three cars retired with engine trouble.

A 1-2 success in the 8-day Tour de France was hard work and mild comfort, but 1971 saw the chastened French team confining their prototype efforts to Le Mans with just one Type MS660. Benefitting from experience in Formula 1, the engine gave 440bhp and the car had a first class chassis, but it retired in the 17th hour, and repeat wins in the Tour de France and Paris 1000km could not allay French despondency. Once bitten, twice shy, Matra again concentrated on Le Mans alone in 1972, leaving Ferrari to clean up the World Manufac-

turers' Championship with a fantastic 10 out of 10 wins. Yet Ferrari abstained from Le Mans, where Matra on their fifth attempt at last won the great endurance race.

Two 480bhp MS670s, driven by Graham Hill/Pescarolo and Cevert/Ganley took the first two places ahead of a Porsche and an Alfa Romeo; an ambition finally achieved although inconclusively with nobody knowing which was fastest—Matra or Ferrari. "We will see next year" said Lagardère, and indeed in 1973 the world saw. The triumphant banshee shriek of Matra's 12-cylinder MS670s resounded over the world's circuits. They won at Vallelunga, Dijon, Le Mans, Osterreichring, and Watkins Glen; they lost one race to Ferrari at Monza, and one to Mirage at Spa, but they emerged as convincing, deserving champions for 1973.

Then they did it all again in 1974 with the further improved MS670C; this had inboard rear brakes, an aerofoil and still more torque from its engine, and scored nine devastating, consecutive victories at Spa, Nürburgring, Imola, Le Mans, Osterreich, Watkins Glen, Paul Ricard, Brands Hatch and Kyalami, in the face of Alfa Romeo, Porsche and Gulf-Ford opposition. Naturally they won the

Championship—their second in succession, and this together with three Le Mans wins in a row decided Matra-Simca that the time had come to withdraw from prototype sports car racing.

They had achieved their aim; "thanks to racing, Matra is known the world over" said Jean-Luc Lagardère, and apart from further engine development for Formula 1 use, the car division thereafter applied its energies to developing the Matra-Simca Bagheera sports coupé.

Specification

Engine: 60° V12; 79·7 × 50mm, 2,993cc; 4ohv per cylinder, operated by 2ohc to each bank; Lucas indirect fuel injection; Ducellier electronic ignition; 7-bearing crankshaft; 450 to 480bhp at 11,200rpm.

Transmission: Two dry-plate clutch; 5-speed gearbox, Hewland or ZF (Porsche for Le Mans MS670B and C), in unit with final drive.

Chassis: Monocoque centre section with tubular sub-frames; independent suspension at front and rear; front by upper rocking arms and lower wishbones with inboard coil springs; at rear by single upper and double lower links, twin radius arms and coil springs; coaxial hydraulic telescopic dampers; Girling hydraulic disc brakes.

Dimensions: Wheelbase, 8ft 4¾in; track, 5ft 0in; approx. dry weight, 1,485lb.

The six-cylinder Porsches

To a marque long experienced in building flat-four engines, and seeking smooth extra power, a flat-six unit is a logical progression. Porsche's Type 356 had grown old by the early 1960s, and its successor, the 911 first announced in 1963, has proved an outstanding car in all its exciting variants, and was still in production in 1979. The greatest change over the 356 was made to the engine which, although still behind the rear axle line, was an 80 × 66mm, 1,991cc flat-six with single overhead camshafts to each bank of separate air-cooled cylinders. It was a compact, sophisticated unit with eight-bearing crankshaft and twin Solex triple-choke carburettors to each cylinder bank, giving an unobtrusive 125bhp at 6,100rpm, with plenty obviously in reserve.

Further innovations included Macpherson strut front suspension, with lower wishbones and longitudinal torsion bars, open rear drive shafts, each with twin universal joints in place of swing axles, and rack-and-pinion steering. Type 356 disc brakes were fitted, while the unitary chassis/body structure followed 356 style, but with 4in extra wheelbase. Some valuable extra space resulted, and over all Komenda the stylist produced a 2 + 2 fastback body of flowing beauty and simplicity, relying not on offensive 1960s styling gimmickry but on purity of shape for its effect.

That "what looked right was right" the 2 litre 911 bore out by its first class performance (130mph maximum), handling and stability. Compared with the 356 it was far from cheap, but it sold well in Europe, the USA and elsewhere, even more so when a bold new body style, the open Targa, was introduced in 1966. This had a broad, flat roll bar in place of a roof, finished in brushed stainless steel, with removable top panel and

a zipp-in plastic rear window, later replaced by fixed glass. As an open car with quick weather protection and built-in roll bar, it quickly caught on, starting a "Targa top" cult eagerly followed by coachbuilders on other makes of car.

The 911 flat-six was a "natural" to use in a new Porsche prototype sportsracer, the Carrera 6, to contest the 2 litre class in the FIA's 1966 Championship of Makes. Power was augmented to 210bhp at 8,000rpm with the aid of twin triple-choke Weber carburettors, 12 plugs, magnesium alloy and titanium in place of aluminium and steel respectively, and other subtle means. This unit was, of course, mid-located in a tubular space frame, and the suspension embodied novel Bilstein pressurised gas dampers. With a fibreglass coupé body only 38·6in high, deep rounded screen, gull-wing doors *à la* Mercedes-Benz 300SL,

and a spoiler on the top edge of the broad, blunt tail, the Carrera 6 was low, purposeful and effective.

It swept the 2 litre Championship with four major class wins plus an outright victory—Porsche's sixth—in the Targa Florio. Ironically, the only time it was beaten was on its home ground in the Nürburgring 1000km, by two 2 litre Dino V6 Ferraris. Homologated as a Group 4 sports car, the "carburettor" Carrera 6 won that category too, although concurrently fuel injection was being tried out with considerable success. Next came the 220bhp 910/6, lighter and more windcheating; this type's great feat in a season when Zuffenhausen was also racing new flat-8 prototypes was to win the 1967 Nürburgring 1000km, a race Porsche had coveted for ten years.

Succeeding the 910/6 despite its earlier designation was the very aero-

Carrera 6: Beauty and efficiency combined in Porsche's bold 1,996cc 210bhp flat 6, termed the 906 by the works. This mid-engined coupé won its class first time out at Daytona in 1966, then won that criterion of hard races, the Targa Florio, the successful Mairesse/Muller car being shown here. The Carrera 6 took that year's 2 litre Championship of Makes

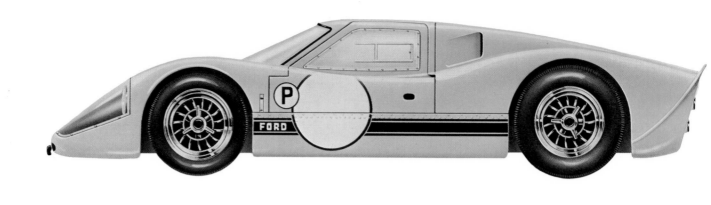

Opposite, top to bottom: *Four rear-engined prototypes from four countries. America's 7 litre V8 Ford Mk. 4, winner at Le Mans and Sebring in 1967; the 1970 Le Mans-winning 4·5 litre flat-12 Porsche 917K coupé; the triumphant 3 litre flat-12 Ferrari 312PB, winner of the 1972 World Championship of Makes; and, the* *winner of that Championship in 1973 and 1974, France's 3 litre V12 Matra MS670*

Above: *First of all sports-racing cars to "go rear-engined", Porsche's formidable competition record surely justified the layout. Bonnier's 2 litre flat-eight Spyder shown here broke its transmission in the 1964 Targa Florio after leading the first two laps, but two other Porsches, four-cylinder 904s, came through to a 1-2-finish*

dynamic Type 907, Porsche's last racing six and distinguished by its long tail and low, stubby nose, all meticulously researched in the windtunnel. No ducts, intakes or vents marred its smooth exterior, which was high-gloss finished, and the *Langheck* (long tail) was also the first racing Porsche with right-hand drive. The shape paid off well at the 1967 Le Mans, with an Index of Performance victory, and speeds of over 183mph on the fast parts of the circuit from only two litres, followed by a 1-2-3 triumph at Daytona early the following year.

Concurrently, a higher performance edition of the road going 911 2 litre, the 911S, appeared, first with 160bhp, rising soon to 170 and then to 180bhp from 1969, when the capacity was increased to 2·2 litres. The cooling shroud of the "S" engine was in red fibreglass instead of black, a badge of distinction like that of the Red Label Bentley of over 40 years earlier. The S also had five-lobe cast-aluminium wheels, improved disc brakes and a potential of over 140mph. Alongside it was the 911E with fuel injection, while a 20-off *rara avis* was the 911R, a kind of "silhouette" 911 of high potency which broke records and won the 1969 Tour de France and Corsican rallies.

All-rounder: Porsche 911 flat-6 variants excelled in rallies, hillclimbs and races of all kinds and distances. This 2·2 litre 911S driven by Bjorn Waldegard only took second place in the 1971 RAC Rally, but the model scored dozens of outright wins in this strenuous form of competition

In deference to the American market, a lever-selected semi-automatic transmission called Sportomatic became optional on several 911s. One such car won the 1967 Marathon de la Route, an 84-hour high speed grind round the Nürburgring, while a 911T, the cheapest of the line, albeit aided by an S-based engine, won Porsche their first Monte Carlo Rally, in 1968, all of which indicated how competitive *any* Porsche can be. In 1971 a 2·4 litre engine became optional, rising to 2·7 litres in 1973, while the Carrera version with front and rear spoilers and other speed equipment acquired a 3 litre engine from 1975, handsomely offsetting power losses suffered by the USA's emission laws, and loping round at a mere 5,500rpm to the old 2 litre's 6,200rpm.

The most sensational development of all, however, has been the 911 Turbo, which was first marketed in 1974. Inheriting racing experience, this 2,993cc flat-six (increased to 3,299cc after 1977) in the basic 911 body and chassis employs that modern "something for nothing" development, turbocharging, in which the exhaust gases are harnessed to compress the air/fuel mixture into the cylinders. The 911 Turbo in 3,299cc form with Bosch K-Jetronic fuel injection and an intercooler developed 300bhp (DIN) at 5,500rpm, imparting rocket-like acceleration (0 to 60mph in under 6sec, 0 to 100mph in 12·3sec) and a maximum speed of over 160mph.

The price, at £26,250 in the UK in 1979, or $38,500 in the USA, is more frightening than the Turbo's gait for

despite its front spoiler and the so-called "whale tail" rear wing on the engine lid, the Turbo 911 is no blaring roadgoing racer but a remarkably tractable and unfussy two-seater coupé, fully equipped and completely safe in sensible hands. Surpassed in performance only by bigger-engined Italian "exotics" such as the Ferrari Boxer and Lamborghini Countach, this Porsche must rank as a future classic of classics in the sports car milieu.

Specification
911 2 litre

Engine: Air-cooled flat-6, rear-mounted; 80 × 66mm, 1,991cc; 2ohv per cylinder, operated by single ohc to each bank; twin triple-choke carburettors; coil ignition; 8-bearing crankshaft; 145bhp at 6,100rpm.
Transmission: Single dry-plate clutch; 5-speed all-synchromesh gearbox; spiral-bevel final drive.
Chassis: Steel unitary chassis/body construction; independent front suspension by Macpherson struts, single lower wishbones and longitudinal torsion bars; independent rear suspension by trailing arms and transverse torsion bars; hydraulic telescopic dampers; hydraulic disc brakes.
Dimensions: Wheelbase, 7ft 3in; front track, 4ft 4½in; rear track, 4ft 3¾in.

911S
General specification as 911, except 2·2 litre engine from 1969, 2·4 litre unit from 1971, 2·7 litre engine from 1974.

911 Turbo
General specification as 911, except engine turbo-charged; 97 × 74·4mm, 3,299cc; 300bhp at 5,500rpm; approx. dry weight 2,884lb.

The parent body lines of the Porsche 911 are obvious in these variants.

Right: A Martini-Porsche works 3-litre Carrera RSR scoring the marque's 14th Targa Florio victory in 1973 at the expense of the Group 5 prototypes. Drivers were Dutchman Gijs van Lennep and Swiss Herbert Muller. The car has the "full treatment", with 280bhp engine, strengthened suspension, front spoiler, plastic fuel tank, racing seats, flared wheel arches to take wide wheels and tyres etc

Centre: The 1974 roadgoing Porsche Carrera RS, with rear spoiler and 2·7 litre 210bhp engine; a very fast but civilised road car, highly popular in the USA

Bottom: The fabulous Carrera RSR, "whale tail" and front chin spoiler prominent, seen on the Karussel banked turn at Nürburgring practising for the 1975 1000km race. With 3 litre fuel injection engine this is an over 160mph racer of obvious road car origins

Flat-12s all: A favoured configuration in Italian
high-performance engines, the horizontally-
opposed 12-cylinder requires less depth (but
more width) than the V12, thus reducing overall
height.

Opposite, top: *Showing that highly successful
exploiter of the layout, the 1972 Championship-
winning Ferrari 312P of Jacky Ickx and Mario
Andretti prior to their BOAC 1000km victory
at Brands Hatch*

Left: *Cutaway of the 4·4 litre flat-12 Ferrari
Berlinetta Boxer road "exotic", in its earlier
365GT/BB form, released at Turin in 1971. The
current version of this veritable "supercar", the
512GT/BB, has the full 5 litre engine*

Above: *Alfa Romeo's prototype flat-12, the
3 litre T33SC/12, enjoyed a grand finale in
1977, when the team, operated by the wealthy
Austrian Willi Kauhsen, won all eight rounds of
that season's rather flat World Sports Car
Championship. Driver here is Arturo Merzario,
winning the first qualifying round at Dijon with
J-P Jarier as co-driver*

Porsche 908

Having graduated from four to six cylinders in sports car racing, it was inevitable that Porsche, in their quest for ever more performance, would move on to the greater piston area and power offered by eight cylinders. Equally inevitably in a Porsche design, those cylinders would be horizontally opposed and air-cooled. The first flat-eight Porsche was, in fact, a 1½ litre 4ohc unit built for single-seater Grand Prix racing to the 1961–65 Formula 1, although with typical Zuffenhausen sense a 2 litre version was simultaneously laid down for use in sports car racing.

Two of these 2 litre engines, measuring 76 × 54·5mm and giving 210bhp at 8,200rpm, were fitted into existing earlier chassis of Type 718 origin, and brought a fierce new exhaust note to echo off the Sicilian mountain sides in the 1962 Targa Florio, a fortnight before the GP Porsche made its debut in Holland. Neither type won its first race, but the sports-racer was destined for greater success by far than the single-seater, which won only a single Championship race, the opposition proving so strong that Porsche took fright at the work and cost of further development and withdrew from so expensive a battlefield.

The 2 litre unit won its first race in the following year's Targa Florio, after which Porsche's first flat-eight design served its time in a succession of special lightweight *Bergspyders* for hillclimbing. These won the European Mountain Championship for 2 litre cars in 1963, 1964, 1966, 1967 and 1968, undergoing periodic improvements

---

Swedish driver Joakim Bonnier drifts the Porsche 718 2 litre flat-eight coupé through some debris kicked up on a curve, while winning the 1963 Targa Florio with Carlo Abate co-driving. This car embodied the same basic engine and suspension design as Porsche's 1962 1½ litre Grand Prix car

Yet another Targa Florio triumph fell to Porsche in 1969, when four 908/02 Spyders swept home in the first four places—the marque's fourth successive win. This is the winning car, driven by Gerhard Mitter and Udo Schutz

which were passed on to other competition Porsches, amongst them the flat-eight Type 910 which, in 2·2 litre fuel injection form, gained Porsche their seventh Targa Florio victory in 1967.

In mid-1967 news came that in 1968 the CSI were to impose new rules restricting Group 4 "sports cars" to 5 litres, and Group 6 "prototypes" to 3 litres. Porsche promptly embarked on the construction of a new 3 litre proto-type, the 908, based on the 907 six-cylinder, but with a new flat-eight engine retaining the 84 × 66mm bore and stroke of the 911 six. This gave an overall capacity of 2,926cc, later increased with an 85mm bore to 2,992cc. The new unit was designed for much quicker assembly and maintenance than the old flat-eights; it had a twin-plane

crankshaft, chain-driven twin ohc to each block, belt-driven cooling fan and dry sump lubrication, and was installed in the 907 type chassis, coupled to a new six-speed gearbox.

Early 908s had multi-tubular space frames in steel, but later ones had argon-welded aluminium tube frames of impressive lightness and rigidity. The independent suspension utilised coil spring-cum-damper units, with double wishbones at the front and single upper and lower arms at the rear, while titanium and other strong, light, exotic and expensive metals figured largely in the specification. Pending completion of the 908s Porsche opened the 1968 season very successfully with 2·2 litre eight-cylinder-engined 907 coupés, scoring 1-2-3 at Daytona, 1-2 at Sebring, and 1-4 in the Targa Florio.

Then came the debut of the full 3 litre 908s in the Monza 1000km, where teething troubles kept them well down the finishers' list. In the Nürburgring 1000km, however, Porsche surprised themselves and delighted Germany by taking the first two places ahead of a

Ford GT40. The 908 engine in Nürburgring form gave 335bhp at 8,500rpm, but it ran roughly, causing much vibration, and this fault, persisting throughout 1968, was attributed to the two-plane crankshaft. Only one further win, in the Austrian GP, fell to the 908 that season, Ford beating Porsche for the Championship.

1968 was, of course, the "year of the wing" in motor racing, and Porsche made some interesting experiments with two moveable tail flaps, spoilers or "elevons", inter-linked with the rear suspension so that under compression of one wheel in cornering the corresponding flap was flattened to reduce down-thrust, while with suspension extended the flaps were raised to increase the down-force. This had been tried on the *Bergspyders* the same season, and also, incidentally, by Nissan of Japan on their Chevrolet-engined proto-type which beat a Porsche to win the Japanese GP in May 1968.

Much winter work at Zuffenhausen brought improved 908 engines for 1969, with a revised flat-plane crankshaft

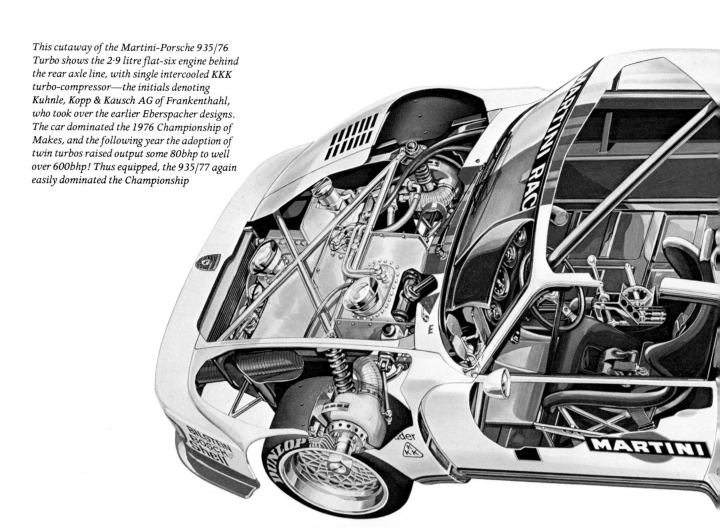

This cutaway of the Martini-Porsche 935/76 Turbo shows the 2·9 litre flat-six engine behind the rear axle line, with single intercooled KKK turbo-compressor—the initials denoting Kuhnle, Kopp & Kausch AG of Frankenthahl, who took over the earlier Eberspacher designs. The car dominated the 1976 Championship of Makes, and the following year the adoption of twin turbos raised output some 80bhp to well over 600bhp! Thus equipped, the 935/77 again easily dominated the Championship

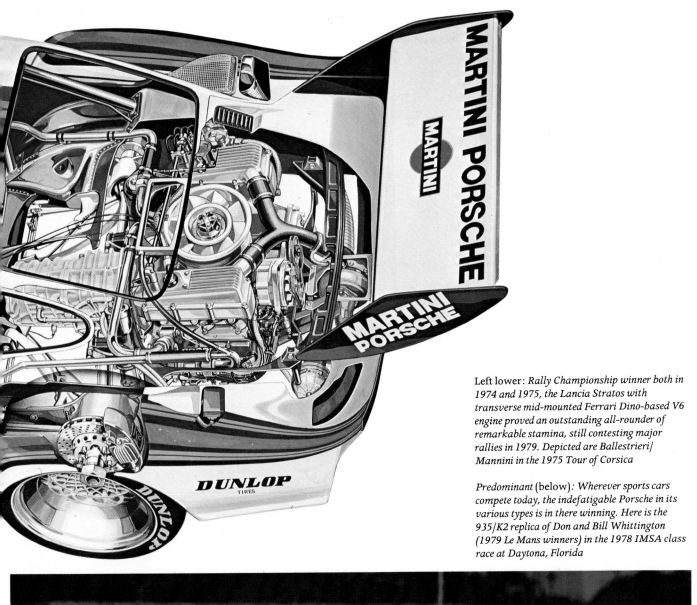

Left lower: Rally Championship winner both in 1974 and 1975, the Lancia Stratos with transverse mid-mounted Ferrari Dino-based V6 engine proved an outstanding all-rounder of remarkable stamina, still contesting major rallies in 1979. Depicted are Ballestrieri/Mannini in the 1975 Tour of Corsica

Predominant (below): *Wherever sports cars compete today, the indefatigable Porsche in its various types is in there winning. Here is the 935/K2 replica of Don and Bill Whittington (1979 Le Mans winners) in the 1978 IMSA class race at Daytona, Florida*

giving a different firing order, and a lighter, improved gearbox with only five speeds. Power output was now 350bhp at 8,450rpm, and revised Group 6 rules removed the irksome windscreen, luggage "boot" and spare wheel regulations, encouraging the use of smaller, lower open bodies. Ever thorough, Porsche built 908/01 *Langheck* (long tail) coupés and 908/02 *Kurzheck* (short tail) spyders for different circuits. Even so, 1969 began badly for Porsche, with mechanical failures both at Daytona and Sebring, but thereafter the low white flat-eight 908s virtually swept the 3 litre Prototype board clean despite the return of Ferrari and the advent of Matra.

Porsche 908s placed 1-2-3-6 at Brands Hatch, 1-2-3-4 in the Targa Florio, 1-2 at Monza, 1-3-4 at Spa and 1-2-3-4-5 at Nürburgring, their intoxicating run of success only ending at Le Mans. Four ferocious new flat-12 Type 917s added to the Porsche challenge on the Sarthe circuit, but their main hopes were vested in the race-proved 908s, their rear flaps now fixed by new FIA rulings. In the most dramatic Le Mans for many

years a *Langheck* driven by Herrmann/ Larrousse fought an epic 23rd hour duel with the Ickx/Oliver Ford GT40. The Porsche was down on power, running out of brakes, and had lost 20 minutes changing a wheel bearing, but it raced wheel to wheel with the GT40 to the end, Ickx beating Herrmann by a few yards.

If victory at Le Mans had again eluded Porsche, their Manufacturers' Championship victory was overwhelming. And while the potent 917s were maturing, the 908s continued nobly to uphold the Porsche name in 1970, now under Gulf sponsorship. Improved cars, designated 908/03 and painted blue and orange, had very light "plastic sandwich" body-work and revised gearbox location ahead of the rear axle, placing the driver further forward. Their svelte bodies were further cleaned up and given a characteristic raised rear deck terminating in a high vertical cut-off, leaving the final drive exposed.

These agile prototypes raised Porsche's score of Targa Florio wins to 11 in 1970, and their Nürburgring 1000km tally to

five, by winning that gruelling race both in 1970 and 1971. It marked their last victory as works cars, for the 917 flat-12s had now stepped fully into the breech and the valiant old 908s bowed out, being sold to private owners who campaigned them successfully in many more races.

Specification (1969–70)
Engine: Rear-mounted, air-cooled flat-8; 85 × 66mm, 2,992cc; 2ohv per cylinder, operated by 2ohc to each bank; Bosch fuel injection; double transistorised ignition; 9-bearing crankshaft; 350bhp at 8,450rpm.
Transmission: Multiple dry-plate clutch; 5-speed all-synchromesh gearbox in unit with final drive.
Chassis: Multi-tubular space frame, steel on early cars, then aluminium; independent front suspension by upper and lower wishbones and coil springs; independent rear suspension by single upper and lower links, radius arms and coil springs; coaxial hydraulic telescopic dampers all round; Dunlop-ATE hydraulic disc brakes.
Dimensions: Wheelbase, 7ft 6·4in; front track, 4ft 10·5in; rear track, 4ft 9·2in; approx. dry weight 1,385lb (spyder); 1,496lb (coupé).

Opposite, top: The "Langheck"—that brilliant driver combination of Jo Siffert and Brian Redman mit Porsche scoring one of their five 1969 victories—the Monza 1000km—with a closed, long-tailed 908/01 for that very fast circuit. Their race average was 128·215mph

Opposite, lower: The "Kurzheck"—by 1970 the 3 litre flat-8 Porsches gave pride of place to the new 12 cylinder 917s. The short-tailed 908/02 Spyders could only manage 4th and 6th places in the wet BOAC 1000km race at Brands Hatch behind three 917s. This is the Larrousse/Koch car

Above: The Siffert/Redman show again, the pair this time winning their first Targa Florio (and Porsche's 11th) with the 908/03 Spyder in 1970

Right: An old soldier serves on—Reinhold Joest's 10-year old Porsche 908, updated to 908/4 specification with 2·1 litre turbocharged engine, easily won the 1979 6 Hours race at Brands Hatch

The Turbo age (right): *The Regie Renault achieved a great ambition by winning the Le Mans 24 Hours classic in 1978, defeating two 936 Porsches. Their instrument of victory, the Renault-Alpine A442 B Turbo, had a V6 4-cam, 24-valve engine of 1,997cc with single Garrett Type T05 turbocharger which raised its "handicap" capacity to 2,796cc. Drivers were Didier Pironi and Jean-Pierre Jaussaud, here leading a Porsche 935 Turbo*

Below: *The brilliant Belgian Jacky Ickx had to rest content with second place at Le Mans in 1978, sharing the Wollek/Barth Martini Porsche 936 Turbo, after his own broke down early. The 1978 936 Turbo spyders 2343 remarkable for their individual cylinder heads, each with four valves and watercooling*

Alfa Romeo Type 33

To a marque so talented, so keen, so Italian and so steeped in motor racing tradition as Alfa Romeo, abstention from the big International events after 1951 surely came hard. It was not so surprising that the executive board of this nationalised Italian concern should have called a halt at that time, for their Type 159 Grand Prix cars had reached the end of their development, and much money had been spent. Yet to settle down to sound, solid production of sound, solid cars without the stimulus of racing to uphold the famous *quadri-foglio* was hard to stomach, especially while the rival Ferraris went from success to success.

The first, limited sanction by the board produced the 3½ litre six-cylinder Disco Volante sports-racing car, which in 1953 took second place in the Mille Miglia, failed at Le Mans and Spa, won at Merano, and then faded out. There-after production-type Alfa Romeos, ameliorated within touring or GT rules, kept the name in the picture, but ten years passed before a proper racing department was opened in 1964, on a trading estate outside Milan. This was called Autodelta, an enterprise originally founded at Udine by Ing Carlo Chiti, a former Alfa man who spent four fruitful years with the Ferrari racing team, and

subsequently returned under the Alfa wing.

In 1967 an all-new mid-engined Alfa Romeo prototype-sports, the Tipo 33/2, was laid down at Autodelta. Designed by Orazio Satta,' this had a two litre over-square 90 degree V8 four-cam engine with Lucas fuel injection and dual igni-tion, a six-speed gearbox, and an all-independently sprung tubular chassis with light-alloy end mounts for suspen-sion. Open and coupé bodywork in fibreglass was used, and the 33 marked Alfa Romeo's welcome return to the International fray with a rasping V8 exhaust note and several two litre class wins in the next two seasons, notably in 1968 at Daytona, Le Mans (4-5-6 overall) and in the Targa Florio (2-3 overall).

Clearly it was an interim model, and the next stage was the 33/3 of 1969, a fiercer beast with 32-valve 400bhp 3 litre engine, Dinoplex electronic igni-tion, and a platform-type frame made from titanium-reinforced duralumin

sheet. Suspension followed current Formula 1 practice, and hip-type side radiators with large intakes permitted a low-profile nose and the customary ugly if purposeful "chopped-off" tail bearing an incipient wing. This car won major 1969 races at Enna in Sicily, and Zeltweg in Austria, and in 1971 reappeared with a new five-speed gearbox, improved aerodynamics and 440bhp, all of which paid off handsomely.

To the huge delight of all *Alfisti*, the great marque from Milan won the Targa Florio again, the Sicilian classic they once dominated, after a lapse of 21 years, and followed it up with other 1971 victories in the Brands Hatch 1000 km and the Watkins Glen 6 Hours, plus high placings elsewhere. The Alfas could not beat the Porsches in total points, but they finished second in the Manu-facturers' Championship ahead of Ferrari. Their International comeback, moreover, proved a handy sales boost for a new road car, the Montreal fast-

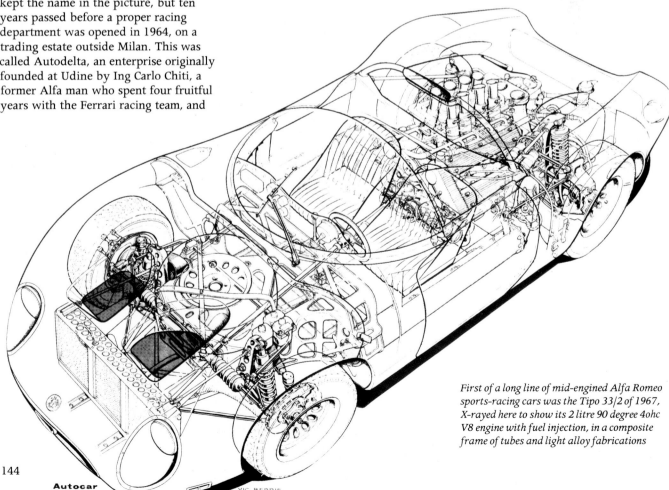

First of a long line of mid-engined Alfa Romeo sports-racing cars was the Tipo 33/2 of 1967, X-rayed here to show its 2 litre 90 degree 4ohc V8 engine with fuel injection, in a composite frame of tubes and light alloy fabrications

Autocar
COPYRIGHT

VIC BERRIS

Above: *Three 2 litre Tipo 33 Alfa Romeos lined up for test at Balocco*

Right: *The improved 3 litre V8 Tipo 33/3 with 32-valve engine and boxed platform chassis, seen at Sebring in 1969, driven by De Adamich and Casoni. The car won that year at Enna and Zeltweg*

Below: *Le Mans 1970, with the Facetti/Zeccoli 33/3 coupé at Arnage. All three cars entered had to retire.*

back, which was just coming into production. Derived directly from the Type 33, its 2,593cc V8 engine was front-mounted in a chassis with a coil-sprung live rear axle. Electronic ignition and a five-speed gearbox featured, and this car could attain 136mph. Between 1971 and 1977 just under 4,000 were built.

Having tasted victory, Alfa and Autodelta produced the 33/3TT, with an all-new alloy tubular frame, slightly longer wheelbase, and gearbox interposed between the V8 engine and the final drive unit. But mastery in the Championship see-sawed; 1972 was Ferrari's big year, and in 1973–74 the Matras reigned, with Alfa Romeo as "also-rans". They had produced another new car, the 33TT/12, with an impressive flat-12 48-valve "boxer" engine, notably oversquare at 77 × 53·6mm, and giving 500bhp at a very high 11,000rpm. This unit was installed in the rather heavy 1973-pattern *tubolare* frame, and the bodywork was characterised by a high airbox over the engine, and prominent tail fins.

Alfa Romeo put a lot of work and hope into their new *Dodici*, but apart from a surprise 1-2-3 first time out, at Monza, it performed disappointingly for the rest of the 1974 season. Then Autodelta "got things right", and the Milanese boxers came into their own in 1975, the flat-12 engines now supremely *au point* and opposition, frankly, minimal with

Matra and Ferrari absent. Of eight qualifying races, the Alfas won seven, at Dijon, Monza, Spa, Enna, Nürburgring, Osterreichring and Watkins Glen, winning the Championship title hands down.

Alfa Romeo were as disappointed as any at the poor opposition, feeling that their cars on 1975 form could have dealt with all rivals. In 1976 preoccupation with preparing Alfa 3 litre flat-12 engines for the Formula 1 Brabham team caused them largely to neglect their prototypes, although they developed a new and much lighter monocoque chassis. The following year brought the blood red boxers back in improved T33SC/12 form; they won all eight races they contested, and "walked" their second Championship, finding time to experiment with a turbocharged version of their boxer. However, its future use was ruled out when the Championship eligibility rules were changed, and Alfa Romeo's prototype racing career was over.

Specification
Type 33/3 V8 (1971)
Engine: 90° V8; 86 × 64·4mm, 2,998cc; 4 valves per cylinder, operated by 2ohc to each bank; Lucas indirect fuel injection; electronic ignition; 5-bearing crankshaft; 440bhp at 9,800rpm.
Transmission: Twin dry-plate clutch;

5-speed gearbox in unit with final drive.
Chassis: Fabricated steel and aluminium boxed structure, titanium-reinforced; independent front suspension by coil springs and wishbones; independent rear suspension by coil springs, single top arms with radius rods, reversed lower wishbones; coaxial hydraulic telescopic dampers all round; hydraulic disc brakes, inboard at rear.
Dimensions: Wheelbase, 7ft 4¼in; front track, 4ft 11in; rear track, 4ft 6⅜in; approx. dry weight, 1,430lb.

Type 33TT/12 (1974–75)
Engine: Flat-12; 77 × 53·6mm, 2,995cc; 4 valves per cylinder, operated by 2ohc to each bank; Lucas indirect fuel injection; electronic ignition; 500bhp at 11,000rpm.
Transmission: Twin dry-plate clutch, 5-speed gearbox in unit with final drive.
Chassis: Multi-tubular plate-reinforced structure, independent front suspension by coil springs and wishbones; independent rear suspension by coil springs, swinging and radius arms; coaxial hydraulic telescopic dampers; hydraulic disc brakes.
Dimensions: Wheelbase, 7ft 8·2in; front track, 4ft 8¼in; rear track, 4ft 9·9in; approx. dry weight, 1,385lb.

Henri Pescarolo practising at Monza in one of the flat 12 33TT/12 Alfa Romeos before the 1975 1000km race, won by Ickx and Merzario with another Alfa. The team was run that year by the Willi Kauhsen organisation

Porsche 917

In the world of single-seater Grand Prix cars, a quoted output of 646bhp for the 1937 supercharged 5·6 litre Mercedes-Benz W125 is frequently cited as the very peak of ferocious power, never yet equalled. Far eclipsing it, however, was the Porsche 917 sports-racing car of 1970–71, an awe-inspiring 5 litre flat-12 commanding 630bhp and a maximum speed of over 220mph—or 1,100bhp and 250mph as a turbocharged 5·4 litre in 1972–73. Big in pace, power, noise and spectacle, the 917 was no "monster" though frequently called one. It was, indeed, a masterpiece of compact, sophisticated design, in a frame shorter in wheelbase than the rival Ferraris, Alfa Romeos or Matras.

Although Porsche had won many major races by the late 1960s, the match-less prestige of Le Mans lured them year after year to the Sarthe circuit. After coming 10th in 1960, they climbed through the years to second and third by 1968, collecting numerous class wins on the way, but never out-and-out victory. For 1969, the Zuffenhausen directorate decided to build big for a Le Mans win, circumstances helping to sway them. Just after the 1968 race the FIA decided to restrict the Manufacturers' Championship from 1969 to 3 litre prototypes and 5 litre "production" sports cars, of which at least 25 examples would have to be built.

Porsche welcomed these rules; by adding four cylinders to their 3 litre flat-8 Type 908, and using many parts of that engine, they could produce a competitive car even though giving away half a litre. Aided by elaborate and expensive computer equipment, design work began in July 1968, followed by the immediate laying down of 25 cars. The first complete 917 appeared at the Geneva Show in March 1969. Long, low and menacing, it already wore its Le Mans *langheck* (long tail), beneath which was a yard of the biggest and most powerful car engine Porsche had ever made—an 85 × 66mm, 4,494cc unit producing 520bhp at 8,000rpm.

The drive to the five-speed transaxle was taken via an output shaft within the crankcase, gear-driven off the centre of the crankshaft. The latter drove the overhead camshafts, two per bank, through a central train of gears in pre-war Alfa Romeo style. The valves, two per cylinder, were sodium-cooled and

Power-house: The magnificent aircooled flat-12 Porsche 917 engine in its first 4½ litre form of 1969. The eight-bearing crankshaft has a central power take-off to drive the output shaft, timing and accessory gears, and the big plastic cooling fan. Initial power output was 520bhp at 8,000rpm

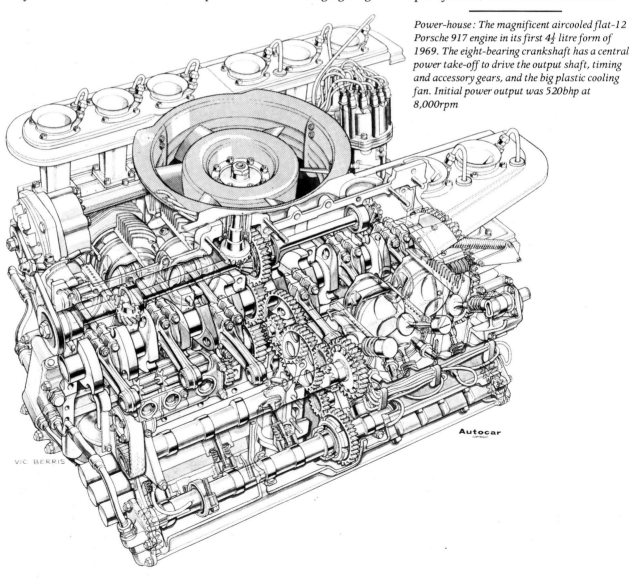

operated by inverted bucket tappets, and Bosch fuel injection was employed. Cooling was, of course, by pressurised air, a large axial-flow plastic fan being installed vertically between the shrouded cylinder banks. The 917's welded multi-tubular space frame was in aluminium rather than steel tubing, very low short or long-tail fibreglass coupé bodywork was fitted, and the wheelbase at 7ft 6·4in was the same as the 908. Although the sale price was given as DM140,000, ie about £14,500 or $35,000, it was estimated that each one probably cost over twice that sum to build.

In its first race at Spa in 1969 the 917 completed just one lap, and managed a precarious eighth in its second race at Nürburgring. Its third race was the ever-vital Le Mans, but Porsche ambitions had to be deferred, both works cars retiring after leading, while a third, privately entered, crashed, killing its driver. Along the Mulsanne straight one 917 clocked 198·4mph, but handling was very tricky and it seemed Porsche really had made a monster. However, they tamed it sufficiently to score their first win in the Austrian 1000km, while another win at Kyalami, South Africa, indicated that the beast was coming to heel.

For 1970, with Le Mans still their prime target, Zuffenhausen reached agreements with JW Automotive, the British stable which won Le Mans for Ford in 1968 and 1969, and the Austrian Team Salzburg, to run separate 917 teams. This enabled the parent factory to concentrate on development, and the body design was radically revised. The front was cleaned up, and the side pods swept up over the rear wheels in a bold wedge form each side of an engine

Above: A 1969 Porsche 917 "Langheck" decked out in the colours of its new sponsors for 1970, Gulf Oil. The cars were run by J. W. Automotive, headed by shrewd race campaigner John Wyer; they won seven races that season, including the Le Mans 24 Hours at which Porsche had aimed for so long

Below: The Gulf-Porsche 917s soon acquired revised bodywork with upswept, cut-off tails. Two of their star drivers, Jo Siffert and Pedro Rodriguez, nearly touch as they sweep into the first corner in the 1970 Spa 1000km race in Belgium. Siffert/Redman won at 149·4mph, while Rodriguez lapped at a shattering 160·5mph!

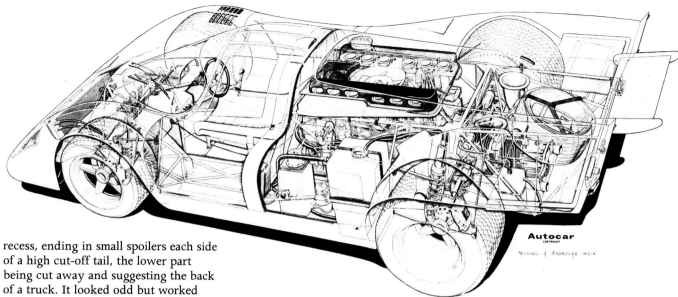

recess, ending in small spoilers each side of a high cut-off tail, the lower part being cut away and suggesting the back of a truck. It looked odd but worked well; wider tracks and bigger tyres also helped towards better handling, and the 917K, thus termed for its short (*kurz*) tail, enjoyed a splendid 1970 season.

Like the 16-cylinder Auto Union of over 30 years earlier, the Porsche 917 proved at its best on fast circuits. It won the Daytona 24 Hours at a 114·86mph average, lost to the new Ferrari 512S at Sebring, and won at Monza and Spa, where one set the lap record at 160·53mph! It also won at Brands Hatch, while seven of the deep-toned flat-12s ran at Le Mans, two clinching the marque's long desired victory by placing first and second, with Hans Herrmann and Dick Attwood the winning drivers. Their car had a 4·5 litre engine, but bigger 4,907cc, 590bhp units had also been introduced, and further "firsts" in the USA and Austria confirmed Porsche tenure of the Manufacturers' Championship.

After further improvements aerodynamically, and with the engine producing 600bhp, the 917Ks romped to a second Championship title in 1971, winning seven qualifying events including a 1-2 *encore* at Le Mans. The Porsche "steamroller" might have rolled on in 1972 had not the FIA ended the 917's Championship career by announcing a new 3 litre top limit. The Germans had another iron in the fire, however—CanAm racing in the US and Canada, run to uninhibiting Group 7 rules with no capacity limit, eminently dollarworthy and prestigious in a most important market. They had already "probed" the race in 1969 with an open spyder, the 917/PA, and the 917/10 in 1971, achieving some good placings but no wins, and for 1972-73 they arranged with the American Roger Penske for the latter to run their cars in the series.

The prime need to combat the big Chevrolet-powered McLarens was more horsepower, and Porsche went so far as

to build an experimental flat-16, but then decided it was unnecessary; the 917 flat-12 with an Eberspacher exhaust-driven turbocharger produced a numbing 900bhp, albeit at about 3mpg of fuel! It was installed in a new space frame car termed the 917/10K (for *kompressor*) on which much of the 917's original grace was lost, the 1972 form with shovel nose and huge rear wing between high vertical fins being aesthetically offensive in the modern manner. But its effect, and that of nearly 1,000hp, could not be denied, and the Porsches notched up six wins to the McLarens' three, Penske's driver George Follmer taking the Canadian-American Challenge Cup.

1973 brought the 917/30, with 7·2in longer wheelbase, altered tracks and a 5·4 litre engine producing a stupendous 1,100bhp at 7,800rpm. Nothing could live with them, and the Penske Porsches won every single CanAm round—eight of them—Mark Donohue emerging as the CanAm champion. Meantime, back in Europe the Finn Leo Kinnunen in another 917 Spyder won four events of the European Interseries contest, a kind of poor man's CanAm run on various road courses, monopolised by Porsche 917s since its inception in 1970. The upshot of this total domination all round was an outburst against the big flat-12s for their "unfair advantage" of turbocharging. An impasse was solved by new CanAm fuel consumption rules from 1974, made in deference to the world-wide fuel crisis, but which effectively excluded Porsche's unforgettable, exquisitely engineered flat-12s. They will live on in motoring history as the most powerful racing cars of any kind, prodigious in acceleration and with a potential maximum speed never realised but estimated to exceed 260mph with suitable high gearing.

Above: *Cutaway drawing of the Porsche 917 in its late 1970–71 917K form, with a small wing mounted on the stern*

Opposite, top: *Martini International took over the Salzburg team 917s in 1971, and gained Porsche their second consecutive Le Mans victory with this "Kurzheck", driven by the Austrian Helmut Marko and the Dutchman Gijs van Lennep*

Opposite, lower: *One of the CanAm Porsche 917/10Ks prepared by the American Penske team for the 1972 race series. With 5 litre, 900bhp turbocharged engine (the K denotes kompressor) the cars won six of the nine races, George Follmer, seen here, emerging as CanAm Champion*

Specification

Engine: air-cooled flat-12 mid-located; 85 × 66mm, 4,494cc (1969); 86 × 70·4mm, 4,907cc (1970–71); 86·8 × 70·4mm, 4,999cc (1971–72); 90 × 70·4mm, 5,379cc (1973); 2ohv per cylinder, operated by 2ohc per bank; Bosch fuel injection; dual transistorised ignition with alternator; 2 plugs per cylinder; 8-bearing crankshaft; 520bhp at 8,000rpm (1969); 600bhp at 8,400rpm (1970–71); 630bhp at 8,300rpm (1971); 900bhp at 8,000rpm with turbo-supercharger on 5 litre engine (1972); 1,100bhp at 7,800rpm with turbo-supercharger on 5·4 litre engine (1973).
Transmission: Triple dry-plate clutch to 4 or 5-speed all-synchromesh gearbox in unit with final drive.
Chassis: Aluminium multi-tube space frame; independent front suspension by upper and lower arms and coil springs; independent rear suspension by upper and lower arms, radius arms and coil springs; Bilstein gas/hydraulic telescopic dampers all round; hydraulic disc brakes.
Dimensions: Wheelbase, 7ft 6·4in (1969–71); 7ft 7·2in (1972); 8ft 2·3in (1973); front track varying between 4ft 10·6in and 5ft 5·7in; rear track, varying between 4ft 9·4in and 5ft 2·4in; approx. dry weight, 1,765lb (1969–70); 1,850lb (1970–71 4·9 litre); 1,763lb (1971); 1,720lb (1972); 1,765lb (1973).

Renault Alpine

The very name Alpine—pronounced, of course, *Alpeen*—suggests mountain roads and rugged rallies, but this remarkable marque from Dieppe can add the *réclame* of outright victory at Le Mans and many other sports car, Formula 2 and 3 race successes to its very distinguished rally record. Founded in 1952 by Jean Rédelé, son of the Dieppe Renault concessionaire, Automobiles Alpine have always been closely associated with the nationalised Regie Renault, and the co-operation of Amédée Gordini, the famous *sorcier* of car preparation and tuning, adds to confusion over a marque of considerable versatility.

Beginning with the 750cc Renault 4CV engine/gear unit, Alpines have

always been rear-engined, advancing through the years via Dauphine, R8 1100 and R16 1500 to more exotic Gordini units, and then to the sophisticated V6 developed at the special Renault-Gordini engine facility at Viry-Châtillon. While Automobiles Alpine have always participated with true Gallic enthusiasm in competition, their bread-and-butter comes from production models, fleet little fibreglass coupés, again Renault-powered, and also built under licence in other countries.

Stepping into the compatriot DB-Panhard's shoes, the little blue space-framed Alpine A210 coupés resumed the tradition of having at least one French winner at Le Mans almost every year. They won the Index of Thermal Efficiency in 1964 and again in 1966, by which time Renault had absorbed the Alpine concern, Rédelé becoming competitions chief. Alpine-Renaults won two classes at Le Mans in 1967, and took both the Index of Performance and Thermal Efficiency categories in 1968. In that year, too, responding to mount-

ing Renault ambition for outright victory at Le Mans, Alpine fielded four new A220 models with 3 litre Gordini-designed V8 engines. They proved disappointingly underpowered, however, with eighth their best placing well behind the Fords, Matras and Porsches.

After another Index of Performance win for the 1100cc car in 1969, the name next loomed large in rallying, where Alpine's fierce little rear-engined A110 *Berlinettes* with 2 litre engines and low coupé bodywork began to nose in among the Porsche 911s, Ford Escort TCs and Lancia Fulvias. After spasmodic successes in 1968 and 1969, Rédelé really made the cars work, for in 1970 the A110s won nine Rally Championship qualifying events and became close runners-up to Porsche. The following year the snarling blue *Berlinettes*—the "French Porsches", rear-engine oversteer included!—found top form, won ten events, and scooped the European title from Saab, Porsche and Lancia.

They took the title a second time in

Wearer of the Blue: Alpine-Renault's neat little fibreglass coupés were consistent performers at Le Mans. The Thérier/Tramont 1,296cc A210 car, seen here at the April Test Day of 1968, won that year's Index of Thermal Efficiency outright, followed by two more Alpines, and also placed 10th overall

Berlinette: From racing, Alpine-Renault turned in 1970 to a successful spell of International rallying. This 1·6 litre Type A110 of Vinatier/Jacob took third place in the snowy 1970 San Remo-Sestrière Rally, which was won by Thérier's sister car. Alpine won the European Rally Championship title both in 1971 and 1973

1973, after which Alpine-Renault returned to sports car racing, their efforts strengthened by sponsorship from the big Elf petrol consortium which had earlier supported Matra. A new sports prototype, the Type A440, was built around Renault-Gordini's highly promising 2 litre Type CH V6 four-cam engine developed at Viry-Châtillon. This featured four valves per cylinder, cogged belt camshaft drives, Lucas fuel injection, wet cylinder liners, electronic ignition and an output of around 270bhp at 9,800rpm.

A tubular space-type frame was used, and this new Alpine *barquette* made its debut in 1973 with small local success. In 1974 it reappeared as the A441, the frame reinforced with sheet aluminium, and the engine now a semi-stressed

member and giving 285bhp. The car made a clean sweep in the European 2 litre Championship by winning all seven qualifying races, after which the 441 was put into very limited production for sale to private stables.

Encouraged by this, Alpine-Renault now aimed for absolute victory at Le Mans—that same prestigious target, so hard to hit, which had lured Ford, Matra, Porsche and others before. Retaining the basic, well-proven A441 chassis, they followed Porsche's lead and turbo-supercharged the 2 litre V6 engine. The use of exhaust pressure to drive a supercharger, which in turn compresses mixture into the cylinders instead of natural aspiration, offered considerably more power but brought problems in train. With a turbo-compressor turning at phenomenal speeds of up to 100,000rpm, enormous thermal problems are created, demanding new technology in metallurgy, cooling, lubrication etc, yet offering huge advantages.

A Garrett T05 compressor was fitted to the engine at Viry-Châtillon, and the

output from the sturdy little four-bearing V6 unit was raised dramatically from under 300bhp to over 450bhp at a shrill 10,000rpm. A heat exchanger was installed between the compressor and the inlets, and Kugelfischer fuel injection was employed, the specification also including a Hewland five-speed gearbox, Koni dampers, Girling disc brakes and Michelin tyres. Fitted into an open *barquette* body, the A442 ran its first race in March 1975; this was round two of the Championship of Makes, at Mugello, Italy, and to the delight of Renault, Alpine and Elf the new turbo beat the Porsches and the home-based 3 litre Alfa Romeos to win the 490-mile race.

Alas, this pleasing début was followed by several failures during the rest of that season, with only two third places and a fourth to show. The year 1976 was little better, Alpine's biggest disappointment being their retirement at Le Mans, on which they based high hopes after the turbo had made the fastest practice and race laps. For 1977 they ran four cars there, but the little 2 litre engines, now

153

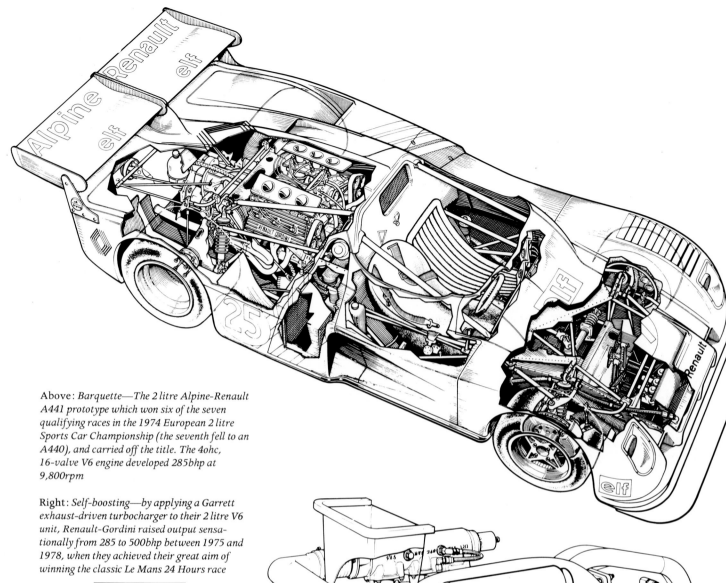

Above: *Barquette—The 2 litre Alpine-Renault A441 prototype which won six of the seven qualifying races in the 1974 European 2 litre Sports Car Championship (the seventh fell to an A440), and carried off the title. The 4ohc, 16-valve V6 engine developed 285bhp at 9,800rpm*

Right: *Self-boosting—by applying a Garrett exhaust-driven turbocharger to their 2 litre V6 unit, Renault-Gordini raised output sensationally from 285 to 500bhp between 1975 and 1978, when they achieved their great aim of winning the classic Le Mans 24 Hours race*

giving a full 500bhp, wilted under the pace, three departing with piston trouble and one with a disarrayed gearbox.

For Alpine-Renault's third straight try at Le Mans, in 1978, no effort or expense was spared; after over 3,250 miles of high-speed testing in France and the USA, they fielded three A442s and a newer 2·1 litre 520bhp A443, all with improved aerodynamics involving longer tails, lateral skirts and controversial full-width canopy screens which cut drag but also driver vision. In a race in which no other make led, and the Renault turbos regularly topped 220 mph down the 3·7 mile Mulsanne straight, one 442 finished first at an average speed of 130·6mph, and another fourth, the pair nicely sandwiching two 3 litre turbo Porsches. Although in its four-year career the turbocharged A442 won only two races—its first and its last—Renault had achieved their aim of an all-French victory at Le Mans, and withdrew from sports car racing to concentrate on Formula 1.

Specification

Engine: 90° V6; 86 × 57·3mm, 1,997cc; 4ohv per cylinder, operated by 2ohc; Garrett turbo-supercharger; Kugelfischer fuel injection; Ducellier electronic ignition; 4-bearing crankshaft; 500bhp at 10,000rpm.
Transmission: Twin dry-plate clutch; Hewland 5-speed gearbox in unit with final drive.

Chassis: Welded tube semi-monocoque with aluminium stressed skin; independent suspension by four-link system front and rear with coil springs and Koni coaxial hydraulic telescopic dampers; hydraulic disc brakes.
Dimensions: Wheelbase, 7ft 6·9in; front track, 4ft 8in; rear track, 4ft 8½in; approx. dry weight, 1,570lb.

*Pour la France: The 1978 Alpine-Renault A442
with 1,997cc turbocharged V6 engine, Hewland
5-speed gearbox and semi-monocoque frame,
seen "ghosted" (above) and in the metal (below),
with the Pironi/Jaussaud car on its way to a
rousing Le Mans 24 Hours victory*

The turbo Porsches

Like Ferrari, Porsche just has to race. Although the illustrious West German sports car makers are always practical about production and profitability, racing is in their blood. It is their test-bed, proving ground and publicity department, and no matter how CSI regulations may writhe from year to year, there is generally a Porsche which will suit them, or can be adapted to do so. Moreover, their racing experience invariably filters through to benefit production models, as in the case of their best-selling Type 911, which inherited invaluable "know-how" gained in turbocharging the flat-12 CanAm 917s, and has become one of the world's most outstanding road cars as the Porsche Turbo.

Although a mock-up 911 Turbo featured at the 1973 Frankfurt Show, the first working examples appeared in competition. Anticipating the "Silhouette" formula for the Manufacturers' Championship, intended for 1975 but postponed until 1976, Porsche built two special 2·2 litre turbo-blown edi-

tions of the 911-based Carrera RSR to contest the 1974 Group 5 3-litre events. Beneath the pretty 911 "teardrop" coupé shape, the engine featured a KKK turbo-blower, magnesium crankcase, titanium connecting rods and inlet valves, dual ignition, and a potential of over 450bhp.

Displacement was 2,142cc, the closest Porsche could get to the FIA's "handicap" for supercharged engines, rated at 1·4 times the unblown capacity. Early problems with the system—so attractive for its "free" drive without power loss —were excessive generation of heat, which Porsche cured with an intercooler, and throttle lag, coupled with sudden access of power which, on the RSR Turbo, came in at around 4,500rpm. These made driving it a tricky business, demanding extra anticipation and much use of the gears to fully exploit the power curve.

Against the seasoned 12-cylinder Matras and Alfa Romeos in 1974 the best these little turbo coupés managed was two second places, one at Le Mans,

the other at Watkins Glen. But they taught much, and the 2·1 litre engines served nobly, fitted into surviving Type 908s from the 1968–71 period and raced by private teams. These old warriors, updated and rebodied, have fought on right to the present time, their victories including the 1975 Interserie race at Mainz, the 1976 Nürburgring 300km, and the 1979 Dijon and Brands Hatch 6 Hours—eleven years after the 908 was born!

When the real production Porsche Turbo, works-designated the 930, appeared at the 1974 Paris Salon, it just begged to be raced. The 95 × 70·4mm, 2,993cc flat-six engine *mit kompressor*, compactly housed behind the rear axle, gave over 250bhp at 5,500rpm with much obviously in reserve. Acceleration was dramatic (0 to 60mph in 6sec) and maximum speed well over 150mph, yet the Turbo was a tractable and practical road car, the early throttle lag problem virtually eradicated. The 911-based torsion bar suspension had modified geometry and stiffer damping, giving a rather hard "sporting" ride, but overall roadholding, braking and handling were fully commensurate with so much extra power. With the engine enlarged to 3,299cc, the Turbo remains on the market today.

The year 1976 brought the inevitable racing versions, three in number and neatly designated 934 for Group 4 (GT), 935 for Group 5 (special production or Silhouette) and 936 for Group 6 (two-seater racing cars). All three have been outstandingly successful, sometimes to the point of boredom. The 934, "mildest" of this tempestuous trio, is the customer's GT racer. By the FIA's yardstick its turbo-blown 2,993cc flat-six engine equals 4·2 litres, and a larger KKK turbo with novel water-cooling for the intercooler made a 485bhp power-pack demanding expert handling. The 911-

The view other Porsches often saw—Herbert Muller at Brands Hatch 1974 with one of the first experimental turbocharged Carrera RSRs, built in anticipation of the "Silhouette" formula. With a single KKK compressor, over 450bhp was on tap, although throttle response was a problem

type torsion bar suspension was augmented by coil springs around the Bilstein gas dampers, and a fibreglass "chin" spoiler, wheel arch flares and "whale tail" rear wing were added to the basic steel body.

Although the larger, more flexible engine improved throttle response, this still demanded a special technique in racing of "ordering up the power" well in advance. The 934's overall effectiveness despite this is emphasised by its achievements; it dominated the 1976 European GT Championship, winning all seven rounds, and it has dominated the category ever since. Elsewhere its successes have been legion, and although the Porsche image has been transformed today by the water-cooled, front-engined, rear-drive 924 and 928 models, the old 911-based Turbos with engine "hanging out behind" continue to win like the classic sports cars they unquestionably are.

The 935 might be termed "a 934 only more so"—more power, more performance, light fibreglass bodywork with an extended, be-spoilered nose, larger rear wing, wider wheels, and 590bhp or more from its 92 × 70·4mm, 2,857cc engine. This formidable Group 5 contender could lap the world's circuits at close on GP speeds, and although challenged by the compatriot BMWs, the 935 won the 1976 World Championship of Makes, run to the Silhouette formula for which Porsche had made

extensive preparations two years earlier.

For 1977 the Zuffenhausen works built still faster 935/77s with twin turbochargers and some 80 more bhp. They also surprised the BMWs and Fords in the 2 litre class with a 1·4 litre 935, besides producing a batch of 2·8 litre 935s for sale to private teams or drivers. Between them the works and private 935s swamped that year's Championship of Makes with seven wins out of nine. In 1978 privateers took the title for

Above: *Over the counter—despite compact dimensions, the customer's turbocharged 2·9 litre Porsche 934 has 485bhp under its throttle pedal. Al Holbert here is performing in a 1976 TransAm race at Mosport, Canada*

Below: *Works only—the 911 body origins are just discernible in this turbocharged Martini-Porsche 935/76 "Silhouette" car with "chin" front spoiler and big rear wing. This is the Rolf Stommelen/Manfred Schurti car winning the Group 5 category (special production) at Le Mans in 1976, placing 4th overall*

Opposite, top: *One season's changes—the Jacky Ickx/Jochen Mass 2·8 litre Martini-Porsche works 935 Turbo winning the 1977 Silverstone 6 Hours race. Alterations since 1976 (see page 157 lower) include twin turbos, reprofiled nose and rear wing brought further forward*
Opposite, centre: *Monopolist—Porsche 935 Turbos won seven rounds of the 1977 World Championship of Makes, and all 8 in 1978. Here is the Stommelen/Hezemans/Gregg 3 litre 935/77A winning the Daytona 24 Hours in 1978*
Opposite, bottom: *Only the roofline, windows and doors confirm the 911 origins of the works 3·2 litre Martini-Porsche 935/78 with its sleek nose and dramatically lengthened tail. Nicknamed "Moby Dick", the car won first time out in the 1978 Silverstone 6 Hours, Ickx and Mass driving*
Right: *Nocturne—the Kremer Racing team 935/K3 Turbo on its way to victory in the 1979 Le Mans 24 Hours. Drivers were Klaus Ludwig and the American brothers Don and Bill Whittington*
Below: *Modern bolide—this sight of the Kremer Team's latest Porsche 935 Turbos in the paddock at Brands Hatch in 1979 epitomises the current stage in sports car racing—coupé tops, exotic aerodynamics, expensive but effective turbocharging, poor aesthetics and shattering performance*

Porsche, losing only one of the eight rounds—and that fell to an experimental 3,211cc factory 935/78, having twin overhead camshafts, special four-valve water-cooled heads, and a blenching output of 750 bhp at 8,200rpm. At Le Mans that year this car was fastest of all through the "radar trap" at a prodigious 227mph! In 1979, Le Mans was won by a specially-prepared 935 built by the Kremer tuning company in West Germany.

The third of Porsche's turbo-super-charged flat-six trio, the Type 936, was a frank open two-seater which surprised Alfa Romeo and Alpine-Renault in the revived World Sports Car Championship of 1976. For a Group 6 sports-racing car it was relatively cheap to build, using up old 917 flat-12 parts such as the five-speed transaxle and many suspension and steering components. The aluminium space-frame, too, was 917-inspired, as was the long-tailed fibreglass bodywork with vertical stabilising fins supporting a large rear wing.

The turbo-blown engine was basically the 1974 2,142cc RSR unit, its com-ponents reshuffled to fit the shallow bay between driver and rear axle. With a blower pressure of 20psi, some 520–540bhp was on tap, and this unexpected newcomer won six of the seven races and walked away with the 1976 Championship title. It capped this, moreover, at Le Mans, dominating the 24 hours race throughout and winning by a margin of nine laps. In 1977 Porsche left Group 6 to the Alfa Romeos, but they could not neglect Le Mans with Renault making tremendous efforts to win. Fate—and Porsche—foiled the

159

Habit forming: Up to 1979 the marque Porsche had won five Le Mans 24 Hours races.
Top: The 1976 winner, the 2·1 litre 936 Turbo spyder driven by Jacky Ickx and Gijs van Lennep; they averaged 123·49mph and led the second car home by 11 laps

Above: The 1977 24 Hours was a repeat victory for the 936 Turbo, with subtle modifications, and Jacky Ickx, this time partnered by Jurgen Barth and Hurley Haywood. Their race average was down to 120·95mph, but the winning margin was again 11 laps

French efforts, and the twin-turbo 936/77 won the race—but only just, for a piston holed on the penultimate lap.

Le Mans 1978 saw the situation reversed. Porsche enlarged their turbo to 3 litres and fitted individual four-valve cylinder heads with water-cooling, as also tried out on the works 935/78. The cylinders were air-cooled as before, and output was 580bhp at 9,000rpm. It availed them not; the 2 litre turbo-charged Renaults were lighter and less thirsty on fuel; they set the pace and won the race, with two 936/78s placing second and third. With 30 years of racing experience, however, Porsche are familiar with such rebuffs, and with counteracting them. Moreover, Renault's victory was also one for the turbo-charging principle which Porsche have exploited so effectively on their modern cars.

Specification
Porsche 934
Engine: Rear-mounted, air-cooled flat-6; 95 × 70·4mm, 2,993cc; 2ohv per cylinder, operated by single ohc to each bank; single KKK turbocharger; Bosch fuel injection; 8-bearing crankshaft; 485bhp at 7,000rpm.
Transmission: Single dry-plate clutch; 4-speed all-synchromesh gearbox in unit with final drive.
Chassis: Unitary steel chassis/body construction; independent front suspension by Macpherson struts, lower arms and torsion bars with auxiliary coil springs; independent rear suspension by semi-trailing arms and torsion bars with auxiliary coil springs; Bilstein telescopic gas dampers all round; hydraulic disc brakes.
Dimensions: Wheelbase, 7ft 5·4in; front track, 4ft 10in; rear track, 4ft 10·9in; approx. dry weight, 2,610lb.

Porsche 935
As Type 934 but with 92 × 70·4mm, 2,857cc engine; 590bhp at 7,900rpm; independent suspension by coil springs; front track, 4ft 11·1in; rear track, 5ft 1·3in; approx. dry weight, 2,295lb.

Porsche 935/77—1·4
As Type 935 but with 71 × 60mm, 1,425cc engine; 370bhp at 8,000rpm; approx. dry weight, 1,650lb.

Porsche 936
Engine: Centrally-mounted, air-cooled flat-6; 83 × 66mm, 2,142cc; 4ohv per cylinder, operated by single ohc to each bank; single KKK turbocharger with twin intercoolers; Bosch mechanical fuel injection; 8-bearing crankshaft; 540bhp at 8,000rpm.
Transmission: Three-plate Borg & Beck dry clutch; 5-speed all-synchromesh gearbox.
Chassis: Aluminium multi-tube frame with open fibreglass bodywork removable in three pieces; independent front and rear suspension by transverse arms, radius rods and coil springs around Bilstein telescopic gas dampers; hydraulic ventilated disc brakes.
Dimensions: Wheelbase, 7ft 10⅞in; front track, 5ft 0¼in; rear track, 4ft 10¼in; approx. dry weight, 1,540lb.